Panchayati Raj and Reservation Policy

Panchayati Raj and Reservation Policy

Study of Impact of Reservation Policy on the Marginalised Sections of the Society

B.M. Sharma

RAWAT PUBLICATIONS

Jaipur • New Delhi • Bangalore • Guwahati • Kolkata

ISBN 978-81-316-0929-3

Published by
Prem Rawat for **Rawat Publications**
Satyam Apts, Sector 3, Jawahar Nagar, Jaipur 302 004 (India)
Phone: 0141 265 1748 / 7006 Fax: 0141 265 1748
E-mail: info@rawatbooks.com
Website: www.rawatbooks.com

New Delhi Office
4858/24, Ansari Road, Daryaganj, New Delhi 110 002
Phone: 011 2326 3290

Also at *Bangalore, Guwahati* and *Kolkata*

Typeset by Rawat Computers, Jaipur
Printed at Chaman Enterprises, New Delhi

Dedicated to my wife
Late Smt. Usha Sharma

Contents

Preface

India is a country of villages, and the concept of holistic development makes it imperative that rural India should be systematically developed. For the development of rural India, the founding fathers of Indian Constitution provided the Panchayati Raj institution with constitution. They inserted Article 40 in the Constitution for this purpose. The Article mandates that the state should organise and empower village Panchayats. The journey of development ever since the commencement of the Constitution indicates that the governments continuously made efforts in the direction which finally resulted in the 73rd Constitutional Amendment of 1993. This significant landmark of the journey constitutionalises Panchayati Raj institutions in the country. It has established an uniformity in Panchayati Raj structure all over the country, and it has developed three tiers of rural local government institutions. It has regularised the elections of Panchayati bodies, and a State Finance Commission looks after their resources and funding needs. To promote popular participation in the functioning of Panchayati Raj institutions reservation of seats has been provided for SCs, STs, OBCs and women. In order to bring women in the mainstream of the society, 33 per cent seats have been reserved for women.

The State of Rajasthan passed the Rajasthan Panchayati Raj Act, 1994, in consonance with the 73rd Constitutional Amendment, and the first elections for these rural local bodies were held in the year of 1994 as per the provisions of this 73rd Constitutional Amendment. The very important and foremost feature of this amendment is to have social change and social justice in the society with the help of reservation for SCs, STs, OBCs and women. It is a very important path-breaking and vital step for the evolution of an egalitarian society.

The reservation makes Panchayati Raj institutions more participatory and representative. All sections of rural society get represented and local institutions look more democratic. Indian society has historically kept a large section of its people away from the mainstream of national life. Reservation has not only inducted these deprived groups to enter into the ruling segment but has also ensured them a life of dignity with human rights. They are gradually developing leadership capability, which portends a bright future.

Reservation for Dalits and women has improved their position and status in the society. There is increased confidence in the downtrodden sections of the society. Women are actively participating in the meetings of Panchayati Raj bodies and their views are given due significance in the policymaking processes aimed at development of their villages. Women are coming out of their houses, canvassing for elections, and asking for votes in their favour. Both the districts under the study are politically very mobilised and aware. The Dalits and women of these districts are also getting mobilised rapidly. It is a field study with the general theoretical framework of Indian democracy as enshrined in the Constitution of India and Gandhian ideology of 'Gram Swaraj'. It is an empirical field study based on primary data and information. For the field study, the two Zila Parishads out of 33 Zila Parishads of the largest State of Rajasthan have been selected. These two Zila Parishads are Jaipur Zila Parishad and Sikar Zila Parishad. Both Zila Parishads have their own specific features. Two Panchayat Samitis from each Zila Parishad have been selected for the purpose. Each Panchayat Samiti supplies five Village Panchayats. From each village Panchayat about 20 respondents have been selected. Thus, the total number of respondents are 400 ($2 \times 2 \times 5 \times 20 = 400$).

The author has prepared a structured questionnaire containing four open-ended sections. The structured questionnaire contains about 60 questions, broadly divided into four sections namely (a) introduction, (b) knowledge testing, (c) role and performance and (d) evaluation and suggestions. The data so collected have been edited and processed by proper coding and tabulation determining relationship between variables like position in power hierarchy of Panchayat Raj bodies, social status, educational attainments, financial upliftment and development. The data have been analysed and the researcher has tried to draw certain research findings and conclusions.

The present study has been divided into six chapters. The first chapter is basically an introduction to Panchayati Raj institutions. The second chapter deals with the history of Panchayati Raj in India in details from ancient times to up until the time of India's independence. The third chapter pertains to the evolution of Panchayati Raj from the time of Independence to the passing of 73rd Constitutional Amendment. Chapter 4 evaluates the 73rd Constitutional Amendment as an important step towards rural government committed to the rural development. The fifth chapter analyses the field study in details. The last chapter provides conclusions and findings of the study.

First of all I convey my sincere thanks to Hon'ble Shri T.N. Chaturvediji, Former Governor, Karnataka and the Chairman of Indian Institute of Public Administration, New Delhi, who has been my friend, philosopher and guide. My sincere thanks are due to my senior teachers, colleagues, friends and students for their valuable guidance and suggestions.

I want to express my gratitude and thankfulness to Prof. P.D. Sharma, Prof. S.L. Verma, Prof. S.L. Goel, Dr. B.L. Arya (IAS, Retd.), Dr. S.N. Singh (IAS, Retd.), Prof. J.P. Sharma, Vice-Chancellor, MLS University, Udaipur, Prof. R.K. Dixit, Dr. Brij Bhooshan Sharma. I also take the opportunity to convey my sincere thanks to the Director of IIPA Shri T. Chatterjee, IAS (Retd.), Registrar Shri Amitabh Ranjan and Dy. Registrar Shri Mithun Barua for their valuable contribution in completing the venture.

I also take the opportunity to express my sincere thanks to the authorities of the library of IIPA, New Delhi and Central Library, University of Rajasthan, Jaipur for their continuous helping hand. I also grateful to all the respondents of various villages under study who have spared their valuable time for data collection during field survey.

I convey my thanks to my son Dr Abhishek Sharma (IRS), my daughter-in-law Smt. Aditi Sharma, who always assisted me in the tabulation work and preparing the tables and diagrams. I also record my sincere thanks to my granddaughter little angel Aaniya for making the environment charming and joyful by her child-like naughty activities.

I thank Shri Pawan Dutt for his painstaking efforts in the typing of the manuscript efficiently.

Last but not the least, I would like to thanks Shri K.C. Rawat, Pranit Rawat and Sachin Rawat from Rawat Publications, Jaipur for their appreciable efforts to bring out this book in record time.

B.M. Sharma

1

Introduction, Nature of the Study, Review of Literature and Methodology

Decentralised governance was a hallmark of the rural society of India during the ancient times. This is evident from the mention of Sabha and Samiti in our scriptures. The recognition of the Panchas, the five representatives of the village community, as the Parmeshwar – the God, also testifies to this fact. The Panchayats comprising these Panchas continued to have an autonomous status in the governance of villages during the ancient period. They performed not only administrative functions but judicial functions as well.[1] Studies on ancient Indian thought and institutions have recorded that their position remained more or less undisturbed during the rule of various dynasties, including Mauryas, Guptas and Vardhans. They are believed to have enjoyed the same status during the regimes of the Rajput rulers. The position of the Panchayats remained almost unaffected even when the Afghans and the Mughals ruled over India. This fact has been verified by Charles Metcalfe, the Provisional Governor-General of India during the period 1835–1836.[2]

The British rule, however, had far-reaching consequences for these institutions of decentralised governance. The centralisation of administration introduced by them undermined the authority and autonomy of Panchayats. Their position was also adversely affected by the creation of officials who were assigned the task of collection of land revenue in the rural society and given the rule of acting as the agents of administration at the grass-root level. This virtually destroyed the traditional Panchayat system.[3]

The financial constraints, however, forced the colonial rulers to create Statutory Panchayats in the second decade of the twentieth century based on the recommendations of the Royal Commission on Decentralisation (1907).[4] But these Panchayats imposed from above could not strike roots on account of the apathy of the villagers, on the one hand, and the hostility of the bureaucracy, on the other. Even the introduction of the Dyarchy in 1921 for the gradual establishment of self-governance in India and the transfer of the function of local self-government from the Governor's Executive Council to the India Ministers in the provinces brought about little improvement in the condition of Panchayats, as the objective situation remained unchanged.[5] The introduction of the Provincial Autonomy in 1937 too failed to improve their status due to the persistence of unfavourable environment.[6]

The dawn of freedom had created the hope that the decentralised governance will be able to achieve its lost glory through the institutionalisation of Mahatma Gandhi's ideal of Gram Swaraj by creating a polity with maximum powers with the Panchayats and minimum powers with the central government, but this hope was shattered by the constitution-makers who framed a constitution that provided for the creation of a highly centralised federal system having no room for Panchayats. However, the strong pressure from the Gandhians did make them to provide for setting-up of Panchayats as the units of self-government in the villages in the non-justiciable Directive Principles of State Policy.[7] Consequently, Gram Panchayats having civil and judicial functions were created in all the states after the first General Elections in 1952. However, these could not assume the form of genuine institutions of decentralised governance on account of lack of powers, resources and autonomy, on the one hand, and the persistence of unfavourable social, cultural, administrative and political situation, on the other.[8] The introduction of the scheme of democratic decentralisation suggested by Balwant Rai Mehta Committee for streamlining development administration led to the creation of the three-tier structure of democratically elected and organically linked Panchayati Raj system in Rajasthan and Andhra Pradesh in 1959 and in other states in the early 1960s.[9]

The experiment of Panchayati Raj underwent three phases. The first phase, 1959–1964, was the development of Panchayati Raj in all the states; the developmental efforts bore fruit due to the commitment of Pandit Jawaharlal Nehru, who was the prime minister of India and the leader of Congress Party which ruled all the states of India at that time. The second phase, 1964–1972, was marked by its decline due to the lack of commitment with national leadership as well as state leadership. The third phase, 1972–1977, marked the virtual demise of Panchayati Raj, a direct result of centralisation and de-politicisation efforts pursued by political leadership at the national level.[10]

From 1977 onwards steps were taken, specifically the recommendations of Ashok Mehta Committee (1978), that revived the hope of revitalisation of decentralised governance to strengthen Panchayati Raj institutions. The recommendations were nevertheless ignored by the Government of India and the political leadership of most of the states. However, these recommendations were implemented in modified form in Karnataka, Andhra Pradesh and West Bengal where the Panchayati Raj Institutions were strengthened and made effective.[11]

Meanwhile, Rajiv Gandhi, who was the Prime Minister of India in 1984, decided to revitalise decentralised governance for ensuring that funds for development are not pilfered during transit and reach the masses. In accordance with the L.M. Singhvi Committee Report (1989), he decided to accord a constitutional status to Panchayati Raj Institutions and make provisions for empowerment of women, Scheduled Castes and Scheduled Tribes through reservations. Rajiv Gandhi introduced 64th Amendment Bill in Parliament for this purpose. It was approved by Lok Sabha but could not secure the required two-thirds majority in Rajya Sabha on account of suspicion in the minds of leaders of opposition parties regarding motives behind this exercise.[12]

Shri P.V. Narasimha Rao, the Prime Minister in 1991, succeeded in getting the 73rd Amendment passed in 1992 by building a consensus in its favour to constitutionalise Panchayati Raj institutions.[13]

The concept of democratic decentralisation has been much discussed and debated by scholars of political science and public administration. Democratic decentralisation has been described and addressed by various names in India such as 'functional democracy', 'grass-root democracy', 'building from below', 'Panchayati Raj institutions' and so on.

The term 'decentralisation' literally means 'away from centre'. Herman Finer explains, 'Decentralisation is a system in which there are many centres of Government, local and central, each with a recognised right of independent existence and functions.' Generally, power is located at one single centre except in a federation. The process by which power is transferred from a higher to lower level is called decentralisation. The Balwant Rai Mehta Committee defines decentralisation as 'a process whereby the government divests itself completely of certain duties and responsibilities and devolves them on to some other authority'.

The underlying idea behind democratic decentralisation is to widen the area of democracy by granting both authority and autonomy to people at lower levels. In simple words, it symbolises an attempt to create democracies within democracy. It implies mass participation of the people at the grass-root level both in decision-making and decision-implementing processes. Most of the writers have limited the scope of decentralisation only to the government structures. Nevertheless, it must be noted that decentralisation, being a useful tool of administration, is also used in non-governmental organisations and other institutions. The term decentralisation also indicates a situation where authority and powers are dispersed from one single centre to a number of centres. *Decentralisation* is not a neutral term. Instead, it is freighted with value connotations. It is commonly advocated as a precondition for the achievement and preservation of the basic values of a free society.

With reference to the institutions of local self-government, decentralisation has a more complex dimension in that it is both political and administrative. Elected functionaries enjoying statutorily defined autonomy have a certain political status. For this, there should be corresponding degree of administrative autonomy.

Administrative decentralisation generally refers to the transfer or devolution of authority from a higher to a lower authority in such a way that the lower authority enjoys a measure of functionally desirable autonomy. This autonomy is less secure in the case of mere de-concentration or delegation. Apart from the formal basis, it depends much upon the human actions – their outlook, style and equipment. The form of power has also to be distinguished from the subject of its exercise. Even in a situation of formal de-concentration it is possible to expect the substance of decentralisation in practice. Technically, however, devolution, which implies a higher degree of autonomy, goes better with decentralisation.

Decentralisation of state power and strengthening of local bodies were advocated by very eminent scholars, thinkers and activists like Mahatma Gandhi, M.N. Roy, Rabindranath Tagore, Pt. Jawaharlal Nehru, J.P. Narayan, M.S. Namboodiripad, Rajni Kothari, Nirmal Mukherji, Indira Gandhi, Rajiv Gandhi and so on.

The growing participation of the people at the grass-roots level is widely favoured as the most effective means of securing socioeconomic development compatible with the aspirations of the public at large and of ensuring percolation of the intended benefits to the poorer sections of society. Mahatma Gandhi fervently advocated the revival of Village Councils during the freedom movement with his philosophy that 'Independence must begin at the bottom.' Thus, every village will be a republic village or Panchayat having full powers.

Genesis and Development of the Concept of Panchayati Raj

The Panchayati Raj is a three-tier structure of rural local government set up at the village, block/taluka and district levels for implementing the scheme of democratic decentralisation recommended by Balwant Rai Mehta Committee to galvanise development administration. The introduction of this system was hailed as a landmark in the history of rural administration of India. It was claimed to be the most epoch-making initiative since the introduction of revenue system by the colonial administration in the nineteenth century. It was remarked that if the launching of Community Development Programme was the most important event in the annals of development administration in the 1950s, the creation of the Panchayati Raj Institutions was the most significant event in the 1960s. It was claimed that its creation aimed at not only cementing the foundations of democracy in India but also sought to democratise and decentralise district administration. On one hand the establishment of the Panchayati Raj system has been perceived as an attempt to revive the ancient institution of Panchayat, and on the other it has been viewed as an effort to realise the Gandhian ideal of Gram Swaraj. If some saw the introduction of this system as an extension of federal system below the state level to the district and the sub-district levels, others described it as participatory democracy.[14]

Various scholars have conceptualised the Panchayati Raj differently. It has been perceived as a local government mechanism on one hand and as a development mechanism on the other. Some perceived it as an administrative mechanism, and others viewed it as a political mechanism. Thus, there exists a great deal of controversy, ambiguity, ambivalence and confusion regarding the real nature of Panchayati Raj system.[15]

The Pre-colonial Period

The pre-colonial period consists of medieval phases. During the ancient phase, village communities were administered by the general body, the Sabha, their council, Samiti, and their representatives, Gramins. A reference to these institutions has been made in the Vedas and other scriptures. The writings of Kautilya also contain evidence showing their existence in the ancient period. In due course of time, the village communities began to be governed by a council of five members, popularly known as Panchayats. These bodies performed the functions of tension management and conflict resolution. The legitimacy of the authority of Panchayat was based on religion and customs. In addition to these Panchayats of village communities, there existed simultaneously caste and sub-caste Panchayats to regulate the code of conduct of their members. Although Panchayats of village communities as well as of castes have been glorified as democratic institutions by those who have taken a romantic view of the rural society of the ancient era, these were dominated by the male landlords of the higher castes owing to its caste-based, patriarchal and feudal character.

Be that at it may, these institutions had complete hold over the rural people during the ancient period. The establishment of a centralised system of administration by the Mauryan dynasty, however, was reported to have reduced their significance to some degree, but their authority was fully restored as a result of decentralisation of administration during the Gupta period. On the whole, the Panchayats remained autonomous institutions of local government in ancient India.

It has been recorded by some historians of medieval India that the Panchayat system remained more or less intact during the regime of the Afghan Sultans of Delhi. The Panchayat continued to administer the village communities. The Sultans did not interfere in their functioning and these remained, by and large, autonomous units under the supervision of an officer of the central administration. Sher Shah Suri also allowed them to continue as such and interacted with these through semi-official functionaries like 'muquaddam', 'patwari' and 'chowkidar'. However, the land revenue, police and judicial system introduced by the Mughals did erode the autonomy and authority of the Panchayats to some extent. However, despite the centralising impact of Mughal rule, the village communities remained autonomous to a considerable degree and continued to be under the administration of Panchayats for the management of local affairs. This testified by Sir Charles Metcalfe, the provisional Governor General of India (1835–1836).[16] He described village communities governed by the Panchayats as 'little republics'.

The Colonial Period

The advent of British colonialism made an adverse impact on the traditional Panchayat system. The colonialists introduced highly centralised land revenue, administrative and judicial systems that almost completely eroded the authority and autonomy of Panchayats. Instead of operating through these, they began to run the rural administration through the officials of district administration who were helped by semi-official functionaries like the 'zaildar' and 'lambardar' appointed by them for the collection of land revenue and for acting as the channel of communication between the village communities and the Raj. However, the financial crisis that the colonial administration had to face on account of the Revolt of 1857 made them realise the need for creating village Panchayats as institutions of local government. This is evident from the account that follows.

Mayo Resolution

The Mayo Resolution, which was adopted by the Council of Governor-General in 1870 during the regime of Lord Mayo, was the first step that was taken by the colonial administration for setting up Panchayats. The objective behind this exercise was to decentralise powers to bring about administrative efficiency in meeting the demands of people and to raise financial resources for local functions. Through this resolution, Panchayats consisting of nominated members were set up to levy and collect taxes for payment to the chowkidars. The Famine Commission of 1880 testifies this in its report. In fact, the colonial regime at that juncture was interested only in reducing the financial burden of provincial governments and not in the establishment of local self-government institutions in the rural areas.

Ripon Resolution of 1882

The credit for laying the foundation of rural local self-government must be given to the then Governor-General of India, Lord Ripon, who was a believer of the ideology of liberalism. The Governor-General's Council on his initiative adopted this resolution. It was the first genuine effort by the colonial administration to create local self-government institutions in India. Lord Ripon hoped to utilise 'intelligent class of public spirited men for local administration'. That is why this resolution provided for the creation of rural bodies having majority of elected non-officials. Although it could not be implemented in its true spirit due to the hostility of the bureaucracy, it did create a favourable climate for the creation of village Panchayat in the years to follow.

Report of the Royal Commission on Decentralisation, 1909

The shift in the policy of the British colonialism from benevolent despotism to that of increasing association of Indians in the administration of their empire led to the appointment of the Royal Commission on Decentralisation by the British government in 1907. It was also prompted by the need for decentralisation of the administration of the continent-sized empire for greater efficiency and economy. The pressure of the moderate leadership of the Indian National Congress too might have influenced this decision.

They were demanding self-government, and the commission recommended that an attempt should be made to constitute and develop village Panchayats for the administration of local affairs. The Morley–Minto Reforms and the Indian Councils Act, 1909, created congenial conditions for the implementation of the recommendations of the commission. This is evident from the enactment of Village Panchayat Act by some of the provinces in the second decade of the twentieth century. However, only negligible progress could be made in that direction owing to the apathy of the rural masses on one hand and the negative attitude of bureaucracy on the other.

Montagu–Chelmsford Reforms, 1919

These reforms also contributed to the development of village Panchayats to some extent. It is pertinent to mention here that the services rendered by the Indians during the First World War (1914–1918) brought about a change in the British policy towards India. Earlier they regarded the Indians unfit for responsible government. Later they agreed to the strategy of gradual establishment of a self-government system in India. It was to be created mainly at the local level and partly at the provincial level. This was what was recommended by Chelmsford (the Governor-General) and Montague (Secretary of State for India) in their report, which was implemented through the enactment of the Government of India Act, 1919. This act introduced 'dyarchy' in provinces and made local self-government a transferred subject, which was assigned to the Indian ministers. These ministers initiated steps to enact laws for removing the defects in the earlier legislations. The village Panchayat Acts made by them were an improvement on the earlier laws. However, these too failed to have the desired result owing to the continuation of the hostility of the bureaucracy towards the village Panchayats.

Provincial Autonomy

The failure of the experiment of diarchy led to the enactment of the Government of India Act, 1935, by the British government after prolonged discussions with the Indian leaders at the two Round Table Conferences held in London. As a result, provincial autonomy was introduced in the place of diarchy. Subject to many reservations and safeguards, all the provincial subjects were handed over to the Council of Ministers responsible to legislative assemblies elected through restricted franchise based on property qualifications. The provincial governments formed after the 1937 elections enacted new laws to develop village Panchayats as local self-government institutions. However, the outbreak of the Second World War in 1939 proved to be a major hindrance in the development of village Panchayats.

Thus, the colonial period witnessed the eclipse of the traditional village Panchayats on one hand and the half-hearted and unsuccessful efforts to create 'Statutory Village Panchayats' on the other. Consequently, these could not become rural local self-government institutions in the true sense of the word.

Postcolonial Period

The evolution of the Panchayati Raj system in the postcolonial period may be divided into the pre-Balwant Rai Mehta Committee Report, post-Balwant Rai Mehta Committee Report, and the pre-73rd Amendment and the 73rd Amendment phases.

Balwant Rai Mehta Committee Report

The issue of the status of village Panchayats in the Indian political system became a matter of great controversy in the Constituent Assembly after independence in 1948 when the Indian Constitution was being made. While the Gandhians wanted India to be a polity with maximum powers at the Panchayat level and minimum powers at the central level, the chairman of the Drafting Committee, Dr B.R. Ambedkar, did not want to give any place to this institution in the constitution. He perceived the village as 'a sink of localism, a den of ignorance, narrow-mindedness and communalism'. He favoured the individual rather than a village as the unit of the constitution. Being a Dalit, he feared that the Panchayats would be controlled by the landlords and the high castes who will use it for the exploitation and oppression of weaker sections of the rural society. However, the Gandhians ultimately succeeded in getting village Panchayat included in Article 40 of the Part IV of the Indian Constitution dealing with the Directive Principles of State Policy. This article laid down that 'The State should take steps to organise village Panchayats and endow them with such powers and authority as may be necessary to enable them to function as units of self-government.' Soon after the implementation of the constitution in 1950, various states enacted Gram Panchayat Acts, which provided for the creation of democratically elected Gram Panchayats. These were given civic, developmental and judicial functions.

In the meanwhile, the Government of India launched the Community Development Programme in October 1952. The National Extension Service Scheme which supplemented this programme was introduced in service areas in 1953 for covering the entire rural areas of the country. These programmes aimed at creating a zeal for development with the rural population. It was hoped that these would bring about a silent revolution in rural society, but this hope was belied as the programmes failed to garner popular support.

The recognition of the failure of the programmes made the Government of India to direct the Committee on Plan Projects of the Planning Commission to conduct an enquiry into the causes of the failure of these programmes and suggest remedies for streamlining them. The committee appointed a study team for this purpose under the leadership of Balwant Rai Mehta in 1957. This team was asked to find out whether the existing institutions of local government, district boards and Gram Panchayat could be used to implement the Community Development Programme and the National Extension Service Scheme in a successful manner. It was directed to suggest not only the ways and means for this purpose but also an alternate system of rural local government.

After an in-depth study, Balwant Rai Mehta Committee submitted its report in 1958. It found that these programmes had failed because of their failure in garnering popular support. The team expressed the view that the existing institutions of rural local government were not fit instruments for streamlining the development administration. It suggested a scheme of 'Democratic Decentralisation' for mobilising human and material resources for this purpose.

To operationalise the scheme, the team recommended the creation of a three-tier structure of democratically elected and organically linked bodies at the district level (Zila Parishad), block level (Panchayat Samiti) and the village level (Gram Panchayat).

The team recommended indirect elections for the bodies to keep the political parties out and to establish an organic link between the three tiers. It expressed the view that the block-level institution, Panchayat Samiti, be made the unit for planning and implementation as it was neither as large as the district in which direct contact was difficult nor as small as a village where the required human and material resources might not be available. The team felt that Panchayat Samiti was an optimum-sized unit in which development machinery was present. Moreover, it argued that the word 'block' was associated with development in the rural psyche. Hence, the team suggested that the Panchayat Samiti be assigned developmental functions. It could also be given the responsibility of implementing the schemes and programmes of the central as well as state governments. It was further recommended that the Gram Panchayat be allowed to retain the civic, development and judicial functions and also assigned the task of implementation of plans and programmes of the Samiti. The Zila Parishad be made a supervisory and coordinating body. The team recommended the association and involvement of MPs and MLAs in the Panchayati Raj Institutions for guiding their leadership and establishing their link with state legislatures and the union parliament. Key functional heads in the government administrative machinery, such as Deputy Commissioner, Collector, District Magistrate and other officials, be made a part of the Panchayati Raj system for ensuring cooperation and coordination between the district administration and the Panchayati Raj institutions. The National Development Council accepted the recommendations of the team in January 1959. However, it was of the view that the states be allowed to make alterations to the scheme taking into account the needs of local situation.

Rajasthan was the first to implement the scheme of 'Democratic Decentralisation' as recommended by Mehta Ccmmittee in October 1959 and create a Panchayati Raj system broadly resembling the model suggested by Balwant Rai Mehta Committee. However, the Government of Maharashtra did not accept this model. It appointed Naik Committee in 1961 to suggest a suitable model. On the recommendations of this committee, the state decided to make the district-level body – Zila Parishad – the unit of planning and implementation. All the developmental departments at the district level were put under its control. The Panchayat Samiti was made only a committee of the Zila Parishad. No changes were made regarding the all the levels. The Collector, MPs and MLAs were kept out of the Panchayati Raj system. Provision was made for the appointment of a senior IAS officer as the Chief Executive Officer of the Zila Parishad in Maharashtra.

Although most of the states opted for the Rajasthan model for their state, they ended up creating their own Panchayati Raj system to suit the unique requirements their rural population. This happened despite the fact that the study teams and the committees that were appointed by other states to evaluate their Panchayati Raj system mostly favoured the adoption of the Maharashtra model.

Post-Balwant Rai Mehta Committee Report

The Panchayati Raj system underwent three stages of evolution: development, stagnation and decay. In the 1960s, particularly during the Nehru era, the Panchayati Raj system witnessed development in almost all the states because of Nehru's strong commitment to make it a success. In the post-Nehru era, it became stagnant as Nehru's successors did not share his enthusiasm towards making Panchayati Raj a strong system of self-governance at the rural level. Later on, the Panchayati Raj lost its authority and power with increasing hostility from both bureaucracy and political leadership, poor quality of leadership in Panchayati Raj institutions, gradual erosion of powers, lack of financial resources, endemic factionalism, conflict between officials and non-officials, apathy of masses and failure of the state governments to hold elections in time.

When the Janata government came to power at the centre in 1977, it appointed a high-powered committee on Panchayati Raj under the leadership of Ashok Mehta, popularly known as Ashok Mehta Committee, for revitalising the Panchayati Raj system. The committee not only recommended constitutional status for the Panchayati Raj institutions but also suggested its restructuring by establishing a two-tier system with the Zila Parishad (the district-level body) at the top and Mandal Panchayat (for a group of villages) at the bottom. It recommended the abolition of Panchayat Samiti and village Panchayat. The committee further recommended more powers and resources for the Panchayati Raj institutions. In place of indirect elections, it favoured direct election. However, before the Janata government could take any action on the report of the committee, it had to quit owing to split in the party in 1979. Indira Gandhi-led Congress government which came to power in 1980 shelved the report.

The Pre-73rd Amendment Phase

The roles of the Left Front government of West Bengal which came into power in 1977 and the Janata government of Karnataka which assumed office in 1983 deserve to be written in golden letters in the history of Panchayati Raj in India during the pre-73rd Amendment phase. The Left Front government not only made institutional changes in the Panchayati Raj system of West Bengal by making amendments in the existing statue in 1978 but also introduced radical land reforms for ensuring genuine decentralisation of powers. Provisions were made for direct elections at all the three levels. The Panchayati Raj institutions were not only given large powers but also assigned the requisite finances through government grants. The government involved them in the implementation of all the schemes and programmes of the central and the state governments for rural development. It also goes to the credit of the Left Front government that it always conducted Panchayati Raj elections in time.

The Janata government of Karnataka also revitalised the Panchayati Raj system of the state in 1983 by genuine devolution of powers and functions. It restructured it on the model suggested by Ashok Mehta Committee report and created directly bodies like Zila Parishad and Mandal Panchayats. Karnataka took the lead in the empowerment of women by reserving 25 per cent seats for them. It also took the lead in the empowerment of scheduled castes and scheduled tribes by giving them reservations based on their proportion in the general population. The chairperson and deputy chairpersons of Zila Parishad were given the salary and status of a minister of state and deputy minister, respectively. The responsibility of making and implementing plans was given to the Zila Parishad. The Mandal Panchayat was made an implementing body.

The 73rd Amendment Phase

The 73rd Amendment of the Indian Constitution (1992) was a watershed mark in the history of Panchayati Raj in India. It was designed to fulfil the strong and long-felt need to accord constitutional status to the system. Ashok Mehta Committee Report (1978), as has already been mentioned, was the first to make this recommendation. L.M. Singhvi Committee Report (1987) also advocated the same. A subcommittee of the Consultative Committee of the Parliament for the Ministry of Rural Development, which was constituted in 1989 under the chairmanship of P.K. Thungan, too stressed the need for giving constitutional support to the Panchayati Raj institutions. The success of the system in West Bengal and Karnataka also prompted the decision-makers to initiate action for strengthening the Panchayati Raj.

It was in this context that the Rajiv Gandhi government had moved the 64th Amendment Bill in 1987 to give a constitutional status to the Panchayati Raj system and remove inadequacies like 'failure to hold regular and periodic elections, prolonged suspension, inadequate representation to the weaker sections like the scheduled castes, scheduled tribes and women, lack of financial resources and inadequate devolution of powers and responsibilities on them'. The bill was passed by the Lok Sabha but failed to get the requisite two-third majority in Rajya Sabha, as the opposition parties suspected that the central government wanted to bypass the state governments by dealing directly with the leadership of Panchayati Raj to mobilise electoral support for the Congress. However, the Congress government headed by P.V. Narasimha Rao was able to get the 73rd Amendment (1992) enacted after building a consensus in its favour.

The 73rd Amendment in the Indian Constitution has not only given constitutional status to the Panchayati Raj but also removed its inadequacies mentioned earlier. It set up a uniform three-tier structure with directly elected members. One-third of the offices and membership were reserved for women. The scheduled castes and scheduled tribes were given reservation in offices and membership. The states were empowered to make reservations for other backward classes (OBC) as well corresponding to their proportion in the population in their respective states. The Panchayati Raj institutions have been given powers over 29 subjects listed in the 11th Schedule of the Constitution of India. The State Election Commissions have been empowered to conduct regular periodical elections and the State Finance Commissions were asked to ensure adequate provision of finances. The new Panchayati Raj thus became effective in all the states and union territories of India.

The Panchayati Raj system emerged after the 73rd Amendment to the Indian Constitution in 1992 and has a long history as discussed earlier in the chapter. The genesis of Panchayats can be traced to the ancient times. Despite some changes in their character in the Mughal era and centralisation of administration, they continued to enjoy considerable authority and autonomy even during the colonial period. The colonial administration, however, destroyed these institutions by introducing a highly centralised system of governance. However, financial compulsions forced the colonial administration to create village Panchayats as local self-government institutions. Thus, Panchayats acquired a democratic character in the postcolonial period as a result of the introduction of universal adult franchise. The implementation of Balwant Rai Mehta Committee report led to the creation of a three-tier structure of Panchayati Raj streamlining development administration in the 1960s. However, the system became weak and shallow without substance due to the erosion of its powers in the 1970s. The 73rd Amendment has revitalised the Panchayati Raj. It has not only resulted in strengthening the base of democracy in India but also led to the empowerment of women and weaker sections. However, the so-called empowerment was more a symbol or tokenism at best rather than a real effective measure because the negative life conditions remained, and continue to remain, largely unchanged. Nevertheless, it was a indeed major step in the right direction with great potential.

Origin of the Study Problem

With these summarised data, the problem arises whether the constitution, election and conduct of these Panchayati Raj institutions have attained the goals enshrined in the act itself. Have the bodies in the context of Rajasthan really been proven to be the third tier of federalism? Have they succeeded in exercising powers granted to them? Or are they merely acting as a dependent politico-administrative department of the government of Rajasthan? What is their actual status on an objective scale of measuring autonomy so that state government might take decisions concerning whether to grant more powers with the provision of an outline for some appropriate procedures to complete them? Whether the reservation granted to the SCs, STs, OBCs and women in the representation of the Panchayati Raj bodies has brought any change worth considering? All this should be tested on the actual experience of the participating and non-participating people living in countryside.

Wide Ambit of the Study

Obviously the ambit of the present study is not confined to the discipline of political science. It is connected with most of the disciplines of social sciences like sociology, economics, public administration and the like. The Panchayati Raj institution under the act aims at total transformation of the society, particularly its weaker sections like women, SCs, STs and OBCs. It aimed at determining to what extent social transformation, popularly known as 'social justice', has taken place? It specifically dealt with, and analyse the conditions of BPL families, strengthening the mechanism of granting loans and credits, distribution of seeds, fertilisers and so on to the small-scale farmers and the like. It was also interested in studying the skills, competences and experience of the officials, public servants and experts who were deputed to monitor the Panchayati Raj institutions. Some such matters were also helpful in the improvement of rural health and hygiene, culture, and upliftment and reduction in the level of migration to urban areas.

Review of Literature

Review of the literature related to Panchayati Raj in India in general and in Rajasthan in particular. Following works have been reviewed as under:

Dalit Women in Panchayati Raj System (M.C. Chalawadi and C.A. Somashekarappa, Prateek Prakashan, Jaipur, 2014), Dalit women constitute the lower segment of Indian society. They have been categorized as the most marginalized among the marginal groups. They are the worst victims of discrimination based on caste, gender and patriarchy. The 73rd Amendment to the Constitution has ensured the participation of women in general and dalit women in particular in the Panchayati Raj Institutions (PRIs) and other Local Self Governments (LSGs). It has given new lease of life to the women with political power which was a distant dream in the past.

But for the enactment of 73rd Amendment Act new vistas of political opportunities are created and political space for women has been opened up to operate in it as the fore-runners of the local community development. In view of this, a study on 'Dalit Women in Panchayat Raj System' has been undertaken to assess and evaluate the relevance and impact of the 73rd Amendment Act on the women in general and Dalit women in particular. In the present study the term dalit is used in the same sense of the parlance of social scientists as well as the literature professionals'. Recently the political authority has started using it to refer to the untouchable poor and niggard people of the Indian society.

This empirical study has been conducted in Koppal District of Karnataka State which is considered a backward district of Koppal in North Karnataka area. Koppal Constitute a part in Hyderabad Karnataka, the region which was covered under the rule of Nizarn of Hyderabad and consequently was pushed to the brink of bankruptcy of all kinds from which it could not come out even after sixty five years of independence. Considering this the government of India has recognized recently the region for a special attention to be provided under the constitutional amendment for its all-round development. This study is based on the details given by 165 dalit women members of Grama Panchayats (GPs).

Role of Women in Panchayati Raj Institutions (Chandrashekhar C. Banasode, Manas Publishers and Distributors, Jaipur 2012), the Balwant Rai Mehta Committee, headed by MP Balwant Rai Mehta was a committee appointed by the Government of India in January 1957 to examine the working of the Community Development Programme (1952) and the National Extension Service (1953) and to suggest measures for their better working. The recommendations of the committee were approved by NDC in January 1958 and this set the stage for the launching of Panchayati Raj Institutions throughout the country. The committee recommended the establishment of the scheme of 'democratic decentralisation' which finally came to be known as Panchayati Raj.

The Union Cabinet of the Government of India, on 27 August 2009, approved 50 per cent reservation for women in PRIs (Panchayati Raj Institutions). The Indian states which have already implemented 50 per cent reservation for women in PRIs are Madhya Pradesh, Bihar, Uttarakhand and Himachal Pradesh. As of

25 November 2011, the states of Andhra Pradesh, Chhatisgarh, Jharkhand, Kerala, Maharashtra, Orissa, Rajasthan and Tripura also reserve 50 per cent of their posts for women.

According to the Ministry of Panchayati Raj's mid-term appraisal of the 'State of the Panchayats 2006-07', 'No less than 10 lakh women are in our Panchayati Raj institutions, comprising 37 per cent of all those elected and rising to as high as 54 percent in Bihar, which has 50 per cent reservation for women'.

Increased political accountability to women comes out only from increasing their numbers amongst decision-makers, although this is necessary and important. It must also be linked to improved democratic governance overall, understood as inclusive, responsive and accountable management of public affairs.

The benchmark generally selected for evaluating women's participation in politics is their representation in term of numbers or percentages. This does not facilitate adequate understanding, because representation does not, in itself, constitute evidence of participation. Thus, several indicators have been identified for determining the status and quality of women participation in the local political process.

Decentralized Governance and Panchayati Raj, (K.K. Srivastava, Kalpaz Publications, New Delhi, 2011), the 73rd Amendment, has been hailed as a major landmark in the history of Local Self-Government in India. Some of the salient features of the Amendment are grant of constitutional status to PRIs, reservation of one third of seats for women in panchayat bodies, holding of elections to panchayats after every five years under the direct supervision of the Chief Electoral Officer, setting up of Finance Commission to review the financial position of panchayats.

In the context of reservation policy for women in Panchayati Raj Institutions, it becomes pertinent to analyse their socio-economic status along with political accountability which was entrusted by constitution to them. The present book is based on the study on decentralized governance and problems of elected women representatives in Panchayati Raj to explore the findings and make remedial measures, lest it should not be known as will-o'-the-wisp in the name of landmark constitutional amendment.

Women and Our Panchayati Raj System, (M.S. Kulhari, Neha Publishers and Distributors, New Delhi, 2011), the book, under review is an attempt to unveil the relationship between the political mobilisation at rural women and its impact on social justice with particular reference to their participation in Panchayati Raj institution.

The Landmark 73rd Amendment to the Constitution India has definitely empowered women in terms of numbers. From the minuscule figure of 2–4 per cent in most of the Indian states, the Amendment has for the time brought 33–40 percent rural women into the sphere of the decision-making process. But, being in large numbers is not enough as reservation provides only the possibility of a voice for women, it does not guarantee it. The awakening of women in India towards a society where justice and brotherhood prevail, can best be achieved by a women to women contact. Even though men have played a pioneering role in the case of women in India, their role has been effective bringing about constitution and legal changes in the status of women.

Women and Panchayati Raj (Ravi Goel, Sonali Publications, New Delhi, 2014), the Balwant Rai Mehta Committee, headed by MP Balwant Rai Mehta was a committee appointed by the Government of India in January 1957 to examine the working of the Community Development Programme (1952) and the National Extension Service (1953) and to suggest measures for their better working. The recommendations of the committee were approved by NDC in January 1958 and this set the stage for the launching of Panchayati Raj Institutions throughout the country. The committee recommended the establishment of the scheme of 'democratic decentralisation' which finally came to be known as Panchayati Raj.

The Union Cabinet of the Government of India, on 27 August 2009, approved 50 per cent reservation for women in PRIs (Panchayati Raj Institutions). The Indian states which have already implemented 50 per cent reservation for women in PRIs are Madhya Pradesh, Bihar, Uttarakhand and Himachal Pradesh. As of 25 November 2011, the states of Andhra Pradesh, Chhattisgarh, Jharkhand, Kerala, Maharashtra, Orissa, Rajasthan and Tripura also reserve 50 per cent of their posts for women.

According to the Ministry of Panchayati Raj's mid-term appraisal of the 'State of the Panchayats 2006–07', 'No less than 10 lakh women are in our Panchayati Raj institutions, comprising 37 per cent of all those elected and rising to as high as 54 percent in Bihar, which has 50 per cent reservation for women'.

Increased political accountability to women comes out only from increasing their numbers amongst decision-makers, although this is necessary and important. It must also be linked to improved democratic governance overall, understood as inclusive, responsive and accountable management of public affairs.

The benchmark generally selected for evaluating women's participation in politics is their representation in term of numbers or percentages. This does not facilitate adequate understanding, because representation does not, in itself, constitute evidence of participation. Thus, several indicators have been identified for determining the status and quality of women participation in the local political process.

Local Government (Jawahar Lal Gupta, Wisdom Press, New Delhi, 2013), in the era of globalization, liberalization and the revolution in information technology the present publication tries to locate local government in the expanding international network of public sector. The book introduces the reader to rural India and urbanization, systems of panchayati raj and its role in rural development. It discusses department of planning and panchayati raj, administration and development along with poverty, politics and panchayati raj. It is believed that the book is not only useful to the students but will also assist local government practitioners, policy makers and social scientists in their thinking with practical guidance for implementing a local government policy.

Rural Women and Panchayati Raj (Manohar Lal Tomar, A.K. Publications, Delhi, 2013), the book has been divided into eight chapters including bibliography and index and each chapter deals with a different topic. A number of topics have been included in those chapters which are more common in the syllabi of different Indian universities. This book has been written in a manner that they can be easily grasped by the students. The book will be useful not only for the students but also for the academicians, lawyers, social workers and others interested in rural women and panchayati raj.

The work under review, *Panchayati Raj in Scheduled Areas* (authored by P.S.K. Menon and Bakshi D. Sinha, published by Concept Publishing Company, New Delhi, 2003), entrusted to the

Institute of Social Sciences, New Delhi, was undertaken from May 1999 for a period of ten months with the following specific objectives:

1. to examine whether the Panchayats in the scheduled areas in the states of Andhra Pradesh, Bihar, Gujarat, Himachal Pradesh, Madhya Pradesh, Maharashtra, Orissa and Rajasthan have been endowed with such powers and authority as may be necessary to enable them to function as institutions of self-government, as envisaged in the 1996 Act, with critical analysis;
2. to study the nature, functions and the role of Gram Sabha to discharge functions specified in the 1996 Act;
3. to suggest measures to achieve the goals envisaged in extending the provisions of Part IX of the Indian Constitution; and
4. to study all other related issues vis-à-vis, Tribal Sub-Plan mechanism, administration and so on, in relation to Panchayati Raj in scheduled areas and make recommendations.

In order to achieve the above objectives, the study critically analyses and evaluates the implementation of the provisions of the Extension Act, 1996 and Conformity State Panchayat Acts, with special reference to the powers of Gram Sabha. It was based on field studies in the states of Maharashtra and Orissa and some of the Panchayats in Rajasthan. The anguish and helplessness in realising that at the grass-roots level matters have not improved, as envisaged, can be expressed both in mild and strong words. The authors observed that out of the eight dates, the provisions of seven states Panchayat Acts in the Scheduled Areas (except Bihar) have been amended in pursuance of the Extension Act of 1996. It may be added that Conformity Panchayat Acts of Maharashtra and Orissa are more or less in conformity with the Extension Act. In short, the functions, powers and responsibilities specified in the Extension Act have been assigned to either 'Gram Sabha and Panchayat' or 'Gram Sabha or Panchayat', except importantly the one relating to following the pattern of the Sixth Schedule in administrative arrangements at the district level.

The Rajasthan Ordinance lacks direction and does not fully reflect the contents and spirit of the Extension Act. All these aspects have been evaluated in this study. Chapter 1 gives the historical perspective; Chapter 2 discusses the implementation of the

Panchayats (Extension to the Scheduled Areas) Act, 1996, with field study results in Maharashtra and Orissa and to a limited extent in Rajasthan; Chapter 3 narrates the comparative analysis of the implementation of the provisions in the Extension Act, 1996, and Conformity State Panchayat Act; Chapter 4 contains conclusions and recommendations.

Panchayat Dilemma People's Power and Poverty (K.K. Sinha, Serials Publications, 2007) is divided into 14 chapters: 1. Panchayat Models in Bihar; 2. Panchayat Elections, 2001: Emerging Scene; 3. The New Bihar Panchayati Raj Act, 1993: A District-Centric System; 4. Task before the Bihar State Finance Commission; 5. Planning from Below; 6. Decentralising Planning; 7. Towards Village Planning; 8. A Model of Spatial Village Planning; 9. The Village Trinity; 10. A Village Plan Model: Antyodaya; 11. A Gramdan Model of Panchayats; 12. Rural Poverty – A Poverty of Governance (An Annexure to Section-11); 13. Elected Representatives versus Officials; 14. Summary and Recommendations and a detailed list of appendices and list of tables have also been given.

People, power and poverty lie at the bottom of democracy, but the system operates from the top. This creates the Panchayat dilemma. Panchayat is said to be the god that failed, but it is also true that it is the last hope of the poor in the villages. Fifty years of planning in India could only serve the rich, and the villages could not organise themselves to claim their share in the national wealth. Generally condemned as inferior groups unworthy of governance, they were never allowed to play a role necessary for their upkeep and development.

However, with a past usage in Bihar, Panchayats have as yet not regained the status of self-governance. A centralist state would not like them to grow except as dependencies. But circumstances force the huge nation-state to allow sharing from below, especially in such functions which are strictly of local concern, lest crimes and corruption overpower the poor. A top-down governance may see the dead animals from the skies like the vultures but cannot see the small ants on the twigs trying to get their food. It is here that Panchayats are seen as micro units of human management at the grass-root.

The Constitutional Amendment of 1993 has hardly brought about any change in the status of village Panchayats, except for mandating elections and creating election and finance commissions. Elections are not sufficient conditions for regenerating Gram Panchayats, but finances do raise basic issues. Unfortunately this has never been properly conceived.

The real danger is the dominance of the district Panchayats to hold the rope and to work as a proxy of the state government under its district officials. The present mechanism of managing district development through DRDAs and DPDCs is a clear example of this. This does not change the character of the village Panchayats from that which the British created. As was the case then, so also now, districts are chosen to administer land revenue and later Zila Boards are supposed to assist them. It is now difficult for the Indian government to go further down from the districts to villages which work as revenue units, called 'Halkas' of about 10,000 population where the Gram Panchayats worked as collection agents. The nostalgia of district governance is a hard nut to crack now.

Flow of village resources to towns and impoverishment of the villages was what has been happening since the British rule. This affected the self-sufficiency of villages and deprived them even of small needs. What ruled in villages are government brokers and Mahajans as the new financiers of village life. Gandhi brought the village situation to light when the British rule stifled the structure in favour of towns as seats of administration and courts. Village poverty could then be taken up only by a Panchayat order, which could revive a will to fight against tyranny, not only of the British imperialism but also of the primitive accumulation of wealth, by the local lords. Gandhi had therefore a modest picture of village Panchayats just providing self-grown food and clothes, a school and a small dispensary, some trees and uncontaminated air, water and roads. The small villages are easily capable of being ordered and organised. Thus, the Gandhian concept of revival of Panchayats was not one of Sanghas or republics at the district levels but of neighbourhoods with widening circles for only fixed to their village roots.

What would create a movement for such small republics was surely some sort of non-violent anarchism against the power-wielding state. Panchayats as effective units must have a supportive government with the will to dilute its power in favour of the village government. This should guide any revival scheme of Panchayats as development units. If not, this will close the possibilities of smaller village groups to have any identity of their own except as commission agents for collecting lands revenue. With such a legacy, the present state governments, even after abolition of the Zamindari system and reduced and marginalised land revenues as a source of state income, do not want to share land management and reforms with villages, thus making them defunct in matters of functions which properly belonged to them. For want of involvement, the village Panchayats feel completely non-participative and moribund.

Bureaucracy at the Grassroots Level in India (Anupama Singh, Kanishka Publishers, 2006) provides that poverty in India, especially in rural areas, has persisted in spite of the continuous efforts made by the government under various plans. There is an urgency to analyse the policies and programmes so as to evolve an effective future policy for rural development.

The effective implementation of rural development schemes is dependent on an efficient bureaucracy at the grassroots and a strong correlation between successful programmes, bureaucracy and people's active participation. These are some of the areas needed to be explored. The main objectives of this study include the following: to study the socioeconomic profile of the bureaucrats and the beneficiaries; to examine the structural deficiencies in the administrative setup at the block level, and in recruitment, promotion and training; to examine the role of bureaucrats with regard to policies, planning and implementation; to pinpoint bureaucratic values, role perceptions, attitudes, orientation motivation and behaviours of officials involved; to assess the performance of development bureaucracy and impact of rural development programmes; to assess the role and participation of citizens in rural development programme.

Certain points are given for improving the atmosphere created while implementing the rural development programmes and behavioural traits of block bureaucracy as well as attitudes of people towards bureaucracy. The official at the lowest echelons should have a high degree of positive attitude towards responsibilities at their work place. Professionalism in officials involved with rural development can be achieved by making the decisions of the administrative machinery compatible with the objectives of rural development.

Rural Women Empowerment (ed.) (S.B. Verma, S.K. Jiloka and K.J. Kushwah, Deep and Deep Publications, 2006) portrays the patterns of decision-making by rural women and their participation in farm and home activities besides other socioeconomic pursuits. This has a definite impact on agricultural production, stabilisation of population policies, social reforms, entrepreneurial activities and so on. The book raises several issues and suggests ways for removing general bias and women's empowerment. The study calls for appropriate extension package to rural communities, including in farming and other sectors, specifically targeting rural women.

The contents of this book include the following:

Part 1: Women Empowerment: Rural Women in Dynamics of Agriculture and Food Security; Towards Technological Empowerment of Women Farmers; Role of Women in Livestock Farming; Invisible Activities of Rural Women; Burgeoning Population: Alarming Signals; Social Development of Rural Women in India; Rural Women's Empowerment; Rural Women Entrepreneurs in the Wave of Economic Development; Need for Developing Rural Women Entrepreneurs; Women in Local Self-governance; Empowerment of Women Representatives in Panchayati Raj; Rural women in Integrated Wasteland Development Project; Empowering Rural Women through Watershed Project; Empowering Rural Women to Give Greater Control over Natural Resources; Women and Peace; Rural Women in Agriculture; Rural Women and Poverty Alleviation.

Part 2: Child Labour Preventive Strategies and Eradication: Child Labour and Preventive Strategies; Child Labour; Panchayats and Child Labour; Practical Solutions to the Child Labour Problem; Child Labour Eradication; India's Tryst with Future; Protecting Children's Rights; Dimensions of Juvenile Problems and Juvenile Justice; Child Labour Is a Disgrace to mankind.

Part 3: Employment Generation: Rural Employment; Gainful Employment for Rural Women; Employment Generation through Community Polytechnics; Strategies for Rural Employment; Rural Employment Generation; Rural Employment and People's Participation; Rural Employment; Employment Generation in Small

Units; Information Technology in Rural Employment; Self-employment in Food Industry; Employment Generation through Forest-based Village Industries.

Local Governance in India: Ideas, Challenges and Strategies (ed. T.M. Joseph, Concept Publishing, 2007) provides that this compendium of 28 papers makes a performance appraisal of the local governance mechanism in India for the first 10 years of its mandatory existence. It throws light on the ideas behind these institutions, the challenges they face and the strategies to contain them. Attempting at understanding local governance, the contributors deliberate on decentralisation and development, people's participation in local governance and the emerging paradigm of local governance.

The book is divided in the following sections addressing a range of topics:

Section 1: Understanding Local Governance: Democracy and Decentralisation; Gandhi and the Contemporary Discourse on Decentralisation; Decentralised Governance: Looking Back and Forth; Four Fs of Decentralisation; Panchayats: Relevance and Potentials; Earth Democracy, Living Democracy: Rebuilding Security in an Age of Insecurity.

Section 2: Decentralisation and Development: Panchayati Raj Institutions and Human Rights in India; Decentralisation and its Impact on Health in India: A Review of Evidence; Sensitising Grassroots Leadership on Health Issues: Experiences of a Pilot TV Project; Rural Poverty, Local Democratic Institutions, and Sustainable Development in India under Globalisation: Issues and Strategies; The New Governance Paradigm: Its meaning and Some Implications for Development; Decentralisation, Employment and Enterprises.

Section 3: People's Participation in Local Governance: From Kallesseri to the People's Plan Campaign: Issues in Governance; Emergence of New Institutions Through Participatory Democracy: An Evaluation of Kerala Experiment; Decentralisation in Kerala: Problems and Prospects; The Institution of Grama Sabha and the Creation of Social Capital in Kerala; Social Capital in Kerala: Mixed Evidence from a Village Panchayat; People's Planning and Kerala's Agriculture; The Missed Linkages.

Section IV – Local Governance at Work: Dynamics and Challenges: The Functioning of Grama Panchayats in Karnataka; E-Governance at the Grassroots: The Case of Belandur Grama Panchayat in Karnataka; The Role of Panchayats and Bureaucracy in Rural Development; Differences and Identities: Women and Political Participation; Party Politics and Functioning of Panchayati Raj Institutions in a Tamil Nadu Village.

Section V: The Emerging Paradigm of Local Governance: The Panchayat's Raj over Global Capital; Democratic Institutions in the Water Sector of Kerala: A Case Study about Water Users Associations and Participatory Irrigation Management from Kerala Community Irrigation Project; Disaster Management and Role of Local Institutions in India; Synergetic Action for Participatory Development; Paradigm Shift in Local Governance: The Synergy between State and Non-state Actors in Kerala.

Governance at Grassroots Level in India (ed.) (S.S. Chahar, Kanishka Publishers, 2005) is an edited work comprising 29 chapters (research papers by various senior bureaucrats, professors and scholars). The book talks about decentralised governance at the grassroots level in India. Local bodies have been constitutionalised through the historical enactment of the 73rd and 74th constitutional amendments, and, thus, the Indian political system is gravitating towards the three-tier federation in India, establishing a third tier (district as third tier of governance). A revolutionary step has been taken in the social, cultural and political scenario to transform Indian society through empowerment of and reservations for weaker sections and formation of district planning committees that leads to planning from below, as doing so will pragmatise the planning process along the lines of policies and directives from the Administrative Reforms Commission. However, even after the passing of a decade since constitutional status was accorded to local bodies their work continues to be riddled with flaws which happen due to lack of political will and shortage of well-trained and dedicated staff at the local level. Thus, democracy or self-governance at the grassroots level has become a crucial area of debate and discussion in both academic and administrative circles, and the present work is an outcome of such debate. The emphasis is on issues and areas pertaining to the actual working of local bodies at the grassroots level. Thus, this book brings together a number of research papers that address the working of local bodies in the wake of the 73rd and 74th Amendments.

Women in Panchayati Raj Institutions (Amal Mandal, Kanishka Publishers, 2003) reveals that with the statutory reservation provision more than one million rural women have now assumed Panchayat seats as members and one-third of them hold the position of chairperson in almost all states and union territories. The induction of women in Panchayat institutions is in sharp contrast to their representation in other political strata as well as in the earlier versions of Panchayat institutions. The very integration of women has evoked conflicts and drama: elation, euphoria particularly in print and public pronouncements on one hand and apprehension and even enmity in social and political parlance on the other.

This empirical study assesses the social and political background of female members in one district of West Bengal, evaluates various facets of their participation and role performance in Panchayat institutions, ascertains the nature of their social acceptability, and informs both the positive and negative aspects of reservation policy for women. The study has brought forth few exclusive and absorbing features: female members neither lack capacity nor do they fall short in demonstrating leadership qualities, and their participation in Panchayats' administrative processes at both formal and informal levels is no less effective compared to male counterparts.

The study's main contention after its appraisal of female members' performance in Panchayats and expectations for women's empowerment is that any well-meaning measure on the part of the government to add teeth to the initiatives targeting women empowerment at the rural level have to take into cognisance the current social situation for women where they are always expected to play a subordinate role to men, the political dynamics, and the functional scope of Panchayats, with all of this not being pointedly propitious for women to make any real, tangible and sustainable progress and get a level-playing field in an otherwise male-dominated society.

Major Issues in New Panchayati Raj System (ed.) (G. Palanithurai, B. Dwarak and S. Narayanaswamy, Kanishka Publishers, 1997) is an edited volume and provides that decentralisation of power is not a mere incident in the political history of India. It is a global movement to release the individual energy for constructive purposes in order to usher in growth and development. The 73rd Constitutional Amendment Act is a consequence of the global movement. It is not for local activities of the citizenry. It is meant to globalise the local activities for benefit of the population at the grassroots; it was instituted to protect the people at the grassroots level and their environment from the exploitation by the big powers.

The enactment of the 73rd Constitutional Amendment Act and the subsequent state-wise Panchayati Raj Acts in India have brought to frontline the significance of the study of grass-root democratic processes. This change in the Indian political system is the result of a growing conviction that merely a big government cannot achieve growth and development in a society without people's willingness and active participation. The turn of events in the provincial polity, administration and society after the introduction of the new act needs an in-depth probe. Of course, Western scholars have paid considerable attention to this subject and have developed theoretical premises in the decentralisation of power and development of the Third World. Yet the experience of the past three years at the grass-root level since the passing of the 73rd Constitutional Amendment Act indicates that there is still a score of problems and hurdles to be dealt with.

As regards giving effect to the implementation of the Panchayati Raj Act, the Tamil Nadu government is in the company of only a handful of state governments which are doing so for reasons best known to themselves. It is with an effort to attempt a break of this impasse, the Gandhigram Rural Institute under the auspices of the Department of Political Science and Development Administration has taken series of steps in sensitising the intellectuals, motivating the voluntary sector and mobilising people by publishing periodicals and organising workshops, seminars, conferences, awareness camps and training camps to train master trainers with the involvement of major NGOs in this region. To some extent this kind of initiatives kept the issue alive among the people in Tamil Nadu. National-level bodies like CAPART, Rajiv Gandhi Foundation, Department of Rural Development, University Grants Commission, and Ministry of Youth through its organisations have helped us both materially and morally to organise such programmes in this province.

Empowering People, Grassroot Organisations and Rural Development (Yatish Mishra, Kanishka Publishers, 2002) provides that right from the time India became independent, there have been efforts to bring people closer to administration at various levels. An impetus was given to these efforts in the mid-1980s when a call was given to empower the institutions and governance at the grass-root level. The culmination of these efforts was the 73rd Amendment Act to the Constitution. The present work seeks to assess the efficacy of these endeavours and the various stages of development and evolution of these institutions broadly known as Panchayati Raj bodies.

The book probes into the reality of and achievements behind this process of administrative decentralisation and grassroots empowerment mainly in relation to the rural and local bodies. The aim of this study is to analyse and understand the role of the grass-roots institutions and their progress towards achieving the cherished goal of good governance.

The year 1991 has a special significance in the political and economic history of India. It was the year when the union government under the leadership of the then Prime Minister, P.V. Narasimha Rao, triggered a phase of transition by introducing the concept of liberalisation and globalisation into the 40-year-old economic policy. It effected a radical change in the economic policy which had remained by and large unchanged since 1951–1952, the year of the commencement of the First Five Year Plan.

The policy adopted in June 1991 was commonly known as the New Economic Policy, under which the government took a series of corrective measures aimed at improving the efficiency and productivity of the administrative machinery, the industrial sector, and agriculture and putting the economy back on the path of sustainable growth with equity and social justice. The measures were taken in the midst of a severe fiscal and external imbalance which had put the country on the verge of collapse.

Even though the liberalisation and globalisation of economy was claimed to be a good concept by the champions of the new economic policy and considered as the need of the hour, particularly in the backdrop of the failure of the controlled and government-guided economy as well as an unprecedented growth of the liberalised economies all over the world, it is clear that it has so far remained ineffective in the Indian situation as far as poverty alleviation is concerned. Given the intrinsic and in-built limitations of the Indian economy and the social system, decentralisation is the most suitable thing to do. The emphasis of the policy for overall growth and development should be about placing greater faith and, accordingly, greater responsibilities on the Panchayati Raj institutions (PRIs) and at the same time gradually reducing the external support and indirect control.

The Panchayati Raj institutions that work at the grassroots level of the social system are a practical and tested form of the decentralisation of the policy and the growth and development machinery. Decentralisation is pursued in reaction to the technical failure of comprehensive national development planning of the poor impact of multisectoral, macroeconomic development planning. It is often seen as a way of increasing the ability of government officials, which enables them to obtain better and correct information regarding local or regional problems. It not only helps them in preparing proper plans for the respective areas but also their proper and effective implementation. It prepares the officials to react more promptly against any unanticipated problems that arise during the implantation of programmes.

In many countries, decentralisation is seen as a method of mobilising public support the various national development planning programmes, and management of such programmes supposedly promotes national unity by giving groups in different regions in a country a greater ability to participate in planning and decision-making and thus increases their share in maintaining political stability.

In countries where the capacity of administration is rated very low decentralisation is sometimes seen as a means of creating a larger number of skilled administrators and managers.

Decentralisation is an ideology associated with objectives such as self-reliance, democratic decision-making, public participation in government and accountability of officials towards citizens. Thus, decentralisation is a political decision and its implementation reflects the political dynamics of a country.

Very little research has been done in the socioeconomic, political and physical aspects of decentralisation. This is the reason very little is known about factors associated with government pressures to develop planning and administrative responsibilities.

Social Justice and Panchayati Raj (B.M. Verma, Mittal Publications, 2002) provides that social justice in Panchayati Raj has undergone a major change of direction in light of the 73rd Amendment Act, 1992. In the backdrop of social transformation, social justice in all its dimensions, that is, fairness, entitlement, equality and impartiality, has been operationalised through democratic decentralisation. The study analyses the process of political re-structuring and the institutional changes in the new paradigm of development and their impact on the efforts towards preservation of human rights and sustaining functional democracy. In order to find out the gap between policy formation and policy implementation, the operational dynamics of the New Panchayati Raj Act has been studied. Furthermore, to achieve the goal of distributive justice, both structural and contextual factors need to be taken into cognizance while the government tries to revitalise the power devolution in favour of weaker sections and this of course calls for the observance of rule of law. For developing a sound substructure of democratic government supported by social development, it is necessary to reinvent a new democratic system that accords significance to both the government and the governed making them equal partners.

The author attempts to test the implicit operation of self-rule in federal polity in the quest of the general investigation of not only the twin policy goals – 'growth with social justice' and 'equitable distribution' – but also the anticipated form and content of democratic vision in politics. The study analyses the performance of bureaucrats and political executives operating at the local level in programmes aimed at the eradication of poverty coupled with efforts made towards designing an integrated system of decentralised administration. The study also suggests new measures for effective development and management of Panchayati Raj institutions. Policymakers, planners and administrators will find this study highly valuable.

S. Baluchamy's *Panchayati Raj Institutions* (Mittal Publications, 2004) provides that the Panchayati Raj system in India has come into existence through a long process of evolution. The Panchayati Raj institutions began to be gradually democratised in structure and were empowered to undertake increasing duties and responsibilities in local affairs, including civil service. Decentralisation is the only way of ensuring radical transformation in self-governance through democratic process.

The Gram Sabha is an institutional form of participatory democracy. In reality, however, it continues to remain defunct even after the introduction of the New Panchayati Raj, with the same old tale of woes, like absence of power, lack of awareness, popular apathy, dearth of enthusiasm and extinction of the glow of freedom. Rejuvenating the Gram Sabha calls for appropriate interventions by concerned experts.

This book is an in-depth study of Panchayati Raj institutions in one of the districts (Dindigul) of Tamil Nadu, India. The study focuses on the knowledge of the Panchayati Raj system; opinion on the adequacy of devolution of powers, resources, decision-making and so on; attitude and support of the state government; nature of the role or the attitude of elected representatives in their work; training for functionaries of PRIs, including their needs, assessment and fulfilment, qualities of leadership and their influence on the functioning of the Panchayati Raj system; reservation for women and scheduled castes; supportive agencies; participatory democracy; and the role and performance of the Gram Sabha. The study is based on personal discussions, observations and available documents.

Sisodia's *Functioning of Panchayati Raj System* (ed.) (Y.S. Sisodia, Rawat Publications, 2005) provides that Panchayati Raj's performance and impact has been a matter of debate and speculation. In almost all states, two or three rounds of elections for Panchayats have been completed. The sizeable presence of underprivileged and poor at the grassroots-level political institutions is a landmark development in the changing dynamics of rural politics. It is also a matter of serious debate as to how this excluded lot after their inclusion in active politics at grassroots would effectively tackle local power equation and set the agenda for development.

Responses from the state governments towards the implementation of Panchayat Raj varied significantly, and it is very difficult to arrive at a consensus or a concrete view about this issue merely on the basis of their functioning during the past one decade or so. A review of the functioning of Panchayat Raj puts forward a mixed scenario with positive and negative characteristics, and there is enough evidence for both positive aspects and impediments and shortcomings; nevertheless, there is room for hope that the significance of Panchayati Raj will improve potentially in the years to come and self-governance at the grassroots level will be strengthened.

This book is divided into six sub-themes: (1) Structure and Functioning of PRIs; (2) Marginalised Sections and Their Participation; (3) Institutional Mechanism and Grassroots Decision-making; (4) Natural Resource Management and PRIs, NGOs; (5) Panchayats and Capacity-building Initiatives; and (6) Decentralised Planning and Finance. It will interest a wide range of readers, including researchers, bureaucrats, policymakers, planners and those concerned with the plight of tribals.

Dutta's *Decentralisation, Participation and Governance* (ed.) (P. Duta, Kalpaz Publications, 2006) is a collection of ten articles focusing on the key issues of local good governance in India in general and West Bengal, in particular. Good governance has been viewed from different perspectives. The World Bank which has popularised the concept in recent times defines good governance as 'the manner in which power is exercised in the management of the country's economic and social resources for development'. In the perception of World Bank there are four major components, namely, public sector management, accountability, legal framework of development, and information and transparency. Beyond this narrow technocratic view, there is another perspective propounded by the *Human Development Report*, 2002, where the emphasis is on democratic governance. This broader human development perspective guides the concept of good governance as developed in this book. The first article seeks to explore analytical and methodological issues in the context of local politics and decentralisation aimed at poverty reduction. It attempts to identify and examine the linkages between local political decentralisation and poverty reduction policies and discusses how to study and analyse them. Although there are references to international experiences, care has been taken to relate the issues to situations in India. This paper was presented at the Conference on Local Politics, Poverty and

Decentralisation organised by the Danish Institute of International Studies at Copenhagen in July 2004.

Democratic decentralisation in India received a new lease of life following two major amendments of the Constitution of India in the early 1990s. We have in India today a new crop of Panchayat and municipal bodies armed with constitutional sanction. As expected in a country of India's size and diversity local self-government experience cannot be even and uniform. There are only a few states where the institutions of local self-government have been working relatively well. However, the overall experience has not been encouraging. There is a view that decentralisation has derailed. While such an extreme view needs to be subjected to scrutiny, there is no doubt that there are challenges to democratic decentralisation in India which have been discussed in Chapter 2. The chapter makes a modest attempt to conceptualise the challenges largely under the framework of political will. It examines the gravity of challenges coming from within and without and their impact on the system of democratic decentralisation. All the arguments have been supported by facts and figures collected from both primary and secondary sources.

The third chapter in the book reviews the policies and programmes relating to the amelioration of urban poverty in India from a historical perspective. Poverty has been understood not in terms of pure economic sense where the emphasis is on income and consumption but in terms of livelihoods, resources, knowledge and rights. The chapter has touched on the impact of structural adjustment programme in the context of poverty reduction programmes initiated at the instance of the Indian State. It has been argued that diversity and complexity of urban poverty require multipronged intervention and at different levels. A case has been made out for development and promotion of people's organisations to deal with poverty issues. The chapter starts with providing a short account of the basic features of urban poverty in India and goes on to discuss the programmes and processes of the involvement of local bodies and stakeholders in the reduction of poverty.

West Bengal is one of the very few states where the Panchayati Raj institutions were given a fresh lease of life by the Left Front government even before the amendment of Constitution in 1993. Panchayati Raj system is guided by the political philosophy of the

Left Front government, although the act was framed by the Congress government. It is true that quite a few amendments have been made to make the act conform not only to the needs of the constitutional amendment but also to the ideological and programmatic commitments of the Left Front. The biggest partner of the Left Front is CPI(M), which adheres to political philosophy rooted in Marxism-Leninism. There is a strong view that the macropolitical stability in West Bengal can largely be attributed to the success of the Panchayati raj institutions in the state. It has been argued that CPI(M) has carved out a pattern of political organisation in rural West Bengal, rare in India, namely, that of involving a penetration in the countryside without depending on larger landowners. The fourth chapter attempts a critical appraisal of the working of Panchayati Raj institutions and the role of other organisations in the implementation of rural development programmes. One of the objectives of the Left Front government is to mobilise the masses. In rural areas Panchayats have become major instruments of mass mobilisation. There is elaborate discussion about this role of Panchayats and their impact in this regard.

Gram Sansad is a new institutional incarnation in West Bengal whose aim is to mobilise masses formally as well as informally. The 73rd Amendment of the Constitution provides for Gram Sabha to ensure participation of villagers in their governance and development. The West Bengal Panchayat Act was amended in 1992 to set up Gram Sabha at the electoral constituency level. However, when the Constitution was amended to create Gram Sabha, the state government decided to constitute another body called Gram Sansad and the Gram Sabha was reconstituted to exist at the level of the Gram Panchayat in terms of the constitutional mandate. West Bengal is one the few states in the country where this kind of institution has been working for some time. Participatory democracy in rural West Bengal examines the working of this body in the state. It also throws some light on the participatory decentralised planning in the state as it started in the form of pilot schemes in selected districts.

Urban governance under the Left Front regime in West Bengal has received a lot of political and administrative attention. The West Bengal Municipal Act has been acclaimed as the best municipal legislation in the country. The Model Municipal Act drafted at the initiative of the Government of India draws heavily on the West Bengal Act and the experiences. The sixth chapter seeks to present an overview of the perspective and practices in municipal administration in West Bengal. The article explains the backdrop and emergence of new institutional mechanisms in the field of urban governance. Attempt has also been made to capture the functioning of these institutional instruments in the next two chapters. The 74th Amendment of the Constitution institutionalises citizen's participation through Ward Committees in urban local bodies with 300,000 or more population. While there are many states that have not yet formed Ward Committees, Ward Committees in most of the states seem to be units of administrative decentralisation rather than those of democratic decentralisation. Against this background the West Bengal government had decided to set up Ward Committees in all urban localities irrespective of the size of population. Chapter 7 analyses the working of Ward Committees in West Bengal in light of the empirical study conducted by the author. The study while bringing out the strengths and weaknesses suggests steps that may be taken to improve the functioning of Ward Committees. The study was funded by UNICEF and Institute of Local Government and Urban Studies, Government of West Bengal. West Bengal was the first state in India to introduce a cabinet form of government in municipal administration in 1994, the idea of which was conceived in 1967 at the sixth conference of the Municipal Corporations in Delhi. In 1988 Maharashtra adopted the model in two cities on a trial basis. Madhya Pradesh followed suit in 1998. However, Maharashtra has gone back to the original arrangement. In Madhya Pradesh, the system is yet to gather adequate momentum. The Mayor-in-Council system has been working in all the corporations in West Bengal. The experience of working of the Mayor-in-Council system in Kolkata Corporation has been dealt with in Chapter 8. Incidentally, the Left Front had been at the helm of affairs when the system started. Later on, Trinamool Congress captured the seat of power, but the Left Front remained in power in Writers Buildings. The interesting experience of these two different phases has been narrated in this chapter.

The idea of Metropolitan Planning Committee in India was conceived by the 74th Amendment of the Constitution as an instrument for the preparation of draft development plan for the metropolitan area as a whole. The state government has been entrusted with the task of framing suitable legislation for this purpose. West Bengal was the first state in India to constitute Kolkata Metropolitan Planning Committee (KMPC) in 2001. Chaired by the chief minister, this body of 60 members has been working for some time. In order to help the KMPC prepare the draft development plan, five sectoral committees have also been constituted. Chapter 9 provides an overview of the structure and processes of KMPC.

The last chapter, though a bit different from all other chapters in the book, fits in well with the central theme of the book. Joint forest management in now widely accepted as a new institutional mode for better, efficient and meaningful management of forests. West Bengal, again, has played a pioneering role in this regard. It was awarded international recognition for its performance in this field. The author did a study on the working of the joint forest management programme in West Bengal at the instance of the Forest Department, Government of West Bengal. The findings of the study have been presented in this chapter.

Palanithurai's *Dynamics of New Panchayati Raj System in India: Panchayati Raj and Multi-level Planning* (Vol. 5, ed.) (G. Palanithurai, Concept Publishing, 2006) is a multivolume series that evaluates the functioning of Panchayati Raj system in India from political, sociological, legal, anthropological and economic perspectives in light of the 73rd Constitutional Amendment. Giving an in-depth understanding of the status of Panchayati Raj in different states, it addresses a wide range of issues concerning empowerment of women and dalits, multilevel planning, finance, people's participation, state–local community relationship, capacity building of Panchayat functionaries, sociopolitical and economic transformation, common resources management, and leadership in Panchayati Raj institutions.

This volume attempts to examine the process and practice of development planning at grassroots level in India with the participation of the people. Touching upon the basics of devolution, namely, transfer of powers, functions and finance in the states, it addresses the bottlenecks involved in the process. The contributors also discuss the relevance or regional information system and development indices in Panchayati Raj, the gap between district planning practice and theory, biomass assessment and optimisation model for energy planning, and the problems in the implementation of decentralisation. The case studies of micro-level planning from the states of Tamil Nadu, Karnataka and Rajasthan make part of the discussion as well. The book will be of great use for researchers, policymakers and development workers.

Mitra et al.'s *Decentralisation, Planning and Panchayati Raj* (S.N. Mishra, S. Mishra and C. Pal, Mittal Publications, 2000) posits that decentralisation of planning process of late has become a matter of worldwide concern. Decentralisation through involvement of local-level representative institutions in the formulation of plans for development as well as their implementation is advocated in the interest of efficient utilisation of resources and for ensuring more equitable sharing of benefits from development. Thus, decentralised planning is not a new concept for India. Although introduced in 1951, it was limited to sectoral programmes at lower administrative levels rather than comprehensive planning for units below the centre or states.

After becoming a part of the Constitution (1992), the planning process at the district levels or below has achieved more significance. This volume analyses the concept and strategy of planning and centralised versus decentralised planning and attempts to test empirically the working of district planning committees vis-à-vis the role of Panchayati Raj representatives and comes out with some revealing findings and meaningful recommendations. This is a very useful book for academics, planners and practitioners.

Arunachalam and Kalpagam's *Development and Empowerment: Rural Women in India* (ed.) (J. Arunachalam and U. Kalpagam, Rawat Publications, 2006) provides that the issues of development and women's empowerment receive critical attention in various debates. Trends and patterns of agricultural development in recent years have not always been favourable to women, especially rural women, who face marginalisation.

An attempt has therefore been made in this book to take stock of the contemporary challenges in rural women's empowerment in India and suggest viable solutions through a process of networking and dialogue to evolve a coherent perspective for the region as a whole. It is towards this end that the book would serve as a launching pad for further discussions.

Palanithurai's *Emerging Dimensions in Decentralisation* (Concept Publishing, 2005) captures the process and implication of decentralised governance established at the grassroots level in Tamil Nadu after the introduction of the 73rd Constitutional Amendment. It analyses the whole electoral process of the local bodies and highlights the achievements of ten Gram Panchayats with the support of the communities on social development issues. Further dealing with the development initiatives of the Panchayats and the people, the book portrays the linkages between the traditional and the formal Panchayats for effective delivery of services to people. Also, it addresses various issues concerning capacity building of Panchayat leaders, performance of dalit leaders and problems of women representatives. The book will be useful for policymakers, development workers and researcher.

Mohanan's *Decentralised Governance and Participatory Development: Issues, Constraints and Prospects* (Concept Publishing, 2005) analyses the constraints and possibilities in participatory planning and democratic decentralisation, with special reference to Kerala. Examining the various aspects of the concept of people's participation, it presents an overview of people's campaign for decentralised planning in the state.

Also, it presents a report on decentralised planning based on extensive field studies at two of Kerala's Gram Panchayats. The political process at the grassroots level has been discussed as well. The book will be of great use for researchers, policymakers and development workers.

Shakuntala Sharma's *Grassroot Politics and Panchayati Raj* (Deep and Deep Publications, 1997) provides a comprehensive analysis of grassroots politics and Panchayati Raj in India. It traces the genesis and growth of village government from the ancient times till today in terms of the evolution of Panchayats and Panchayat leadership as well as Panchayat elections and voting behaviour. A unique feature of the book is its discussion focusing on the interaction between caste, class and power in rural areas. The profile of rural leadership and analysis of rural power structure throw a new light on the working of Panchayat system. It investigates and analyses various aspects of grassroots democracy and politics in terms of performance of Panchayats, patterns of rural power structure and links between rural leaders and higher political leadership.

The book is divided into Introduction, Panchayati Raj-Historical Perspective Post-independence Period, Legal Framework, Leadership Profile and Rural Power Structure, Suggestions, and so on. The book will be of immense interest to academics, policymakers as well as general readers and scholars and students of political science, public administration and rural development.

Arun Sharma and Rajagopal's *Planning for Rural Development Administration* (Rawat Publications, 1995) contends that rural development is a comprehensive subject but that in no sense is it complex. Rural development administration, woven into a multi-agency system, often makes development issues more intricate. Consequently, an administrator spends a long part of his tenure in figuring out procedural paths to bridge the divide between programme implementation and end benefits. The book asks a key question: Are we following the right path to rural development when using a blend of theoretical, applied and management concepts? The book attempts to create a prolific dialogue out of this long-debated issue. The discussions presented in this book unveil the other side of rural development administration; it talks about what is required for making structural adjustments in ensuring that every effort is a milestone.

P.S. Das's *Decentralised Planning and Participatory Rural Development* (ed.) (Concept Publishing, 2005) provides a summary on the outcomes of discussions and deliberations that took place on various aspects of decentralised planning and participatory rural development in two national seminars organised by the Department of Economics with Rural Development, Vidyasagar University, Midnapore, West Bengal, under the UGC-sponsored DRS Scheme during 30–31 March 2000 and 1–2 March 2001. The book contains 15 chapters, which are papers presented by distinguished participants in these seminars. The chapters discuss issues like people's participation in the local-level development planning and governance with case studies from different states, problems of integration of physical and financial planning in the decentralised planning framework, decentralised planning and women empowerment, experiments in rural development planning at the village and the Gram Sansad levels, Gram Panchayats and rural development, micro-credit planning, and the Panchayats and NGOs. All the chapters are based on individual or group research carried out in different areas in decentralised planning and rural development. The book makes a significant contribution to the understanding of the actual status of decentralised planning and various aspects of development and empowerment in the states on India, particularly in West Bengal.

Mishra and Mishra's *Decentralised Governance (Macro and Micro Perspective)* (S.N. Mishra and Sweta Mishra, Shipra Publications, 2002) posits that governance as a concept remains underdeveloped and therefore remains exposed to a variety of interpretations. However, for the purpose of present book, a simplistic meaning of governance has been taken which concerns with the problem of management of the affairs of the state. When one talks about governance one must have in mind political institutions within which management is exercised with the focus on how democratic institutions function, authority and working of judiciary, administrative system and culture, role of civil society and underlying sociopolitical dynamics which condition the functioning of such institutions.

In this broader framework, the book systematically analyses the functioning of democratic institutions at the grassroots level and the historicity, functioning and work culture of decentralised administrative setup as well as the nuances of development mechanisms. To support their findings, authors have taken into account both the macro and micro picture of the system as it operates. Although microanalysis deals with the scenario of two districts only, the findings presented appears to have the scope for applicability for the whole of the country as the human nature and politico-administrative set up remains almost the same throughout the country.

This is a useful work for those who are interested in the study of functioning of grassroots institutions vis-à-vis development programmes. It may be of equal interest for general readers interested in studying the rural scenario as well as for academics, public administrators and practitioners.

B.S. Khanna's *Rural Local Government in India and South Asia* (Deep and Deep, 1999) posits that rural local government institutions have evolved gradually in the South Asian countries such as India, Bangladesh, Pakistan and Sri Lanka during the last two decades of the previous century. In Nepal this has been taking place since about the middle of this century. There have been many ups and downs in their evolution over the years, especially in Bangladesh and Pakistan in their post-independence period. Recently however there has been an increase in the recognition and significance of their role in the processes of democratisation and development in these countries. This has motivated governments to introduce reforms and rejuvenate these institutions to function vibrantly in local decision-making and management of certain local services and affairs. There are however large variations in the progress made so far in this direction.

This book provides a national perspective of evolution and contemporary status and functional empowerment of these institutions in each of the five South Asian countries. Part 1 relates to India and Part 2 to the other four countries: Bangladesh, Pakistan, Sri Lanka and Nepal. Part 3 provides a comparative perspective of these institutions across the countries. It also includes a few suggestions for general discussions regarding further enhancement of efficacy of these institutions.

J.K. Soni's *Governance of Panchayati Raj* (Authors Press, 2005) provides that Gram Panchayats had been in existence in ancient India, administering justice, looking after the affairs of villages and promoting community life. Panchayati Raj system in India is inevitable. The Panchayati Raj institutions (PRI) are the prime instruments of de-centralisation at the grassroots-level programmes.

Panchayats are meant to secure the participation of rural people in various activities of the rural sector. People's involvement through Panchayats in planning would result in better and more efficient planning because they have a better perception of their needs, which would be useful in the identification and selection of schemes and formulation of programmes that are of local importance.

This book is an effort to present an assessment and panorama of Panchayati Raj with special emphasis on women empowerment and education as tool of development. This book will be of immense use to teachers, policymakers, researchers and students of various disciplines in India and abroad.

Panchayati Raj in India: Emerging Trends across the States (R.P. Joshi and G.S. Narwani, Rawat Publications, 2005) finds that Panchayati Raj, as a system of governance at the grassroots level in

India, has been rightly conceived as the most viable and proper mechanism of realising the twin goals of democracy and decentralisation. The current debate is not on its desirability but on strengthening it by identifying its weaknesses and taking care of the lacunae which are still there in spite of its enhanced power through the historical 73rd Constitutional Amendment Act. It has now been almost a decade since Panchayati Raj in India became constitutionalised in the true sense of the term and was also given a status which triggered a debate on 'district government' and the creation of a third tier of federal polity in India. Likewise, empowerment of women and weaker sections, through a well-devised system of reservation, has not only brought about a change in the sociopolitical culture of these sections of society but has also led to a virtual transformation of the rural scene where people have increasingly become aware of their rights and have started demanding their share in power. In fact, rural India today has become the embodiment of a new revolution which seeks to provide a much-needed direction to the polity and thereby making democracy and decentralisation vibrant and feasible for those who deserve it most.

Governance of India: Issues and Perspectives (ed.) (R.N. Prasad, Concept Publishing, 2002) provides that governance is purposive and development-oriented administration which concerns the improvement of quality of life of the people. Governance is also considered a citizen-friendly, citizen-caring, responsive, goal and result-oriented administration. It requires effective participation of people in state, civil society and private sector activities that are conducive to human development.

The book is a collection of 13 chapters which were already published as articles and deals objectively with some of the burning problems/challenges/issues and perspectives of Indian governance, such as those in the social, political, economic and administrative spheres, arising out of the failures of state and nation-building. The book, in order to resolve the conflicts/problems confronting the Indian governance, emphasises a major structural shift and institutional change in the existing socioeconomic model of development on capitalist lines, exploitative social and property relations, and the pursuit of market economy framework. The positive role of the state in resolving social, political and economic conflicts is emphasised. The book, in a nutshell, stresses on the concept of humane governance.

The book will be helpful both for academic and practical purposes of governance. It provides policy insights for the future and will be highly useful to policymakers, public administrators. political leaders, social activists, social scientists, teachers, researchers, students of social sciences and all those committed and interested in resolving the emerging problems/challenges/issues/ conflicts of the Indian governance – state and nation-building.

Empowerment of People: Grassroots Strategies and Issues (ed.) (R.V. Ravi, V.N. Reddy and M. Venkataraman, Kanishka Publishers, 2004) analyses and concludes that empowerment is a process focused on the capacity building of the people to help them initiate, sustain and own the development. In this process, people are enabled to have access, participate and control the decisions of various aspects/activities of welfare as well as development programmes. In our country, efforts on the part of both government and non-governmental bodies in recent times are aimed at increasing the 'power resource' of the people for their sustainable development. The process of empowerment includes enhancement of economic, political, social and psychological capabilities of the people to help them achieve sustainable development.

This volume is a documentation of the perspectives, review, research findings and experience related to the empowerment strategy that has influenced the socioeconomic, political and psychological capabilities of people. The chapters are contributed by academics, social scientists, social workers and development consultants. The chapters are grouped into four major areas: women empowerment, self-help group movement, rural development and social development.

The book is divided into four parts:

Part 1: Empowerment of Women includes the following chapters: Empowerment of Women – A Perspective, Strategies for Women Empowerment; Empowerment of Women – Difference between Theory and Practice; Participatory Development of SC Women: A Micro Perspective; Men's Perception on Women Empowerment – A Micro Study; Women Education in India – An Overview.

Part 2: Self-help Movement contains the following chapters: Empowerment of Rural Women through Self-help Groups: A Perspective; Empowerment of Rural Women through Self-help Groups – A Study in Tamil Nadu; Women empowerment and Self-help Groups: A Participatory Approach; Role of NGO in Promotion of Self-help Groups – A Case from Andhra Pradesh.

Part 3: Empowering for Rural Development includes the following chapters: Effect of Occupation on Poverty: A Micro Study; Housing for Weaker Section – A Study in Andhra Pradesh; Empowering Rural Poor through Information Technology; Empowerment of Fishing Households through Technology; Rural Development Bureaucratic Culture vis-à-vis Education; Decentralised Planning and Empowerment: The Role of NGOs; People's Participation in the Grassroots Democracy.

Part 4: Social Development Issues includes the following chapters: Social Security Mechanisms for Vulnerable Community with Special Reference to Devadasis; National Social Assistance Programme in Rajasthan: Existing Facts; Case and Politics at Village Level – A Case Study; Relative Deprivation among the Elderly; Working Man Complex and Cultural Continuities into Retirement: A Study on Retirees; Impact of Economic Reforms on Women's Quality of Life.

Objectives

In brief, the aims and objectives of the study are as given below:

1. To study the actual form, working and the effect of the Panchayati Raj institutions constituted as a result of 73rd Constitutional Amendment Act as adopted and improvised by the state government of Rajasthan.
2. To compare the profile, achievements and difficulties of the Panchayati Raj institutions.
3. To ascertain the transformation of socioeconomic and political conditions of the weaker sections in rural areas of Rajasthan, particularly female members of the Panchayat and those belonging to SC, ST, and OBC categories.
4. To study the efforts made by the Panchayati Raj institutions for the development of rural areas.
5. To survey the attitude of the people of village towards the Panchayati Raj bodies and members working for them.

6. To look into the attitude, attainments and deficiencies of the officials working under the elected authorities of Panchayati Raj bodies.
7. To evaluate grants, help, guidance, and control provided by the state and central government for Panchayat Raj institutions.
8. To ascertain which type of persons or segments of communities have benefited more than others.
9. To ascertain the role and impact of political parties, caste, money, tradition and so on in the election/nomination of the members of Panchayat Raj bodies.

Conceptual Framework

The concept of democratic decentralisation has been much discussed and debated by scholars of political science, public administration and other social sciences. Democratic decentralisation has been described and addressed by various names in India, such as 'functional democracy', 'grass-root democracy', 'building from below', 'Panchayati Raj institutions' and so on.

The term 'decentralisation' literally means 'away from centre'. Herman Finer explains, 'Decentralisation is a system in which there are many centres of Government, local and central, each with a recognised right of independent existence and functions.' The Balwant Rai Mehta Committee defines decentralisation as a 'process whereby the government divests itself completely of certain duties and responsibilities and devolves them onto some other authority'. The underlying idea behind democratic decentralisation is to widen the area of democracy by granting both authority and autonomy to the people at lower levels. It implies mass participation of people at the grass-root level both in the decision-making and the decision-implementing processes.

Decentralisation under the 73rd Constitutional Amendments

The 73rd Amendment of the Indian Constitution (1993) was a watershed in the history of Panchayati Raj in India. It was designed to fulfill the strong and long-felt need to accord constitutional status to the system. The 73rd Amendment has set up a uniform three-tier structure involving directly elected members. One-third of the offices and membership have been reserved for women. The scheduled castes and scheduled tribes (SCs and STs) have been given reservation in offices and membership. The states have been empowered to make reservations for other backward classes (OBCs) as well in proportion to their population in the concerned state. The Panchayati Raj institutions have been given powers over 29 subjects listed in the 11th schedule of the Constitution of India. The State Election Commissions have been empowered to conduct regular periodical elections and the State Finance Commissions have been instructed to ensure adequate finances. The new Panchayati Raj has been institutionalised in all the states and union territories of India. The 73rd Amendment has not only resulted in broadening the base of democracy in India but also led to the empowerment of women and weaker sections. However, empowerment is more formal and tokenistic than real because the conditions in the ground reality remain largely unchanged. Nevertheless, it is a good beginning with great potential in the field of decentralisation. The research proposes to empirically study whether the 73rd Constitutional Amendment has facilitated the establishment of democratic decentralisation which in turn has resulted in the political, economic and social upliftment and empowerment of the downtrodden sections of the society and has accelerated the pace of developmental efforts in rural India.

Hypotheses

The study prepared a set of questions and hypotheses to test and evaluate developments in the study area, namely Panchayati Raj, and these are listed as follows.

Questions

1. Whether reservations granted to SCs, STs, OBCs and Women in the representation of Panchayati Raj bodies have brought any qualitative social change (social transformation) in their life?
2. What has been the impact of reservation policy on development efforts?
3. What has been the impact of reservation on empowering these classes (status of these classes)?
4. Is there any change in the social prestige of these classes after they received reservations?
5. Have the Panchayati Raj institutions succeeded in exercising powers granted to them?

6. Are Panchayati Raj institutions merely acting as a dependent politico-administrative arm of the Government of Rajasthan?

Hypotheses

1. Panchayati Raj institutions led to the empowerment of weaker sections, particularly SCs, STs, OBCs and women after the passing of the 73rd Amendment of the Constitution.
2. Panchayati Raj institutions in Rajasthan became stronger with more decentralisation of powers particularly in fields such as finance, agriculture, irrigation and police (law and order) at least partly.
3. Panchayati Raj institutions are in a position to accelerate the pace of developmental efforts in rural areas, specially after introducing reservation for dalits and women.
4. Greater protection to weaker sections, including women, resulted in more empowerment of Panchayati Raj institutions in Rajasthan.

All these hypotheses were tested based on the study data gathered by the author from the operations and workings of Panchayati Raj institutions in Rajasthan.

Methodology

It is a field survey with the general theoretical framework of Indian democracy as enshrined in the Constitution of India and the Gandhian ideology of 'Gram Swaraj'. It is an empirical field study based on primary data and information. For the field study two Zila Parishads out of 32 Zila Parishads of the State of Rajasthan were selected. These two Zila Parishads are Jaipur Zila Parishad and Sikar Zila Parishad. Both Zila Parishads have their own specific features. Two Panchayati Samitis from each Zila Parishad were selected for the purpose of this study. Each Panchayati Samiti governs five village Panchayats, and from each village Panchayat approximately about 20 respondents were selected. Thus, the total number of respondents is 400 ($2 \times 2 \times 5 \times 20 = 400$).

The author has prepared a structured questionnaire (schedule) containing four open-ended sections. The structured questionnaire contains about 60 questions broadly divided into four sections: (a) introduction, (b) knowledge testing, (c) role and performance and (d) evaluation and suggestions. The data thus collected have been edited and processed by proper coding and tabulation for determining the relationships between variables like position in the power hierarchy of Panchayat Raj bodies, social status, educational attainments, financial upliftment, and development. The data were analysed, findings were made and conclusions were drawn.

Relevance, Anticipated Outcomes and Proposed Outputs from the Study

The Panchayati Raj institution under the 73rd Constitutional Amendment Act aims at total transformation of the society, particularly in weaker sections like women, SCs, STs and OBCs. The present study is an interdisciplinary study with its scope primarily covering political science and public administration but it does extend its scope to sociology and economics and investigates the growth and development of the tree of Panchayati Raj institutions.

The study is very relevant and path-breaking. It contributes to theory by giving an idea about the functioning of Panchayati Raj institutions at the ground level. The study aimed at studying the impact of the 73rd Constitutional Amendment Act on the empowerment of rural people in general and those belonging to SC, ST and OBC categories and women in particular and whether changes as envisaged were taking place. Study findings show that reservation policy has contributed a lot in the efforts made for development in all walks of life in rural India.

Notes

1. George Mathew, 'Panchayati Raj in India: An overview' in George Mathew (ed.), *Status of Panchayati Raj in the States and Union Territories of India*, Concept Publishing Company, New Delhi, 2000, p. 3.
2. Dalia Goswami, 'Evolution of Panchayati Raj in Haryana', M. Phil. Dissertation (unpublished), Directorate of Correspondence Courses, Kurukshetra University, Kurukshetra, Haryana, 1999, p. 9.
3. Hugh Tinker, *The Foundation of Local Self Government in India, Pakistan and Burma*, Athena Press, London, 1954, p. 36.
4. For details, refer to 'Royal Commission upon Decentralization in India, 1907 Report', *Committees and Commissions in*

Pre-Independence India (1836–1947), Vol. 4, 1903–1912, Mittal Publication, New Delhi, 2001, pp. 79–100.

5. Mathew, *Panchayati Raj in India*, pp. 4–5.
6. Ibid., p. 5.
7. Goswami, 'Evolution of Panchayati Raj', pp. 26–28.
8. H.D. Malaviya, 'Village Panchayats in India', Economic and Political Research Department, All India Congress Committee, New Delhi, 1956, pp. 1–10.
9. Mathew, *Panchayati Raj in India*, pp. 6–7.
10. Ibid., pp. 7–8.
11. Ibid., p. 8.
12. Arun Ghod, '64th Amendment, a Major Step towards Decentralization', *Hindustan Times* (Delhi), 25 May 1989.
13. Goswami, 'Evolution of Panchayati Raj', p. 77.
14. S. Bhatnagar, *Rural Local Government in India*, Light and Life Publication, New Delhi, 1978.
15. T.N. Chaturvedi (ed.), *Panchayati Raj*, Indian Institute of Public Administration, New Delhi, 1987.
16. R.L. Khanna, *Panchayati Raj in India*, The English Book Depot, Ambala Cantonment, Punjab, 1972.

2

Panchayati Raj in India

From Ancient Times to Attainment of Independence

Today Panchayati Raj system seems like an integral part of local self-government. But when did it really originate and what was its original form is too difficult to research and assess. It can be vaguely hypothesised that local institutions originated with the commencement of civilised social living of human beings. The term 'Panch' literally means five, and the organisation of five leaders called as Panchayat is an ancient institution. The vicissitudes of Indian history put the institution to test, and somehow it has survived and revived itself in the modern times.[1]

In this sense Panchayats have been in the main stream of Indian life since early ancient times, but what we see today is the result of several efforts which our political leaders have made after independence. The concept is not new, but the philosophy, structure and working of Panchayats have been attuned to the democratic and federal structure of our Constitution.

The terms 'Panchayat' and 'Raj', if translated literally, mean government of five representatives. In Sanskrit literature the company of five persons has been called as 'Panchayatan'. It is a group of wise people and what they speak is justice. Celebrated Hindi story writer Premchand called them 'Panch Parmeshwar'; that is, god speaks through the Panchas.

Gradually the spiritual and ethical connotation of the term changed, and today it is an elected body with five or more members who look after the development of a small rural place. Mahatma Gandhi defined a Panchayat as a representative body of five people elected by the residents of the village.[2]

Panchayati Raj in Ancient India

Panchayati Raj in its institutional form owes its origin to the recommendations of Balwant Rai Mehta Committee constituted for the introduction of democratic decentralisation in the year of 1957. It may be called a revival of the ancient system. History says that Panchayats have been functioning effectively during the Hindu period of Indian history. Commenting upon them Sir Charles Metcalfe (1830) called them '"mini village Republics," who were autonomous and self-sufficient with their living relations with the outside world.'[3] Panch, Panchayat and god seem to be synonymous in Sanskrit literature, and their universality is writ large on every page of ancient history. The social system builders gave extraordinary stress upon primary institutions like village, joint family and Panchayats, so that social life can have smooth sailing. The village had to be a complete, independent, self-sufficient and total unit of social life.[4]

The small states in ancient India were called 'Janpads'. The Janpads have several 'Vishes', whose leaders were named as 'Vishaptis'. A Vish could have several villages, and 'Gramani' was the head of the village. He used to consult elderly people of the village and acted on the advice of the best people available. This was the original form of a Panchayat. Agriculture and animal grazing being the prime vocations of villagers, the villages were more important than cities. The means of transportation were poor, and the villages were forced to be self-sufficient. Distribution of land, management of irrigation, vigil over pastures, organising fairs and festivals and local justice were the primary functions of Panchayats, and the Panchayats could manage them well. Security realisation of land revenue was the job of the 'Gramani' who was accountable to the Panchayat of his village.[5]

The Vedic age talks about rural government because urban administration was non-existent in an agricultural society. The village Panchayat was a local rural institution and had responsibilities of local administration and rural justice. The Vedic recitations pray for rural affluence. The term 'Gramani' appears in Vedic literature which mentions about large and small villages as key units of administration and economy.[6]

The Republican traditions of Vedic age talk of glories of rural life. The 'Rastradhaksha' has been addressed as 'Rajan' (king). The king was elected by the people and public opinion was decisive. The heredity was a factor in elective monarchy, but merit was always prescribed for the Yuvraj or the Prince successor. If the ruler did not have a worthy successor, any other able person could ascend the throne.

"विप्रं विप्रासोऽवसे देवं मर्तास उत्तये। अग्निं गीर्भिर्हवामहे।"[7]

Yajurveda also reiterates as follows:

"आ त्वाऽहार्षमन्तरभूर्ध्रुवस्तिष्ठाविचाचलत्।
विशस्त्वा सर्वा वांछन्तु मा त्वद्राष्ट्रमधि भ्रशत्।।"[8]

People used to elect a king on the basis of his virtues. He was usually a brave soldier, a brilliant man of rare virtues. His versatility was debated, and elections were conducted using ballot papers.

"ये धीवानो रथकाराः कर्मारा: ये मनीषिणः।
उपस्तीन्पर्ण महयं त्वं सर्वान्कृण्वभितो जनान्।"
"ये राजानो राजाकृतः सूता ग्रामण्यश्च ये।
उपस्तीन् पर्ण मह्यं त्वं सर्वान्कृण्वभितो जनान्।"[9]

The election of the Vedic King was done objectively. His powers came from the people. The king could not last in his throne if found guilty of violating public morality. The 'Sabha' and 'Samitis' were the representative institutions of people. The Yajurveda mentions:

"स विशोऽनु व्यचलत् तं सभा च समितिश्च सेना च सुरा चानुव्यचलन् ।
सभायाश्च वै स समितेश्च सेनायाश्च सुरायाश्च त्रियं धाम भवति य एवं वेद।।"[10]

Atharvaveda mentions that there were no kings in the early times. Hence the concepts of Grahpati, Sabha, Samiti, Panchayat and Cabinet were born.[11] A.P. Sambh Dharamsutra shows that some kind of local government was functioning in the Vedic era.[12] The Vedic India remained under self-controlled republics for centuries and a variety of committees, sabhas and assemblies remained in existence in one form or the other.[13]

A sociological study of rural system indicates that there was 'yagya' system in rural India. The importance of yagya gave birth to 'Yajmani System', which was quite relevant for the Panchayats. The barber, cobbler, ironsmith, potter and goldsmith had their specialised jobs in community life. Each one had a specific place in the social system of the country. All had their respective caste Panchayats, which played a significant role in running the rural social system of the village. Each group has a social status and was dependent upon the other for its recognition. Economic system was based on exchange of goods and services. The person could be rich or poor, and the social system ignored the economic inequality. The entire society controlled the means of production, and individual ownership did not disturb the system of production. The entire village controlled production, and the system functioned around agricultural production from the land. 'Lord Indra' called it an 'Agricultural Civilisation'. The king used to get a fixed part of agricultural produce in lieu of the security to the individual persons and their farm and animal wealth. The entire agricultural produce of the land was put on a Chaupal, and shares were allotted to different groups, including the share of the king. The land was ploughed collectively. The two characteristics of the system need a mention here:

1. The quantum of land revenue was commensurate with the actual produce from the land;
2. The king and the farmer had a direct contact without any middleman or a feudal land lord.

The system ensured social protection, and the minimum wants of all classes were adequately satisfied. Atharvaveda authenticates it:

"विराडवा इदमग्र आसीत् तस्या जाताया:
सर्वविभेदिय मे वेद भविष्यतीति।।"[14]

Thus, Panchayats strived to unify the society. The members of these Vedic Panchayats viewed every body without discriminations. All were the children of God and equal in their rights and dignity:

"एकोदेव: सर्वभूतेषु गूढ़: सर्वव्यापी सर्वभूतान्तरात्मा।
कर्माध्यक्ष: सर्वभूताधिवास: साक्षी चेता केवलोनिर्गुणाश्च।।"[15]

The Panchayat decisions were usually unanimous. The office bearers were objective and selfless. This feature made them unique. The following mantra of Ishoupnishad testifies:

"ईष्ठावास्यमिदं सर्वं यत्किण्च जगत्यांजगत्।
तेन त्यक्तेन भुंजीथा मा गृधः कस्यस्विद्धनम्।।"[16]

Ramayana and Mahabharat present detailed accounts of village management. There was a 'Mukhiya' or a 'Headman' in every village, and the administration took orders from him. Usually each village had only one-man administration. He was a hereditary official but unworthy successors could be removed. He was a non-Brahmin. It was an important office. His duty was to protect the village and the villagers. There were village volunteers for his support. With the help of guards and other officials he used to levy and realise direct taxes. The files and other documents were kept as records, and revenue realisation was a major part of village administration. He was also an ex-officio Chairman of the Panchayat, and rural problems were discussed and resolved under his leadership.[17]

Bhisham says in the 'Shanti-Parva' of Mahabharat: 'The King should appoint a "Gramadhipati" in every village and each "Gramadhipati" may be given charge of ten, twenty or hundred villages under their care. These Dashagramadhipati 'दशग्रामाधिपति', Vishgramadhipati 'विशग्रामाधिपति', Shatgramadhipati 'शतग्रामाधिपति' were arranged in hierarchy and used to hear appeals from lower functionaries. Any complaints or problems used to reach the king through an elaborate appeal system and thus all the 'Adhipatis' in their respective sphere were performing the functions of the state.[18]

Ramayan talks of village administration and its role in national governance of the empire. The term used is Rajkartarah 'राजकर्त्तारः', which literally means the kingmakers. After the death of King Dasrath, these kingmakers assembled in Ayodhya. They were known as:

समेत्य राजकर्त्तारः सभामीयु द्विजातयः

There were small Janpads during Ramayan era. They were known as village republics.[19] The Poet of Ramayana calls the leaders as Gramani 'ग्रामणी'.[20] Historian Altekar says that 'Perhaps this Gramani was the Gramadhipati. It was a prestigious office, and mostly the rich persons from Vaish community wanted to hold these offices. The king used his authority through these Gramadhipatis. He was a police officer also. Taxes were collected by him. The Gram Sabha called all the residents and their dues were worked out by the Gramani. A 'Vradh-Sabha' was an advisory body. The Gramani was something akin to the office of the Patwari, and he used to preside over the 'Gram Sabha'.[21]

The Smritis also mention about local institution. Manu finds it desirable to organise the state at various levels to have effective administration.[22] He suggests 10, 100 and 1000 village groups as the unit for rural organisation. They come close to modern Panchayats, Samitis, Tahsils and Parishads. According to Manu Smriti village is the smallest unit under a Gramik 'ग्रामिक'. As the hierarchy ascends the Gramiks take charge of clusters of 20, 100 and 1000 villages. The prevalent term were Gramik 'ग्रामिक', Dashamgrampati 'दशग्रामपतिः', Vishtigrampati 'विशतिग्रामपतिः', Shatiadhipati 'शतीअधिपति' and Sahstradhipati 'सहस्त्रधिापति'. The functions were magisterial and providing security of the people against crimes. The tax collections were deposited in the treasury. Manu calls these officials as Rakshak 'रक्षक' of the people.

Although Yagyavalakya Smriti is relatively silent about monarchy and public administration, there are numerous references about public institutions working in the empire for public good. It talks about Karyachintaks 'कार्यचिन्तक', who were expected to be Dharmagya 'धर्मज्ञ', Shuchi 'शुचि' and Alubdh 'अलुब्ध'. Whatever was earned collectively must be surrendered to the state. Violation of this custom was punishable, and the penalty was 11 times of the amount involved in the case.[23]

Kautilya in his 'Arthshastra' gives details of local institutions. He divides the state administratively into two parts: (1) Pur and (2) Janpad. A Pur comprised city, fort or capital while the Janpad consisted of the rest. How should a Janpad have its layout, Kautilya has given details. The smallest dwelling was called 'Gram', and a cluster of ten villages had an office called 'Sangrahan'. He suggests that 200 villages should be organised into Kharvtak 'खार्वटक'. The cluster of 400 villages was called 'Dronmukh' and 800 villages could have a 'local institution.'

"अष्टशतग्राम्या मधये स्थानीयं, चतुश्शतग्राम्या द्रोणमुखं,

द्विशतग्राम्याः खार्वटिकं, दशग्रामीसन्ग्रहणं स्थापयेत्।।"[24]

Kautilya wants the 'Samaharta' 'समाहर्त्ता' to organise 500 villages and appoint a Gop 'गोप' to manage the institutions. He was supposed to keep the census record of the villages and all other information relevant to village economy. Saletore writes that Kautilya's village besides being an economic unit had to function as a political and judicial unit also.[25]

Mauryan Age

This epoch (324 BC–236 BC) of Indian history was basically agricultural, and the job of the rural administration was to manage the farmland and its produce. The average population in a village was 100–500 families. The natural boundaries were formed by rivers, hills or forests. The usual distance between villages was one or two kos 'कोस'.[26] The rural staff comprised of (a) Head, (b) Accountant and (c) Sthanics like veterinary doctor, horse trainer and medical officer in each village. They were given land for which they paid no rent. They were not owners because selling of the land was prohibited.[27]

The government officials controlled the villages. Although Chandragupta had a centralised empire, the rural communities enjoyed reasonable autonomy. Thus, villages were self-regulated. The historians have recorded about Mauryan village as under.

Every village had a Sabha. The members used to enact laws after conducting debates with members of the community. Criminals were punished under due process of law, and judicial system was stable and fair. The Sabha was a multifunctional body. All social and religious matters were brought to its notice. Recreational facilities were organised for the village by the Sabha. The meetings of Sabha were held under a tree, and all old, experienced and family representatives used to participate. The entire population lived in liberty in these autonomous village Republics of the Mauryan Kingdom.[28]

The Mauryan rulers exhibited their foresightedness and political acumen in organising village Panchayats. The empire followed a policy of decentralised administration and local justice. The Panchayats realised their taxes with the aid and support of local elders. This eliminated the possibilities of popular revolt. The Panchayats had effective powers in civil matters, amounting to thousands of rupees. This local network relieved the higher courts of case leads. Some villages had separate committees for temple management, which was otherwise under the Panchayat committee of the village. The religious property was well looked after and worship could be observed in peace and harmony. The Panchayats used to plan schemes for public good especially in the area of irrigation and dams. The Gram Sabhas could levy additional taxes. Generally there were six committees each having five members in every village.

1. The first committee looked after industries and arts.
2. The second committee welcomed outside visitors or guests.
3. The third committee maintained records of birth and death in the villages.
4. The fourth committee governed trade and commerce activities and monitored the generation of local produce.
5. The fifth committee was an inspection committee whose function was to keep the old and new goods separately and sell them without adulteration.
6. The sixth committee assessed one-tenth part of the produce as land revenue to the coffers of the state.[29]

The later Mauryas (200 BC–300 AD) continued with the system. The head of Vradha Sabha was the head of the village Panchayats.[30]

Gupta Period

The Gupta rulers continued with the Mauryan legacies. A.L. Bhasam[31] has given a detailed account of this period. There were traditional heads in villages in the North as well as in the South. The heads and accountants were de facto rulers. The village watchmen used to assist these administrators. Historian Altekar writes:

> The village administration was under the charge of a Head. Below him there was a clerk who used to maintain records. A non-official body assisted the Heads. ...The village-Sabhas during the Gupta period were known as 'Janpads'. The functions of the Head were – Security of the village, resolution of rural conflicts, collection of government revenue, organisation of public trusts etc.

The Sabhas in South India were more active in the areas of land management and revenue collection. The rural conflicts pertained to lands, animals and so on; as historian Majumdar writes, 'The Royal Official dispensed justice with the help of Gram Sabhas. In some maters the Sabha was the final body to deliver justice and pass judgments.'[32]

According to Majumdar 'Kuram' (group of villages) was the lowest rural unit in South India. They had their Heads, and the Mahasabhas (Urs) used to help them.[33] In some villages all the residents assembled in the Sabha. In some the Brahmins or VIPs were elected by ballot papers. The small committees of the Sabha also functioned as per needs. A government official called 'Adhikarin' used to direct these autonomous units.

The 'Makiya' and 'Lekhakar' were the key functionaries from Vedic times, and their roles were varied and significant. The Gram Sabha continued into the entire Maurya and Gupta periods with minor revisions or adjustments. Research demonstrates that ancient India had a more extended, effective and successful local governments than their counterparts during British period.[34]

The Panchayats in ancient India were total institutions, and all the problems of villages and villagers were handled by this institution. A.S. Altekar writes, 'The village has been the hub of Indian life since early times. The number of towns and cities was insignificant in ancient India.'[35] K.P. Jayaswal accepts the presence of 'Gram Sabhas'. His study based on records and archival documents confirm that Gram Sabhas were the vehicle of expression of national life in all sorts of actions and daily functions.[36]

Decentralisation was the buzzword of political life. Self-government was practised, and the lowest unit of the village was covered through these Panchayats or Sabhas in the empire. The cluster of villages had autonomous associations. Thus, ancient India can be called a system of mighty rural democracy. The demarcation line between the state and the society was clear. The political changes did not disrupt the social system. The Indian culture could survive through these rural republics and self-governing village system. The political upheavals passed of quietly. The outside relations were very restricted. The autonomy of this system permitted several characteristics that made them perennial. They contributed to the security of villages and villagers. Even when there were conflicts and wars, the land was never damaged and farms were respected as holy places exempt from enemy behaviour. The scorched-earth policy was never followed, and the enemy's land was neither damaged nor destroyed by the winning villages. Even trees were not denuded. The village system as a political unit was different and separate from the social system in all respects.

The Vedic age gave autonomy to villages. The later emperors established empires, but the villages remained as before. The Maurya emperor controlled minute details of empire, but the village government was immune from such interventions. Thus, the village government kept languishing, although a wide diversification was felt in different parts of the country. The village continued as a social and administrative unit. In North India 'Gramani' was the head. Later on he was called 'Gramak'. In middle ages this village headman had names such as: (a) Pattkeel (पट्टकील) in Malawa, (b) Gramik or Grampati in North India and (c) Gramkoot in the South. The term 'Patel' is a slang of Pattkeel. The root term of Gramkoot is Gamot. Some stone inscriptions used the work 'Mahattar'. In Konkani language it is still called 'Mahatte'. These were five Panchas or officials under this head. In Mahabharat the names of these five were: (a) Samahartta (समाहर्त्ता), (b) Sannidhata (सन्निधाता), (c) Ganak (गणक), (d) Lekhak (लेखक) and (e) Sakshi (साक्षी).[37]

The powers of the people were respected even during the medieval period of Indian history. There was a Sabha or a Mahasabha in each village which administered the rural affairs. The organisation differed because of time and space. They were like small kingdoms and did all those jobs which states do.

Sukraneeti, a document of tenth century AD, refers to Panchayats as an institution. According to Sukra the members of these Panchayats were elected. Their powers were legal as well as administrative. The state officials respected the Panchayat members. The major functions of Panchayats were distribution of land, imposition of taxes and collection of land revenue. Sukraneeti describes the central structure also and references are also available about urban and town institutions. Sukra prescribes the appointment of Sahsadhyaksh (SP) and Bhaghar (Revenue officer), Lekh, Shulk Grah and Dwarpal in every village and town.[38]

Beni Prasad points out the differences in the administrations of North and South. According to him local administration was the most significant variable in the two administrations. South has a systematic form of local institution, but North India allowed the local officials to be controlled by the senior officials of the state. The guilds were more active in South than in the North.[39]

Elphinstone classifies the native system of South into villages and towns. They had all the elements of a government and could protect their members. Even if the upper layers of government were removed they could survive as local government in their own right.

In South India the Tamil Mandalan (Province) was divided into Kottam (District) Nadu (Taluq) and Ur (village). Village was the smallest unit and was managed by several committees. The important committees were (a) Tank and Lakes Committee, (b) Garden Committee, (c) Justice Committee, (d) Temple Committee and (e) General Administration Committee.

References are fond about (a) Gold Committee and (b) Currency Committee. The village had Sabhas and Mahasabhas. The temple courts were the venue for the meetings. The elderly wise people (भद्र) of the village were members of the Sabhas. The village was further divided into wards and ward Panchas were elected by a ballot system. Education and property were qualifications for elibility.[40]

Radha Kumud Mukherjee based his book *Local Government* on ukkal inscriptions. His research demonstrates that the village ukkal was administered by a Sabha or Mahasbha. The main central Sabha had several committees and included, for example, (a) Annual Committee (संवत्सर वारियम) It was the most powerful and prestigious committee. It was elected in the first instance and had 12 members, and (b) The Tank Committee comprised of 6 members, (c) The Gold Committee also had a membership of 6 persons, (d) The Garden Committee consisted of 12 members, (e) The Pakhwar Committee supervised the five Panchayats, and (f) The Justice Committee was a larger one with heavier responsibilities. There were 30 wards for election purposes, and ballots were used to conduct election of these committees. The elections were held annually, and the eligibility of candidates required the following: (a) ownership of 5 acres (one-fourth Veli) of land paying land revenue, (b) domicile in his own house, (c) age between 35 and 70 years and (d) must be well-versed in Vedic literature.

It explains that South India had a really well-developed system of rural government. Chola emperor Rajrai I (985–1013 AD) encouraged the villagers to have public meetings of Panchayats and managed their own affairs. The literature talks about such meetings in which the young and old used to sit together. The village had a town assembly working through committees. The central committee used to conduct polls, and the names of candidates were written on ballot papers in public.

A.S. Altekar studies the stone inscriptions of the Chola dynasty (900–1300 AD) and found that Gram Sabha and their committees were highly developed and active in the Tamil empire. Ur and Agrahar were the grassroots institutions, and the latter one was dominated by Brahmins. Some villages had very active Gram Sabhas. The scholarly members were methodical, and discussions in the meetings were of a high order. Altekar found that some provinces during the Gupta Period had village committees for special functions. They were called Panchmandali (पंचमण्डली) in Madhya Pradesh and Gram Janpad (ग्रामजनपद) in Bihar. The village Janpads of Nalanda had their seals, and the letters sent by Nalanda officials bore the marks of these seals on the documents. Altekar's documents about Pallv and Vakatak villages (250–550 AD) where village elders called 'Mahattar' were administering the area with and without committees. The inscriptions of Gujarat and Daccan (600 AD) demonstrate that village elders had their executive committees which were called as 'Mahattradhikarinah' (महत्तराधिकारिण:).[41]

In fact, the stone inscriptions of South are more elaborate and authentic than the ones found in the North. The institutions of Sabhas and committees were a common experiences in the Janpad of South India. The inscriptions of North are confusing and even silent about the nature and functions of the various institutions. Perhaps the judicial functions are more pronounced in the North as indicated in the 'Smritis'(स्मृतिन:). The detailed functions of these institutions are missing.

Thus, the Gram Sabhas and Panchayats in the ancient India had a variety of functions. Some of them have been enumerated as follows: realisation of land revenue, ownership of fertile land, management of temples, and delivery of justice (it was a special functions of the Pugh). In South some more functions were assigned to these bodies. For instance, they managed tanks and gardens, advanced loans to residents, managed trusts, provided famine relief and supervised welfare activities in the area.

Radha Kumud Mukherjee in his research specifically of South India lists the following functions of Gram Sabhas: (a) safety and security of public property against external aggressions and internal disorders; (b) land management, especially village property and use of land for public purpose; and (c) charity, public works and currency control. There was a village office to conduct these activities, and this office maintained accounts and detailed records of land and public property.[42]

Mughal Period

The rural system of village government continued during the Mughal Period (1556–1749 AD). The autonomous units of Maurya and Gupta periods remained active and functional. The empires rose and fell, but the traditional headman, accountant and watchmen kept doing their jobs. The village remained the basic unit of governance, although the Mughals and the Marathas introduced minor adjustments here and there. The traditional officials of the villages worked under the headman. Later on he was called as 'Patel', who used to collect revenue. In Madras area he was magistrate and civil judge also. The accountant used to make entries of land ownership, and maintenance of records was his responsibility. Similarly, the Chowkidar played the village policeman.[43]

S.V. Samant opines that rural Panchayats performed judicial functions and supported the Mughal administration as their routine duties. According to him, the interests of Muslim subjects were intertwined with Hindu interests in rural life and the Panchayats' decisions were upheld by the Muslim rulers of the state. This testifies the fact that the Mughal state derived its strength from village councils, and the local government continued as a prop for the empire in the early years.[44]

Thus, the spirit of Maurya and Gupta periods influenced the Muslim period of Khilaji's and Lodi's. These rural officials are found in the regimes of Allahuddin Khilji and Mohd. Bin Tuglak. The Sultan found the Patels, Chowkidar and Lekhakars useful and did not disturb their work.

The Delhi Empire during the middle ages was administratively organised into several parganas and divisions. The province was called 'Inta'. Allahuddin named it as 'Suba'. In the later period the head of the pargana became 'Aamal' or 'Mushrrak', and the village headman came to be known as 'Lambardar' and 'Patwari'. The lowest unit, that is, the village, was administered by Lambardar, Patwari and Chowkidar. They divided the revenue and law and order work between themselves, and their responsibility was collective. The Panchayat even during sultan period was autonomous and self-sufficient because the military rule could not reach villages without roads and other means of transportation.

The Rajasthan archives have the same story to tell. The Panchayats worked through executive committees. They were called as 'Panchkuli' (पंचकुली), and their head was known as Mahant (महन्त). The donations offered by native rulers and others were announced in the meetings of the Panchayats.

The Meenas, Gurjars and Bheels were the original inhabitants of Rajasthan. The Rajputs, Yadavs and Yaudhey (यौद्धेय) came in the sixth and seventh century AD. They kept fighting with the original inhabitants for domination for more than 250 years. Here also the Bheel Meenas and 'Hulpos' (हुल्पो) had an organised Panchayati system with long traditions. The Gram Sabha was a powerful and established institution. It took critical decisions and they were binding on the entire population of the village. The Rajputs were a warrior community, and they remained engaged in wars to demonstrate their military prowess. Naturally Gram Sabha was an irrelevant institution for the Rajput community.[45] A stone inscription of Bheenmal in Western Rajasthan enumerates the list of donor members to Panchakul in the year 1266 AD. It states, 'We offer this donation, but its use will be made by the officials who will adorn the village positions':

"यस्मात्पंचकुलः सर्वो मंतव्य इति सर्वदा।
तस्य तस्य तद श्रेयो यस्य-यस्य यदा पदम्।।"

It conclusively proves the existence of Panchayats. The meetings were called for public decisions, and smaller committees carried out day-to-day work with mutual consultations. The local jobs included village surveillance, resolution of petty conflicts, and management of education and entertainment.

The Gram Sabha had three major roles:

1. Land control was not individual but collective. The pastures were the property of the village and Gram-Sabha managed the land distribution and possession.
2. Village forests belonged to the village and village body ensured their full use in the interest of the village itself.
3. The guests visiting in village for trading purposes paid taxes which spent on the development of village dwellers.

The Head was called Grampati, Mahttama (महत्तमा) or Mahattara (महत्तरा) was his associate. The village council of elders helped the Grampati. The Gram-Sabha listened to criminal and civil cases and their powers were reasonably wide. The Grampati used to negotiate and settle the issues of village revenue to be deposited to imperial treasury. The security personnel and other officers were supervised by this headman and he kept all the records under his personal custody.

Huges Tinker writes that despite of the democratic structure of rural administration the individual headman ran the village life during Mughal period. It was one man rule and representation in Panchayats was neither de jure nor de facto. The Panchayat members were aristocrats or Brahamins who hailed from well to do families. The landless and marginal farmers were sidelined in the composition of these local bodies. Of course in south India the Sudras had their representation and the composition and functioning of Panchayats were more democratic than their counterparts in the north. The villagers participated in these Panchayats but it shall be an exaggeration to call them democratic. Tinker evaluates them as effective units in the area of justice. According to him even caste-Panchayats discussed public issues in public and the members present were more than conscious about their onerous responsibility.[46]

The British Period

Historian Lord Harley believes that village Panchayats in India have breathed their last much before the advent of the British rule. He writes 'Perhaps there was some interganum between 6th and 9th centuries when Panchayats were vibrant and alive. It was in few selected areas that Panchayats performed their functions actively. In fact some old people of the village attended these Gram-Sabhas and their activities were more or less ritualistic'. He opines that the Panchayat system had collapsed much before the Englishmen took over the reins of administration.[47]

Eighteenth century seems to be the time when the main stream of local institutions got dried up. The reason can be the disbelief of the British colonials in Indian ingenuity. But then later on they accepted the facts of history and made efforts to revive them also. The ground reality forced them to encourage the bureaucracy and replace local bodies by local officials. These officials were interested in keeping their alien masters happy rather than serving the people. The British administration damaged the self-sufficiency of rural life and the Panchayati system developed dysfunctionalism.[48]

The centralised government of the British preferred to direct the field units from headquarters. 'Village' was absent in the British scheme of things. The rulers had direct contact with the tenants on land and this pushed the village structure in background. The assessment and realisation of land revenue performed by Gram Sabhas was taken over by officials and the official bureaucracy was supplanted in place of local democracy. This deprived the village from its income and the headmen and other officials were reduced to the status of salaried public servants.

S.B. Samant finds the same situation in the judicial field also. The newer courts established ruined the village court system of Panchayats. The Panchayat decisions were not recognised by the British courts. The religions and traditional practices were given up in preference to legal enactments. Social legitimacy weakened and legal supremacy established impersonal rule of alien masters. The legal concept of British Justice suppressed the native institutions. The traditions were ridiculed and community control over Panchayati justice waned and ultimately got lost or adjusted to the changed conditions of time.

The British policy encouraged migration from villages to the towns. The education system adversely effected the self-sufficient community life of the village.[49] The colonial system not only destroyed the legitimacy of rural life but made it subservient and dependent on the government officials. In the earlier years the village was a source of land revenue but the later rulers thought that the roots of the colonial power should reach to villages. In place of using feudals or officials like Patwari and Aameens for the support of rulers it was felt that the rural populace should cooperate and people should look to the government for the resolution of their problems. But then when the British rule became firm and settled, the English rulers returned towards village government by reviving the Panchayats. The resolution of 1802 is indicative of this fact which resulted in the recognition of Madras Presidency urban local government. This policy was extended further and in 1816 the rural local bodies were endowed with the judicial powers of delivering local justice.

The age of representative institutions in India commenced in 1870 when Lord Mayo got his local government resolution passed for urban and rural areas. It was a landmark in the history of local self-government. The resolution enlarged the powers of presidency or provincial governments to spend more money on education, roads, health and public works. It provided an opportunity for the expansion of local activities and people began to take interest in areas which are managed by local bodies today.

The Mayo resolution stressed on popular participation by Indians in their own administrative affairs. It was the reversal of a policy which aimed to fulfill the colonial interests of the British raj. The resolution says that the government will develop local bodies as an instrument of self-government. The Taxation Enquiry Commission of 1953–54 has very aptly said, 'the need to associate Indians with the administration spared the British government to establish self-governing institutions in India on a permanent basis (It facilitated taxation and its realisation from the people). Lord Mayo conjectured about the development of local bodies. But it was a secondary objective. The real reason was to milch the local sources of revenue and effect economy in administration through decentralisation.'[50]

The year of 1882 added a new chapter to the evolution of local self-government in India. Lord Rippon who has been hailed as the Father of local self-government in India brought another Resolution which not only reiterated the Mayo theme but made it workable and practical in Indian conditions.

The 1882 Rippon Resolution expanded the network of local bodies in all the villages under the British rule. They were provided a democratic base and a very commendable progress could be made in this regard. Lord Rippon desired that the elected non-officials should constitute majority in the local bodies and they must enjoy workable and minimum autonomy. Two local bodies were assigned to each district and they were given the name of District Board and Tahsil or Taluka Board. The village Panchayat in this arrangement was conspicuous by its absence.

The following principles were enunciated in Rippon Resolution, in fact these were the premises on which the future local bodies could be based or developed:

1. Most of the members and Chairmen of local bodies should be non-official members.
2. The state control over local bodies should be indirect, not direct.
3. The local bodies should have adequate financial resources for their activities. The specific allocation should be made for from provincial budgets.
4. The local employees will work under the control of elected representatives. Even the officials sent on deputation should be regarded as local employees and they should work under the control of the local government.
5. The interpretation of 1882 local resolution should be made by provincial governments as per their local conditions.

The reactions upon the 1882 Resolutions were not very encouraging. The progress in the field was not only slow but halting.[51] The provincial governments took little or no interest in executing the Rippon resolution. Still union Panchayats were constituted in Madras and Bengal in the year 1884 with a jurisdiction on a number of villages. Lord Rippon made consistent efforts, yet the entire experiment proved to be a terrible disappointment in the long run.

Although the Rippon scheme of local reforms was incomplete but a sincere effort could have yielded results. Several provinces enacted legislation in compliance to the resolution, but the provincial bureaucracy was too strong to change. It frustrated the Rippon reforms.[52] The British ICS officers regarded the resolution a mere whim of the Governor General and saw to it that it did not work. Notwithstanding the non-cooperation of provincial government, several other factors contributed to the failure. Firstly, the financial resources of the boards were too meager to undertake useful public work. Secondly, the government officials had a heavy control bordering on the humiliation of elected representative. So good people avoided these positions. Thirdly, the nominated members were seen with an eye of suspicious. Fourthly, even the elected members were corrupt and were involved in nepotism. All this created a situation because of which the grand objectives of Lord Rippon got frustrated.[53]

In 1907 the Royal Commission investigated the causes of failure of Rippon efforts and found that the institutions created under the 1882 reforms could achieve only negligible results. The then Secretary of state for India expressed his regrets for the failure of Rippon scheme of decentralisation. The congress party in its 24th session at Lahore in 1909 passed a resolution appreciating the honesty of the Secretary of state in accepting the failure of Rippon scheme. The congress reiterated its demand for autonomy of rural and urban local bodies and pressurised the government to advance in this direction. The congress hoped that the government of India will take steps to get the elections completed and ensure adequate funds for their functioning.[54]

The Royal Commission felt that villages in India constitute a primary field unit and cover a vast area of Indian territory. A large administrative power centre exists in the rural areas.[55] These villages used to enjoy autonomy in the past, but it gradually got eroded because of the establishment of civil and criminal courts, organisation of revenue and police departments, means of communication and development of individualism and Rayaatwadi system of the new government. The village Headman (Patel or Mukaddam) accountant and chowkidar are useful officials. Government pays them regular salary and they do possess a feeling of serving their own fellowmen in the villages.

The commission recommended that Panchayat administration should be restored as a primary unit in the village. But it accepted a variety of institutions at local level. The commission recommended that village Headman should be the ex-officio chairman of the Panchayat. It was suggested that Gram Sabha members should be informally elected under the supervision of government officials. The term for Panchayats was left open and the following functions were recommended for inclusion in the Panchayat list:

1. Petty civil and criminal cases
2. Rural Hygiene and small matters

3. Construction and maintenance of school buildings and management of teachers.
4. Management of fodder depots and pasture lands
5. Management of rural markets of local importance.

Superficially it was all fine but the provision of putting Panchayats under district officials destroyed the reformatory positive spirit of the report. The nationalist leaders criticised the report on the ground that dependence of village leader on government officials will end decentralisation. The Indian national congress rejected the report and launched protest movements under the leadership of Mahatma Gandhi and Pt. Jawahar Lal Nehru.[56]

Some provinces did try to implement the report but without any substantial achievement. The reason was obvious. Like the central British government, the district officials were not prepared to part with power. The doubted the integrity and capability of local leaders. It is true that the suggestions of 1909 commission were not implemented, but none the less their significance survives undiminished even today.

The Recommendations of the Royal Commission (1909) were reiterated in the local self-government resolution of 1915. The recommendation pertaining to local district boards were accepted. The Boards were given majority of elected members, but the electoral Boards remained unchanged.

The contribution of Indians in winning the First World War was gratefully acknowledged by his majesty's government. Considering the demand of democratic institutions some what sympathetically, the Secretary of state for India Montague made a policy declaration on 20 August 1917. The Secretary said 'The policy of his Majesty's government, with which the government of India is in perfect accord is to increase the participation of Indians and to promote a gradual development of self-governing institutions as an integral part of the empire. It will establish self-government in instalments.[57]

In May 1918 before the advent of Mont Ford Reforms, the government of India passed a resolution stressing upon the need of a separate law for Panchayats. The resolution said 'the purpose of local self-government is to train people in self-management of local affairs. This political education should be preferred in contrast to administrative efficiency. The local institutions should represent the people whose affairs they seek to manage. These affairs should be assigned to them and their powers should be real rather than mere nominal. Their mistakes should be condoned so that they may learn. The control should be minimum.' It further added 'the development of village Panchayats should be ensured by a separate law, unrelated to municipal and village Boards.' The expansion of the Boards was recommended and it was stressed that chairman should be elected non official representatives. The Panchayats were to be developed as institutions expressing the rural aspirations in a spontaneous manner. The resolution set guideline for future.[58]

The Mont Ford Reforms of 1919 inaugurated a new era of local self-government. It was a transferred subject in the diarchy of provincial government and elected representative ministers were in-charge of the department. But finance being a reserved subject, the responsible ministers were not free to act in their respective spheres. Still several provinces made new enactments for the reorganisation of their local institutions. The non-official majority was introduced in all the local bodies. The number of voters increased and the local institutions were endowed with wider powers of tax imposition. But the national struggle for freedom restrained the British government to experiment and the local bodies became the casualty. People also became negative and the faith in local self-governance was shaken from both the sides.

In 1920 the British government passed 'United Provinces Village Panchayat Act'. It empowered the district officials and Janpad civil servants to create Panchayats in their areas. In UP alone hundreds of new Panchayats were created but they were too weak and have been called as shadow Panchayats.[59]

Between 1919 and 1920 the provinces of Madras, Bombay, Bihar and Bengal passed their Panchayat enactments. Punjab and Assam followed suit in 1922 and 1925 respectively. It was a landmark development.[60] Some provinces created temporary judicial Panchayats, which were representative and represented the corporate structure of the village. They were given a wide jurisdiction in civil matters of litigation in the village.

In 1927 the Simon Commission was dispatched to India. One of its purpose was to examine the working of local governments. The progress made under dyarchical reforms of 1919 was to be evaluated for future installments. The commission surveyed the scene and identified the strong and weak areas of local governance in the twenties. The commission acknowledged that several resolutions have been passed but the concept of responsible government in local bodied was far from being satisfactory. Some provinces did make undoubted progress, but failure was writ large on most of the institutions in majority of the provinces. The commission found the overall progress some what satisfactory.

The Government of India Act 1935 conceded provincial autonomy by shifting diarchy to the centre. This positive initiative influenced the growth of local self-government in a meaningful manner. The scope of district boards got expanded and the collectors became the executive heads of district boards. This made the district board powerful and they ceased to be mere advisory bodies. Executive duties were assigned to them. Under provincial autonomy congress party came in power for the first time in 1937 and local institutions were established and got some what strengthened.

It was an opportunity but lost because of the following reasons:

1. Absence of an able salaried official like Town Clark in the rural councils.
2. Obnoxious control of provincial governments over the representatives of local bodies.
3. Large size of the district
4. Inadequacy of financial resources
5. Absence of public spirit among voters

The Indian national leaders were in agreement with the critical evaluation of local bodies by Simon. D.P. Mishra who was the Minister for local self-government in UP and Barar in 1935 raised his voice against the deplorable situation. He said 'the activities of our local institutions in UP and in the country presents a pathetic situation. The local institutions have become synonymous with the incompetence. The interparty conflicts which are more personal than partisan, are bitter and deep. Our council members spend their time, energy and even money on the appointment, transfers and dismissals of trained officials.

The Minister deployed the system of responsibility at lower levels and suggested reforms based on earlier recommendations of committees. He felt concerned about the officialisation of local administration and desired for popular participation. He suggested that political representatives should adjust themselves with government officials so that politics and bureaucracy may join hands to work in public interest.[61]

To revive self-government D.P. Mishra presented a scheme of decentralised administration. This scheme made district the key unit and municipalities and Panchayats could be organised within the circle boards and urban areas. This division into blocks could be used as units of local self-government in place of administrative divisions of the Raj.

The elections under the Act of 1935 constituted popular ministries in the provinces in 1937. The Indian minister undertook law making to facilitate the election of true representatives in local institutions. But unfortunately the outbreak of Second World War in 1939 dampened their enthusiasm. The congress ministries resigned and the Governors took over. The period from 1939 to 1946 has been called the 'Dark Age' of local self-government. The officials took their Vendetta and totally rejected the concept of Panchayats in any form. The situation in 1946 took a dramatic turn and partition followed. All this explains the state of local government in back waters.

Notwithstanding the adverse factors the idea of Panchayati Raj survived and remained a strategic factor in our freedom struggle. Mahatma Gandhi was the Chief architect of this edifice which he wove in the struggle for freedom.

Indian Constitution and Panchayati Raj

The Constituent Assembly was constituted under the Cabinet mission plan and started functioning in undivided India in 1946. Two committees were created for preparing the draft plan for union and state governments. They were called Union Committee and Provincial Committee. These committees do not talk about Panchayats or about the views of Father of the Nation towards local governance. Granville Austin found that even the minutes of the committee meetings are meaningfully silent about Panchayats and Gandhism. Perhaps a Gandhian Constitution was not even presented in the agenda. The Drafting Committee did not discuss the concept of Panchayati Raj and naturally the draft constitution did not even mention the term in proper perspective.

The constituent assembly debates present the paradoxical picture of Panchayats. The Gandhian Protagonists talked about Panchayats as nursery to self-government. They stood for autonomy, financial resources and revival. M.A. Ayyangar and N.G. Ranga tabled their amendment that state governments shall establish Panchayats in a cluster of villages to train villagers and make them effective with adequate functions and powers.[62] On the other hand Dr Ambedkar opposed the idea tooth and nail. He hated the rural system to the core and said on the floor of the Assembly 'What is a village, a *cesspool* of localism, ignorance parochialism and casteism. I am happy that the draft constitution rejects the concept of rural autonomy and individual has been accepted as the unit of government.'[63]

Several members expressed their dismay and reminded Ambedkar about Panchayats of pre-Mughal India. But nobody came forward to present Mahatma Gandhi's perspective of autonomous village republics. During freedom struggle it was asserted time and again that the fate of rural India can be reconstructed only through Panchayats. They were regarded as tools of economic development. The Gandhian members harped upon the undemocratic components of centralisation, which leads to Fascism. Gandhiji wanted Panchayats to train villagers in democratic decentralisation.[64] The consensus in the constituent-assembly was that centralisation will prove disintegrative and too much power with the centre was not the goal of freedom.

The view could be heard in a partial manner when K. Santhanam's amendment was accepted on 22 November 1948. Article 40 was added to the Directive Principles of State Policy, which inter alia states 'state will try to develop village Panchayats and endow them with powers, so that they become units of self-government'. Henry Meddick writes 'the constitutions expected three goals to be achieved through Panchayats (a) Promotion of participation of people in the democratic process of the nation. (b) Rural participation for rural development and (c) Reduction of responsibility of the state government.[65]

This situation of 1950 has gone a long way in twenty first century. The next chapter provides the study of the developments of last sixty years after getting freedom.

Notes

1. B.B. Majumdar, *Problems of Public Administration*, Pustak Mahal, Patna, 1951, p. 205.
2. M.K. Gandhi, *Gram Swarajya*, Navjivan Trust, Ahmadabad, 1965, p. 7.
3. Sir Charles Metcalfe, 'Select Committee Report of House of Commons', 1832, vol. III, 84, p. 331.
4. R.C. Majumdar and H.C. Raichaudhuri, *Advanced History of India*, Macmillan, London, 1948, p. 29.
5. T. Raghukul, *Loktantra*, UP Hindi Academy, Luknow, 1972, p. 458.
6. S. Parmatma, *Pracheen Bharat mein Rajneetik Vichar Aur Sansthyen*, Meenakshi Prakashan, Meerut, p. 45.
7. Rigveda, 8/11/06
8. Yajurveda 12/11
9. Atharvaveda 3/5
10. Atharvaveda 6/7
11. Yajurveda 6/2, 12/6
12. Atharvaveda 8/107
13. B.K. Sarkar, *The Political Institutions and Theories of Hindus*, pp. 51-52.
14. Atharvaveda, ch.8, Mantra 10.
15. प्वेताएवतसोवनिश्त्तद, ch.VI, Mantra 11.
16. Ishoupanishad, Mantra 1.
17. K.D. Bajpai, *Vishwa ke Rajneetik Darshan ka Itihas*, Vidhannidi, 1992, Delhi, p. 17.
18. Shantiparva Mahabharat, ch.87, 319.
19. Ramayan, Ayodhya kand, Sarg 67.
20. The Panchayats, GoI, 1956, p. 4.
21. A.S. Altekar, *State and Government in Ancient India*, Motilal, Banaras, 1955, p. 309.
22. Manu Smriti, ch.VII, Sholak 114-115.
23. R.K. Mukherjee, *Hindu Civilization*, Bhartiya Vidya Bhavan, Bombay, p. 187.
24. Kautilays, 'Arthashsthra', Prakash 17, ch. I.
25. B.A. Saletore, *Ancient Indian Political Thought*, Asia Publication, Bombay, 1963, pp. 419–425.

26. H.D. Malaviya, *Village Panchayats in India*, All India Congress Committee, New Delhi, 1956, pp. 7–72.
27. Ibid., p. 72.
28. S.K. Vidyaalankar, *Maurya Samrajya ka Itihas*, Indian Press, Allahabad, pp. 210–211.
29. Mountstuart Elphinstone, *History of India*, John Murray, London, 1906, p. 68.
30. A.S. Altekar, *State and Government in Ancient India*, Motilal Banarasidass, Delhi, 1962, p. 331.
31. A.L. Bhushan, *The Wonder that was India*, Grove, New York, 1959, pp. 104–105.
32. Altekar, *State and Government in Ancient India*, p. 342.
33. Majumdar, *Problems of Public Administration*, p. 194.
34. M. Venkatarangaiyya and M. Pattabhiram, *Local Government in India*, Allied Publishers, Delhi, p. 1.
35. Altekar, *State and Government in Ancient India*.
36. K.P. Jayaswal, *Hindu Polity,* The Bangalore Printing and Publishing Co., Bangalore, p. 12.
37. S. Parmatma, 'Pracheen Bharat', p. 256.
38. Sukraneeti, ch. II, Shlok 121–122.
39. B. Prasad, *Theory of Government in Ancient India*, Central Book, Allahabad, 1974, p. 500.
40. Altekar, 'State and Government in Ancient India', pp. 200–204.
41. Mukherjee, *Hindu Civilization*, pp. 164–165.
42. S. Parmatma, 'Pracheen Bharat', p. 455.
43. C.M.P. Cross, *The Development of Self Government in India*, Chicago University Press, Chicago, 1922, p. 27.
44. S.V. Samant, *Village Panchayats*, Local Self-Government Institute, Bombay, 1957, p. 15.
45. Altekar, *State and Government in Ancient India*, pp. 171–173.
46. Tinker Hugo, *Foundations of Local Self Government in India*, Lalwani, New Delhi, 1967, p. 19.
47. Lord Hailey in Hugo Tinker, 'Preface'.
48. S.R. Maheshwari, *Bharat Mein Sthaniya Shasan*, Laxmi Narain, Agra, 1990, pp. 25–37.
49. D. Zamora Mario, *The Panchayat Tradition*, Reliance, New Delhi, 1990, p. 20.

50. Report of the Taxation Enquiry Committee, 1953–54, Vol. III, Delhi, GoI, 1955, p. 336.
51. Shiriah, *Panchayati Raj: An Analytical Survey in ICD Survey*, Hyderabad, 1976, p. 31.
52. S.R. Maheshwari, *Bharat Mein Sthaniya Shasan*, Laxmi Narain, Agra, 1990, p. 19.
53. Raghukul, *Loktantra*, p. 460.
54. Malaviya, *Village Panchayats in India*, pp. 220–221.
55. Ibid.
56. Mario, *Panchayat Tradition*, p. 23.
57. C.S. Mishra, *Bharat ka Sanvedhanik Itihas*, Law Dept., GOI, Delhi, 1983, p. 6.
58. R.V. Jhathar, 'Evolution of Panchayati Raj in India', JSSI Eco Survey, Dharwar, 1964, p. 26.
59. Hugh Tinker, *Foundations of Local Self Government*, 1954, pp. 129–145.
60. R.P. Dhokalia, *Village Panchayats in UP*, Allahabad, 1951, p. 6.
61. Shiranna, *Panchayati Raj Reform and Rural Development*, Chug Publication, Allahabad, 1990, p. 40.
62. G. Austin, *The Indian Constitution*, Oxford University Press, Delhi, 1972, p. 34.
63. Ibid.
64. Ibid.
65. Henry Meddick, 'Panchayati Raj', *Journal of Local Administration Overseas*, No. 4, October 1962, pp. 204–205.

3

Panchayati Raj in India

From Attainment of Independence to 73rd Constitutional Amendment

Attainment of independence in 1947 added a new chapter in the history of local self-government in India. In 1948 the Union Minister for Local Self-government invited a conference of state ministers for local self-government at Delhi. Inaugurating this conference Prime Minster Pandit Jawaharlal Nehru said, 'local self-government constitutes the backbone of a real democracy and this is the way it should be. We often tend to think about the government above rather than government below. But if you do not build the foundation, the edifice does not last.'[1]

The new Republican Constitution of India was adopted on 26 January 1950. Local self-government was included in the State List of Seventh Schedule. One of the directives in Chapter IV said, 'it will be the duty of the state to organise Panchayats in such a manner that they become the units of self-government.'[2]

Pandit Nehru eulogised the Panchayati Raj system on the floor of the assembly and said, 'Panchayats form the basic foundation of the governmental edifice. We do not want to weaken this support base in our own interest.'[3] He was a great advocate of democratic decentralisation. In his own words, 'if you decentralise you will reach to the villages. They are the smallest unit of government.'[4] Minister for Rural Development in Pandit Nehru's Cabinet, M.S.K. Dey, opined that 'village Panchayats are the real institutions of the people. They have to attend the basic needs of social order and fulfil the social and community obligation's.[5] He argued that if we want to get rid our villages from the malaise of bureaucracy, feudalism, capitalism or religious bigotry, then we should strengthen the base i.e. the Panchayati Raj'.[6]

This thought process continued in India and even Indira Gandhi, who encountered National disasters of high magnitude maintained that 'Panchayats have played a vital role in keeping the foundations of India democracy strong. We have high hopes from this system and they can be fulfilled only when the weaker sections of rural life come forward to participate in their own governance'.

First Five Year Plan and Panchayati Raj

The draft outline of Five Year Plans was prepared to facilitate an all-round development of the country. The first plan was prepared and implemented for the period from 1952 to 1957. This plan highlighted and gave priority to rural development. The Planning Commission stressed upon the need of Rural Development agencies and their establishment at village and block levels. The Commission believed that 'if Panchayats could be associated with the living process of rural development, then they will generate a meaningful participation of the people and will fulfill their civil role with satisfaction'.[7]

The First Plan draft talks about democratic decentralisation. It says 'the government of India and state governments have democratic institutions under the constitution but the local institutions have organic link and failed to establish a democratic administrative structure. They are the tools of local growth. Hence it is all the more important to democratise them. This way they can establish good relations for good governance at every level. Their relations with Panchayats, Zila Parishads and divisional local boards are quite relevant in the development process.'[8]

Thus, the first Five Year Plan makes a plea for creating the structures of rural local development at each level. As many as 34,000 Panchayats were established during the first plan period (1952–1957). Thus, the member of Panchayats increased from 83,000 to 180,000 in 1957.

Second Five Year Plan and Panchayati Raj

The Second Five Year Plan extended the scope of community development programmes and National Extension Service. They identified the functions and roles of Panchayats. Cooperative effort for economic growth was stressed, and the commission openly said, 'Panchayats are the agencies of rural leadership and they provide direction to development. Development of Panchayats should be a vital component in community development and National Extension Service programmes.'[9]

Community Development Programme

The community development programme was launched on 2 October 1952 to promote democratic decentralisation. Pandit Nehru, while inaugurating the programme, said, 'Majority of people of India live in the villages. Any reform that seeks the development and welfare of these villagers should not only be welcomed, but enthusiastically encouraged to yield fruits.'[10]

The Planning Commission concretised this philosophy by developing community development programmes in a manner that it may become a Nodal agency for rural as well as urban social welfare.[11]

The community development programmes aimed to resolve rural problems at village level within their limited resources. It was good as well as necessary. Food, housing, raiment, health and ethical behaviour are not isolated problems. All of them had to be solved as a package. If the disease afflicts the whole body, partial treatment does not cure. No one solution can rid rural life from its historic and organic ailments of collective nature. The community development programme aimed to induct qualitative transformation in the lives of villagers. They must accept this indivisible and holistic nature of change. The programme was designed to generate and strengthen the will to change. One aspect of it was reform in agriculture and extension of cottage industries to eliminate rural poverty and unemployment. In addition, education facilities were to be provided for people of all the age groups. Housing problems were to be solved along with healthy entertainment facilities to lead a happy and healthy life of joy and fulfilment. Thus, community development was a multipurpose programme to stir the country side which has been stagnant for centuries or generations.

A multipurpose functionary was the characteristic feature of this programme. It has handled a variety of problems like agriculture, veterinary diseases, garden maintenance and forest records. The junior-most functionary in community development programme was expected to assist the farmer with his specialised training in a variety of areas. Till now different departments used to second their officers in the field. These officials made piecemeal suggestions and created more problems rather than solving them. Now this one officer was responsible and trained. He could help the farmer directly and quickly. The need of this village official was felt by Finance Commission in as early as 1949. The commission wrote: 'In our opinion India needs an extension service which can bridge the gap between researchers and the user of rural services. This service should be on the pattern obtained in UK. We feel that there can be an extension officer or a group of workers for a cluster of 40 to 45 villages. He should work on a Demonstration Farm. The departmental officials and the farmers may remain in continuous contact to this multipurpose functionary who will act as a friend, philosopher and guide to the farmers. His contact will help the villagers to solve their problems.'[12]

Community development programmes introduced greatest number of people to greatest good or highest welfare of the people. The programme aimed to accomplish welfare projects that pertained to all the population group, men, women and children, of a particular area. The programmes included the following functions:

1. Fertilisation of arid and barren land
2. Provision of improved farm equipment
3. Management of educational facilities
4. Administration of public health
5. Training of farmers and farm workers
6. Promotion of cottage industries
7. Construction of rural houses
8. Organisation of cooperative societies.

Commencement of National Extension Service

After a year-long experience of community development schemes, another programme called National Extension Service was inaugurated for rural reconstruction. It was relatively smaller in scope, but the purpose was the same as that of community development programme. The scheme and projects were spread all over the country. Hence, a permanent agency was needed to monitor and coordinate these programmes. The first Five Year Plan has emphasised upon it. The Balwantrai Mehta addressed the problem in details. It recommended that a block should be constituted by combining the Tahsils or Talukas. This block administration should be the hub of welfare activities in the area. This situation was studied, and a permanent extension service was established in the country. The block was made the lowest unit, and appropriate administrative activities were assigned to it. Block as a development unit was created for a three-year period with a budget of ₹ 5.50 lakh. The later stage of intense development was called as community development block, and a budget of ₹ 15 lakh was allotted for another three years. The last or the highest state of development in this scheme was also conceived and an amount of ₹ 30,000 was added every year to support the growing needs development schemes. All these stages worked in a similar manner except that more money was made available at the later stage. The scheme was to be extended to the entire country towards the end of Second Five Year Plan. As these blocks developed the community development scheme became the general scheme for development of villages.[13]

The National Extension Service commenced in 1953 and its network covered the entire country in a decade's time. There were three criteria to select the area for National Extension Scheme. They are listed below:

1. The block should be headed by the block-level officer to manage the block-level functions and activities.
2. The block should not coincide with the ordinary administrative unit.
3. While delimiting the boundary of a block, special needs of members of SC and ST communities may be taken care of.

Administrative Structure at Block and District Level

The administration of Community Development Blocks was assigned to the bureaucracy in the field. There were some minor changes in the organisation so that the integrated rural reconstruction programmes may get reflected in it. The work policy of the block was to be distinguished and both BDO and VLW were a part of the programme. The VLW was the last link of the administrative chain, and he was conceived as a multifunctional rural worker for 5–10 villages. A block usually had 300 villages and the BDO was its chief administrator. He was an ordinary administrator, and his job included coordination between various technical officials in the block. The district-level coordination was the responsibility of the collector.

Administrative Structure at State Level

There was a common administrative authority for National Extension Service and other development programmes at the level of the state. Most of the states had a Development Committee for policy formation which was presided by the Chief Minister or the Minister concerned. The Development Commissioner was the ex officio Secretary. He was the head of the block which had various secretaries of technical departments, and while coordinating their work he was specially responsible for the execution of projects under the scheme.

Administrative Structure at Union Level

Although community development programmes fell in the jurisdiction of the state, the union government offered them all sorts of physical, financial and moral support. The Central Committee of the union government included members of the Planning Commission. The committee laid down the policies and supervised the work of the administrators of the projects. The project officer was a new officer who supervised, directed and coordinated community development work in the entire country. The committee sought reports from him and officers below reported to him in matters of finance, training and personnel. Similarly, technical officers in the departments of health, education, irrigation, industries, housing and so on advised him and he in turn supervised and controlled them on behalf of the union government.

The administration of community development was entirely in the hands of bureaucracy. The revenue official played a special role. The bureaucracy did not allow people to be partners, and the distrust kept the system formal without rural involvement. The committees could accomplish nothing, and people kept distance from bureaucratic pronouncements. Prof. Rajni Kothari found that the large army of officials and their tall claims of community development could not bridge the gulf between people and government. The programme failed because it was organised and run like any government department. The villages did not develop, but the bureaucratic machinery of community development workers were indulged with fat salaries. The official attitudes did not change, and the people kept waiting for the officials without any substantial achievement.[14]

The bureaucracy rode roughshod over community development administration. The local people who knew and who were to be served were treated as beneficiaries of the Raj. People's participation was used as a rhetoric, and people were neither trusted nor invited to learn by trial and error.

The UN Community Mission testified that 'Community Development in India is a government's official agenda without popular support and involvement.'[15] R. Bendix corroborates this view that community development programme is an euphuism and it suffers from bureaucratic bottlenecks. The mentor of this scheme believed that civil service alone can implement programmes, but paradoxically they talked that people alone can do it. People were to come forward, but they were always relegated to the background.[16]

The study team of Administrative Reforms Commission (ARC) suggested that democratic decentralisation had its relevance only at the hustings. The team made a plea for elected representative institutions at the locals levels so that they may be vested with adequate powers and functions. The local institutions are not departments, nor can they be administered under any contract. The elected institutions are a part of the government.[17] The Mehta Committee recommended that the existing Boards and Blocks should be abolished and replaced by new institutions which should be elective, powerful and functional. They should be responsive and responsible.[18] The hub of this chain should be in the middle and their size should be such that they may be active to fulfill the demands from below and dictates from above. Block was identified as the key tier from where the development assignments may be administered at all the three levels.[19] The organisations above should coordinate and create conditions conducive for development at below. Popular participation in all these institutions can be ensured or encouraged only by elective principle and committee mechanisms. People in general should be galvanised through democratic institutions and rural local government given to the people without control of the state. Balwant Rai Mehta called it Panchayati Raj and the three tiers he recommended are as follows:

1. Village Panchayat at village level
2. Panchayat Samiti at middle level
3. Zila Parishad at top level.

The Mehta Committee strongly argued that democratic decentralisation could yield maximum results only when these elective institutions are introduced at all the three tiers in a simultaneous manner. Piecemeal experimentation would kill them through governmental evaluations.

Implementation of B.R. Mehta Committee Report

All the states of India welcomed the Mehta Committee report and Panchayati Raj institutions were created to enhance popular participation and to rectify the deficiencies of community development programme. They were intended to act as institutional agencies for socioeconomic change in rural reconstruction. The main objectives of Panchayati Raj reforms are as follows:

1. Ensure popular participation of maximum people in socio economic development
2. Decentralise administration at the lower level of the villages
3. Create local self-government institutions through a democratic process in rural India.

The National Development Council in its meeting in January 1959 approved the three-tier system of Panchayati Raj. However, the council suggested that the Panchayati Raj institutions should be attuned to the local conditions of the state. The National Development Council was of the view that the external structure and key areas may have uniformity, but complexities should be avoided so that the variety of local situations may get reflected as 'unity in diversity'. India is a vast country and Panchayati Raj will have to grapple with unanticipated and varied problems of long-range implications. Naturally, these institutions should be given authority to experiment and evolve a variety of patterns of local governance. The major purpose is transfer of power to the people. Once this is ensured, the questions of size, functions, constraints and so on can be sorted out based on the needs of the target local population. The

National Development Council also endorsed it as a matter of policy and wanted the Panchayati Raj to work in unison with the state governments as envisaged in the Constitution.

A uniform pattern of Panchayati Raj for the whole country is ruled out by the very size and cultural diversities across the country. Hence, some basic principles were evolved on the basis of consensus to implement the Mehta model within the frame work of unique needs of different states. These principles are listed below:

1. From village to District, the system should be three-tier, and each tier should be linked with one another.
2. The functions and authority should be transferred to people in a genuine manner.
3. Adequate resources should also be transferred to these institutions so that state governments do not starve them to untimely death.
4. All programmes of popular welfare and economic development should be linked and put under the care of these local institutions.
5. The three-tier system should be so organised that it may be revised and further strengthened or remodelled with the passage of time.[20]

All the states established Panchayati Raj institutions in accordance to these principles. The then Prime Minister of India, Pandit Jawaharlal Nehru, inaugurated this Panchayati Raj system at Nagaur in Rajasthan on 2 October 1959. Andhra Pradesh followed suit. Then the other states switched over to the system by 1962. By the year 1965–1966 the Panchayati Raj institutions were established in all the states, except for Kerala, Jammu and Kashmir, and Nagaland.

The states' option for Panchayati Raj accepted the importance of Gram Sabha. It was being felt that the Panchayati Raj institutions function at each level but the ultimate responsibility should be to this village body in a continuous manner. It was conceived as a body of village elders. Different states suggested different kinds of compositions. For instance in Rajasthan, Bihar and Orissa all the adult residents of the village were made the members of Gram Sabha.[21] Other states included only the Panchayati voters whose names appeared in the voter list for State Legislative Assembly.

The State of Rajasthan was the first to launch Panchayati Raj institutions all the way to cover village, block and district levels.

The Naya Panchayats were also constituted for 5–7 Panchayats in the area.

The National Development Council quite enthusiastically accepted the B.R. Mehta's report and all the states showed interests in the reform almost the way they implemented the community development programmes. In the 1950s, Andhra Pradesh, Gujarat, Maharashtra and Rajasthan experimented with the three-tier model with varying emphasis. The popularity of the reform can be measured by the fact that thousands of Panchayats could be established all over the country in three years' time. The states like UP, Maharashtra and Andhra prepared to make Zila Parishads the hub of rural development. However, in several other states Panchayat Samiti or Taluka Panchayat was made the key institution under the active supervision of district bodies. The political system responded to this local reform, and heads of Samitis and Parishads soon became rural representatives which the Constitution later legitimised.

Experience of early years demonstrates that the generation of freedom fighters in almost all the states had a desire to do something worthwhile as their duty to the motherland. To them politics was not a means of livelihood. But as time passed succeeding generations began to see community development programmes as an opportunity to make money. The development campaigns began to fail. The genuine leaders of the older generation like Balwant Rai Mehta felt that institutionalisation of Panchayats may fill the vacuum and people may feel the difference between a new democratic order and old bureaucratic mischief. The need for facilities in the villages generated pressure on these leaders, and in the 1960s they tried to revive that fervour through local institutions. The senior leaders of Congress sitting in Assemblies and Parliament patronised the junior leaders and sincerely cooperated in their efforts of rural reconstruction. The intentions of senior leaders can be gauged by the fact that senior administrative officers of IAS, IPS and RAS cadres were appointed as BDOs and the collector was the Secretary of the Zila Parishad.

As much as 99 per cent of villages and villagers have been covered by Panchayati Raj by 31 March 1965. The total number of Gram Panchayats, Panchayat Samitis and Zila Parishads were 212,398, 3,489 and 247 in the country, respectively.[22] Millions of officials and non-officials were trained in various training centres. A project of this magnitude is bound to have difficulties that can be both expected and unexpected.

The first problem was that these village leaders were not only uneducated but illiterate without any capacity to read or write. There was no experience of working in public offices. It was natural that they were likely to be victims of caste, class, family or groups and could not function objectively as public servants.[23] Another difficulty was that the tradition of confidence and cooperation between official and non-official members was conspicuously absent. The officials were used to command or order and the juniors 'just' obeyed them sheepishly. The introduction of Panchayati Raj made a world of difference which the two could not comprehend. The officials, being more educated, did not concede equality and the non-officials had the feeling that they were mere subordinates who are there to take orders and that position didn't sit well with them. Petty issues hurt their ego and created controversies. For instance, there would be a tussle as to who should keep the key of the jeep – the Pradhan or the BDO. It was found as one of the apples of discord in the field. The third problem was the financial crunch. The grants in aid from the state governments were inadequate, and state officials like collectors and commissioners got opportunities to get the grants processed or delayed as they wished. Because of this, self-respecting leaders of masses did not contest elections and the officials misbehaved with political leaders of lesser merit.

Because of these problems the Santhanam Committee recommended the powers of local taxation to these bodies. It also recommended the enactment of a code of conduct for the officials and the elected non-officials.

The post-Nehru era witnessed a steep decline in public life. The state-level leaders began to think that the local Panchayati Raj leaders do not represent the people. On the other hand, Panchayati Raj leaders began to challenge state leaders who in their judgment were far away from people. Naturally, therefore, the state became relaxed and neglected the financial needs of Panchayats. This conflict between the state and local leaders of Panchayati Raj impacted adversely upon the growth of nascent institutions which started wilting even before they blossomed.

The state leaders became apathetic and postponed the Panchayati elections for years. Powerful local officials abused resources. Privileged groups spoiled the image of Panchayati Raj, and people lost faith in the viability of the Panchayati Raj institutions.[24]

Leaving Maharashtra and Gujarat, other states provided very few opportunities to projects handled by Panchayati Raj bodies. Block administration of Panchayat Samitis by and large failed to run development administration. Political leaders and bureaucratic officials weakened Panchayati Raj institutions in order to serve their personal ends.

All this contributed to the ritualisation of Panchayati Raj. People felt that rural government of bureaucrats has become strong in the name of rural local self-government.

In 1962, union government constituted a committee under the chairmanship of an MP from Rajasthan, Sadiq Ali, to study the execution of Panchayati Raj Acts. Its report in 1964 outlined the problem areas. The Naik Report in 1963 and Bhandari Committee report in 1964 further identified the bottlenecks in the development of rural local institutions. A high-power committee under the chairmanship of Shri Girdhari Lal Vyas in Rajasthan also submitted detailed suggestions to rejuvenate Panchayati Raj institutions at all the three levels.

The 1977 general elections defeated the Congress party. The Janata Party formed the government, and it made a bold bid to resuscitate the spirit of decentralisation through Panchayati Raj institutions. It appointed the Ashok Mehta Committee to diagnose the malady and suggest a workable prescription.

Thus, the finding that Panchayati Raj institutions' were indeed working over two decades is an indicator that future can be optimistic for Panchayati Raj institutions but not without introducing reforms in a sustained manner. The initial stage witnessed enthusiasm and sincere efforts. Then came the period of apathy and hostility. States kept beating the dead horse, and the situation remained disappointing till 1965. The period 1965–1969 proved to be the lowest ebb for Panchayati Raj institutions, and financial support from the state literally stopped. Administrators were corrupt and abused resources made available for rural development. Till 1976, it can be said that the structure of Panchayati

Raj got crystallised but its working remained ineffective. The institutions collapsed, and the period from 1969 to 1977 is called the *dark age* of Panchayati Raj.

Ashok Mehta Committee

This committee was constituted on 12 December 1977 with 14 members from various political parties. Its objective was to suggest measures for strengthening Panchayati Raj. The committee submitted its report in August 1978. The 300-page report submitted contained 11 chapters and provided numerous recommendations.[25] Senior members like M.S. Namboodiripad, M.G. Ramachandran and S.K. Dey recorded their notes of dissent to some of the recommendations made and their comments.

The Mehta report maintained that it is wrong to believe that Panchayati Raj has been a failure. The report specifically recounts the achievements of Panchayati Raj system. It is a potential process to fertilise the Indian soil with democratic seeds. It has served as a bridge between the bureaucracy, the elite groups and the masses. It has produced a leadership which, besides being new and modern, is a protagonist of social change. It has generated development awareness among rural people. However, its shortcomings and frailties are obvious. The report suggested some remedial measures, including the following.

Decentralised System

Administrative decentralisation implies functional decentralisation. If millions and millions of people are to be involved in their economic development, micro-level projects need to be implemented and monitored in a decentralised way. People's supervision or public audit is another way to stay sensitive and respect public aspirations. The report writes, 'In our view the structure and working of Panchayati Raj institutions should be determined by the future functional needs of rural development management. Its personnel and financial resources should also be tailored accordingly.

Establishment of Mandal Panchayats

The Ashok Mehta Committee championed the two-tier Panchayati Raj. The decentralisation should begin at the level of the district. A high level of technology for developments is available here. The second tier should be below the district and Mandal (block) will be an appropriate tier for a Mandal Panchayat. The report inter alia mentioned, 'We recommend a two-tier system of Zila Parishad and Mandal Panchayat. We are aware that the two tiers are already in existence but the institutional frame we are suggesting will take some time in getting a shape. Wherever Block Panchayat Samitis exist they may be converted into executive Committees of the Zila Parishads and later on their functions may be handed over to Mandal Panchayats. The Block structure may be retained during transition as per needs and status of development in the state. The village committees may help Mandal Panchayats and urban bodies for some time. It is also advisable to form a "village Panchayat Sangh" till the Mandal Panchayats of the district come to a takeoff.'[26]

This system was already in existence in some states. The district bodies were to be democratised and endowed with functions and powers. A Mandal Panchayat for a population of 15,000–20,000 was novel and unique. According to Mehta Committee the Mandal Panchayat alone could strike a balance between the technical needs of development and possibilities of popular participation in rural development programmes.

Partisan Elections

Ashok Mehta openly and boldly argued against the Gandhian view of party-less democracy. He firmly believed that partisan elections of Panchayati Raj institutions will rid them from petty parochialism of castes and sub-castes. He defended reservation of seats for social justice at each level. The report makes a plea for reservation of women for the seats at the Mandal and the district levels. The Panchayat elections should be conducted by state's Chief Election Commissioner to ensure free and fair poll at the hustings.

Evaluation of Ashok Mehta Report

B.R. Mehta Committee and Ashok Mehta Committee constitute two major landmarks in the history of local self-government in India. They have their distinctive ideological structures to suggest the framework. To some extent Ashok Mehta borrows the basics from B.R. Mehta report, but there are some areas in which the two deliberately disagree and keep different perspectives. B.R. Mehta accepted block-level organisation as the basis of Panchayati Raj structure whereas Ashok Mehta argued for district-level decentralisation. The block remains a standard unit, but development has to be planned at the level of the district to get coordinated with the state.

Ashok Mehta Committee took a narrow view because of its stress on functionalism. It regarded Panchayati Raj institutions as mere means of administration which should assist the state in rural development. It could not conceive of decentralisation as a third tier of government. Naturally, the Ashok Mehta Committee could not devolve powers and functions to make Panchayati Raj institutions autonomous and adequately powerful.[27]

The Ashok Mehta Committee did not envisage Panchayats as developmental agencies. Mehta did not accept village as a key unit, and his report ignores the village Panchayat as a dynamic institution capable of transforming the lives at the bottom level. According to him, this tier is too weak to serve as the base of Panchayati Raj edifice.

Critics accuse the structure of Panchayati Raj for its several failings which flow from the institutional design. The fact of the matter is that it was neither analysed nor sympathetically experimented upon. The committee had its doubts about the capability of our rural people and the use of technology in rural development. So it opted for a two-tier system.[28]

Mehta Committee recommended Mandal Panchayats without village Panchayats at the base. If it was accepted, the entire structure of Panchayati system would have collapsed; pointing out this lacuna, Sidh Raj Dhadha, a member of the committee, stated, 'I have no objection to Zila Parishad and Mandal Panchayat, but the committee did not discuss the role of "Gram Sabha," which in my judgment provides the ground floor for the edifice.'[29]

Partisan election of Panchayats was a suggestion practical and desirable. Political parties enable popular participation, and they can be made responsible also. Local institutions should reflect popular aspirations and opinions. Hence, the committee quite boldly brushed aside what J.P. and other Gandhites were preaching since the days of freedom struggle.

Social audit was also a desirable proposition. This will make local institutions accountable, and leaders will encounter informed people. It will improve performance.

The Ashok Mehta Committee accepts growing urbanisation inevitable. Rural people should have facilities like roads, drinking water, medical facilities, education and employment. It will arrest their migration to cities. The present situation caused conflicts between villages and cities. The rural and urban local bodies have different kinds of structures. They are not interrelated. As development efforts expand the facilities, this distinction is fast disappearing. It all the more requires a clearer enunciation of the functions of the two sectors. India will ultimately need to create a local system in which the rural and urban population may have their basic minimum needs met and the two segments may get merged eventually.

Resuscitation of Panchayati Raj in post-Mehta era (1978–1989)

It is the period when the Seventh Five Year Plan was searching directions in which development should move forward. The Ashok Mehta report naturally attracted the attention of the commission, and the recommendations of Panchayati Raj were translated into financial outlays and resource mobilisation. Several states had a change of party governments, and when Rajeev Gandhi took over the reins as Prime Minister of India the Panchayati Raj had an ally in his leadership. Yet there were doubts and dangers. The states like Rajasthan, Gujarat and Maharashtra have already gone more than half-way. West Bengal and Karnataka also emerged as strong proponents of Panchayati Raj system.

The Left alliance in West Bengal amended the 1973 Panchayat Act and the Panchayati Raj established by Jyoti Basu is still considered as a bold experiment that shaped the identity of district administration in its role in rural development. The district collector in West Bengal is the chief executive of the Zila Parishad. The land reforms programme called 'Operation Barga' has added to the stature of Panchayati Raj. People gave credit to local leaders and the state government used Panchayati Raj institutions to bring land reforms and land management in a state where Marxism had its roots in the discontentment of the landless.

In 1985 Karnataka launched a very strong Panchayati Raj system by combining democratic decentralisation with decentralised district development. It was a revolutionary step taken by the then Chief Minster C.M. Hegde. The District Development Agency was transferred and merged with Zila Parishad. The departments were put under the Zila Parishad, and a senior official higher than collector was made something like the chief secretary of the district in the district body. As much as 40 per cent of the funds allocated to the plan head and 50 per cent of the funds allocated to the non-plan head were transferred to Zila Parishads under the Gadgil formula. The Mandal Panchayats were established in place of village Panchayats (for a population of 20,000–25,000) as recommended by Ashok Mehta Committee.

The state of Karnataka had not only allotted adequate resources but also transferred planning and development functions along with personnel administration to Panchayat Raj institutions at both levels. Only sensitive areas like law and order and police were not transferred because of their criticality and non-political nature. The collector looked after revenue affairs and acted as district magistrate in law and order administration. Partisan elections were accepted, and the popular participation in development projects at lower levels proved highly beneficial to the people.

Karnataka had nine Zila Parishads. The Pramukhs in these nine Parishads were the secretaries of committees for functional departments. These secretaries working for different areas, such as agriculture, health, education, public works, and industries, were under the supervision of Zila Parishad, and the elected members evaluated their day-to-day working. The division of subjects was clear and specific without any diarchy or double control. There was an inter-district Parishad to resolve problems through coordination and distribution of funds in the state budget. The State Finance Commission did the job of resource distribution on a continuous basis.

All the Panchayati Raj bodies in Karnataka were directly elected. The Mandal Panchayats and Zila Parishads were popular bodies of people. The members of parliament and legislative assembly from the field or districts were nominated as members of Zila Parishads. As much as 25 per cent reservation of seats were provided for SC, ST and women on the basis of their proportion in population. If not elected, every Panchayati institution was to have minimum two seats for these deprived groups. The Karnataka experiment proved that Panchayati Raj institutions can play the nursery of leadership for higher institutions of Indian democracy. The powers of supersession were given to higher bodies, that is, to Zila Parishad for Mandal Panchayats and to state government for Zila Parishads. The Zila Pramukh and Up-Zila Pramukh were given the salary and status of a state minister and deputy minister of the state cabinet. This was an official recognition of the significance of local government. The collector looked after regulatory functions only, and the development part was supervised by a senior IAS official who was appointed as the secretary to Zila Parishad. He acted under the political supervision of the elected head. It was the first significant attempt to place career bureaucracy under political leadership for developmental tasks at the district level.

In 1986, the Telugu Desam party's government in Andhra Pradesh enacted the Panchayati Raj legislation and created Mandal Praja Parishad, Zila Praja Parishad and District Development Review Boards in each district. Here also the Mandal model of Ashok Mehta was prepared to replace the Balwant Rai Mehta model of three-tier system.

Rajasthan conducted elections of Panchayati Raj bodies in 1978 after an interval of 18 years. Special efforts were made to revive these bodies in 1981. Other states like UP, Bihar and MP revived the three-tier structure. Gujarat and Maharashtra strengthened the Zila Parishads by endowing them with extra powers and appointing IAS officers as their secretaries. This added to their stature and functional capacity.

Report of the Working Group on District Planning – 1984

The Planning Commission constituted an expert panel under the chairmanship of Hanumanth Rao. It was asked to suggest ways how district plans can be formulated at the district level. The panel concluded that the development plans being centralised have been insensitive to local needs and resources because of the absence of popular participation. The panel deplored that the implementation of developmental scheme have fallen short of targets during the past 40 years. The expert panel recommended decentralised planning from below. The process was to be reversed. The report had a great impact on plan formulation in the states.

G.V.K. Rao Committee – 1985

The Ashok Mehta Committee revised the structure, administrative nature and financial regulations of working in Panchayati Raj institutions. As chance will have it the Janata Party government went out of power much before the committee recommendations could be implemented. The Congress (I) returned to power in 1980. Mrs. Gandhi did not accept Ashok Mehta Committee's report and appointed another committee under G.V.K. Rao to reorganise Panchayati Raj institutions in view of the increasing need of decentralisation. Rao prepared his report in consultation with Planning Commission. It recommended a bold system where by a district-level agency for development was to be created. The committee was of the view that economic development and social justice cannot be imposed upon the people by making bureaucracy accountable for the change. The local people have to come forward, participate and formulate and execute their own plans.[30]

The committee made a plea for the reactivating the Panchayats and urged upon the government to provide support and facilitation so that they can effectively remove people's grievances. There is imminent need for electing Panchayat members in time.[31] The committee recommended that district should be the basic unit for policy, planning and programme implementation. The Zila Parishads should create executive agencies so that the development programmes can be implemented in the field. According to Rao, the Zila Parishad should constitute subcommittees on the basis of proportional representation to promote participatory democracy. The Panchayati Raj institutions below should do monitoring of development and play an effective role in rural reconstruction. The committee felt that the concept of a district budget should be put in effect at the earliest opportunity.[32] The district development projects should be executed at the block level for which the block-level organisation should be strengthened.[33]

L.M. Singhvi Committee – 1986

This report was prepared and presented by the efforts of Union Rural Development Ministry in 1986. The Singhvi Committee reviewed the decentralised development and recommended for the reinvigoration of Gram Sabha. The Sabha was to include the entire adult population of the village, and it was called the Reincarnation of Direct Democracy. It also suggested the constitutionalisation of Panchayati Raj institutions. The committee opined that a separate chapter on Panchayati Raj institution be added to the constitution, so that their basic structure may be protected from intrusion by other bodies of the state. The committee also suggested for the provision of Nyay Panchayats with a jurisdiction on a group of villages. About the participation of political parties, the committee remained meaningfully silent and wanted a practical decision in consultation with parties concened. It prepared a concept paper on 5 November 1986 where in it was reported that Panchayati Raj institutions have been victims of apathy, conceptual confusion and lack of political will for prioritisation. The union government have also ignored them in giving their due.

Collectors' Workshops

From December 1987 to June 1988 the Personnel and Administrative Reforms Department (Training Division) of the union government organised five workshops for collectors and district magistrates in the country. These workshops were conducted in Bhopal (December 1987), Hyderabad (February 1988), Imphal (April 1988), Jaipur (April–May 1988) and Coimbatore (June 1988) and contributed to the creation of a consensus that Panchayati Raj institutions have a special role in making development programmes and administrative system congruent to popular aspirations. The government officials initiated this idea and supported that subjects at the district level may be enumerated in a district schedule and it should be incorporated in the Constitution itself. The subjects suggested for the schedule are as follows:

1. Agriculture
2. Animal husbandry
3. Minor irrigation
4. Social welfare
5. Health and family welfare
6. Primary education
7. Drinking water

8. Social forestry
9. Rural roads
10. Rural electrification and
11. Unconventional energy.

Sarkaria Commission – June 1988

The commission in its report on union–state relations favoured the concept of constitutionalisation of Panchayati Raj institutions. Agreeing with L.M. Singhvi Committee recommendations the commission argued that entry '5' of the state list can be revised or amended for Panchayati Raj functions. The Panchayati Raj laws were to have uniformity in all the states. This can be attained by choosing any one of the following options:

1. The Panchayati Raj laws under Article 263 based on the consent of interstate councils can be the model bill for presentation to the state assemblies.
2. The parliament can make a law in this regard under Article 252 (1) with the consent of state assemblies.
3. The parliamentary enactment of uniform import may be modelled on Articles 172 and 174 for application in the whole country.

Later on P.K. Thungan Committee (1989) made several suggestions in this regards. This committee stressed upon (a) constitutionalisation of Panchayati Raj institutions, (b) holding of elections with regularity and (c) making the Zila Parishads as agencies of planning and development.

In the later part of 1980s the significance of Panchayati Raj institutions was reiterated in the context of decentralised planning and rural reconstruction. Prime Minister Rajeev Gandhi actively participated in the workshops and encouraged deep discussions in the collectors conferences. The consensus that emerged made it apparent that Panchayati Raj institutions alone can promote decentralised development in the country side.

Several inadequacies and challenges were also identified. Some of these dilemmas are presented in the following:

1. Will constitutionalisation of Panchayati Raj be a workable proposition in the politico-economic milieu of rural India?
2. Should there be reservation of seats for SCs, STs and Women?

3. How can periodicity and regularity of elections be ensured?
4. Should the Panchayati Raj system be uniform in all the states?
5. What should be the functions and what resources are to be procured and from where?

To resolve these dilemmas the Rajeev Gandhi government piloted Amendment 64 in May 1989 on the floor of the parliament. This amendment though passed by Lok Sabha could not survive in Rajya Sabha owing to the non-availability of two-third support. Consequently, the 65th Amendment for urban-local bodies also fell and both bills fell short of majority and couldn't pass muster.

Later in 1990, the Congress government came out with the 74th Amendment. However, the ninth Lok Sabha got dissolved and the bill couldn't be passed. Again in 1991 the Congress government of Shri P.V. Narasimha Rao brought the 72nd Amendment for constitutionalisation of Panchayats. The bill was passed by the parliament in December 1992.

The Lok Sabha constituted a select committee for the review of 72nd Amendment. This committee comprised members from various political parties representing several states. Shri N.R. Mirdha was the chairman and the committee examined all the pros and cons and allied details for the perusal of the parliament. After having satisfied itself with the report of the Mirdha Committee, the Lok Sabha passed the bill on 22 December 1992. The Rajya Sabha followed suit and the bill became an act as 73rd Constitutional Amendment. The legislatures of 17 states endorsed the amendment, and it could come on the Statute Book on 24 April 1993 for enforcement in the country.

The evolution of Panchayati Raj and the passing of two amendments represent the culmination point commencing from the Ripon Resolution. For a country of India's size and diversity, it seems like a great leap forward, converting the classical two-tier federalism into a three-tier structure of neo-federalism. This can further take rural India to the exalted and ideal structure of district government. Some conceptual clarity can help if prevailing confusions or hurdles can be overcome with optimism.

Notes

1. S.R. Maheshwari, 'Bharat Mein Sthniya Shasan', op. cit., p. 23.
2. Constitution of India, Article 40.

3. J.L. Nehru, *Community Development and Panchayati Raj*. Delhi, Ministry of Information and Broadcasting, 1963, p. 104.
4. *Nehru on Panchayati Raj and Cooperatives*, Government of India, Delhi, 1964, p. 27.
5. S.K. Dey, *Panchayati Raj: A Synthesis*. Bombay, Asia Publishing, 1965, p. 104.
6. V. Singh, *Desh ki Rajneetik Vyavastha Men Panchayaton ka Yogdan*. Bhopal, MP
7. Planning Commission, *The First Five Year Plan*. New Delhi, Government of India, 1952, p. 133.
8. Ibid.
9. Ibid., pp. 66–70.
10. Maheshwari, *Bharat Men Sthaneeya Swarajya*, p. 54.
11. Ibid.
12. Estimate Committee Report, Lok Sabha Secretariat, Delhi, December 1956, p. 8.
13. *Report on Democratic Decentralisation*. Bombay, Government of Maharashtra, 1961, pp. 27–28.
14. Rajni Kothari, *Politics in India*. Delhi, Orient Longman, 1970, p. 95.
15. *Report of a C.D. Mission*, UN, New York, 1959.
16. R. Benedix, *Nation Building in Citizenship Transaction*, New York, 1964, pp. 266–283.
17. B.R. Mehta Committee on CD and NE, Delhi, 1956.
18. H. Khan, *Government in Rural India*. Bombay Publishing House, Bombay, 1969, p. 26.
19. B.R. Mehta Committee Report, p. 5.
20. R.K. Tilak, *A Digest on Panchayati Raj*, p. 465.
21. Sadiq Ali, *Study Report on Panchayati Raj*. Rajasthan Government, Jaipur, 1964, p. 44.
22. *Times of India*, Year Book, Delhi, 1967, p. 34.
23. Tilak, *A Digest on Panchayati Raj*, p. 472.
24. S.L. Varma, 'Panchayati Raj from State to Centre', *Political Science Review*, Department of Political Science, University of Rajasthan, Jaipur, January–June 1989, p. 112.
25. *Report of the Committee on Panchayati Raj institutions*. Delhi, Government of India, 1978.
26. Ibid, p. 178.
27. Maheshwari, *Bharat Men Sthaneeya Swarajya*, p. 137.

28. Ibid., pp. 173–174.
29. Ibid.
30. Report of G.V.K. Rao Committee, Delhi, 1985, p. 1.
31. Ibid.
32. Ibid.
33. Ibid.

4

The 73rd Constitutional Amendment

A Step Towards Local Government

The 73rd Amendment of the Indian Constitution (1992) was a watershed in the history of Panchayati Raj in India. It was designed to fulfil the strongly felt need for according constitutional status to the system. Ashok Mehta Committee Report (1978) was the first to make this recommendation. L.M. Singhvi Committee Report (1987) also advocated this step. A subcommittee of the Consultative Committee of the Parliament for the Ministry of Rural Development, constituted in 1989 under the chairmanship of P.K. Thungal, too stressed the need for giving constitutional support to the Panchayati Raj. The success of the system in West Bengal and Karnataka also prompted the decision-makers to initiate action for strengthening the Panchayati Raj.

It was in this context that the Rajiv Gandhi government had moved the 64th Amendment Bill in 1987 to give constitutional status to the Panchayati Raj system and remove its inadequacies like 'failure to hold regular and periodic elections, prolonged suspension, inadequate representation to the weaker sections like the scheduled castes, scheduled tribes and women, lack of financial resources and inadequate devolution of powers and responsibilities on them'. The bill was passed by the Lok Sabha but failed to get the requisite two-third majority in Rajya Sabha as the opposition parties suspected that the central government wanted to bypass the state government by dealing directly with the leadership of Panchayati Raj to mobilize electoral support for the Congress. However, the Congress government headed by P.V. Narasimha Rao was able to get the 73rd Amendment (1992) enacted after building a consensus in its favour.

The insertion of two amendments in the Indian Constitution symbolizes a revolution in the structural frame of Indian polity. All efforts made by the then government to get these amendments passed confirm their belief in grassroots democracy. It was a welcome step which had opened the gates of long-range change process in the working of Indian democracy at the level of the district and below. It was bound to strengthen the foundations of democracy which has been a fiefdom of the elites and a manipulative phenomenon of political relations at the top. A true democracy has to be a bottom-up affair, and Panchayati Raj is an admirable initiative in this process. The size and diversity of the country make two-tier structure of government inadequate, and mere union parliament and state legislatures cannot govern the country effectively. Democracy at the doorstep of people is a need, and people can participate and control only when they have true representation in the rural and urban local institutions. Through these institutions they can manage their own affairs, with 73rd and 74th Amends marking a beginning in this direction. The process once started will obliterate the distraction between villages and cities and the present-day double government system for two kinds of Indians will come to an end. The two kinds of local institutions represent the two kinds of lifestyles and facilities which are a legacy of the British Raj. At the local level a uniform government system will create a mainstream society and democracy that will become a government for all. Continuous efforts are needed in this direction. The concept of a district government will go a long way in bridging the existing gulf and the inequality created by colonial masters among rural and urban populace.

The 73rd Constitutional Amendment and Local Self-government

The 64th Amendment introduced by Rajeev Gandhi was taken up by P.V. Narasimha Rao, who got it passed by the parliament as the

73rd Amendment in December 1972. This amendment added a New Chapter IX captioned as Panchayats. It includes provisions from Articles 243 (a) to 243 (o). It was enforced on 25 April 1993. Its major provisions are as follows:

Definitions

1. District means a district in the state.
2. Gram Sabha is a body of the village within a Panchayat whose members are enrolled as voters in the village concerned.
3. 'Middle level' means the level between the village and the district which has been declared as such by a declaration of the governor of the state.
4. Panchayat will include any institution constituted as local self-government body under Article 243 (b) under any name.
5. Panchayat area means the geographical area of the Panchayat.
6. Population means people who have been enumerated in the earlier census and whose figures have been published.
7. Village will include any one or a group of villages included in the declaration of the governor.

Gram Sabha

The Act provides for the constitution of Gram Sabha, which will have powers and functions as assigned to it by the law made by the state legislature.

Composition of Panchayats

1. Every state will have Panchayati institutions at the village level, middle level, and district level as provided in the provision of the act.
2. The middle-level Panchayats will not be constituted if the population is more than 2 million people.

Structure of Panchayats

The amendments provide that states will enact Panchayati legislation within the prescribed provisions of the act. Nevertheless, the population of the Panchayati area and their elected seats will be uniform in the entire state. All seats of Panchayats will be filled by elected representatives. The entire area will be so distributed that the proportion of seats and population in all Panchayat wards will be somewhat equal. The state legislative assembly will provide for the middle-level and district-level tiers. The Panchayat heads will represent at the middle tier and if there is no middle tier then heads will be represented at the district tier. The members of Lok Sabha and Members of State Vidhan Sabha who hail from these Panchayat areas may be represented in these bodies. The members of Rajya Sabha and State Vidhan Parishad, if they are registered as voters for the middle tier and district tiers, they may be made members for representation in Panchayats.

All these heads of Panchayats directly elected or otherwise will have the right to cast their votes in Panchayat meetings. The state assembly will prescribe the system of election of local Panchayats, but the head of the middle and district tiers will be elected by elected members from among themselves.

Reservation of Seats

The Constitutional Amendment lays down that:

1. every Panchayat will have reserved seats for SC and ST members. The reserved seats will be in the same ratio as will be obtained in the population of SC and ST in the concerned Panchayat of the area. Such seats will be allotted by rotation in different constituencies of Panchayat elections.
2. one-third of the reserved seats will be further reserved for women belonging to SC and ST groups of the area.
3. these one-third reserved seats will include seats of women members belonging to SC and ST groups of society. These seats will be allocated by rotation to different constituencies in the Panchayat bodies.
4. The state legislative assembly will make provisions for the post of heads of these bodies belonging to SC, ST and Women. The proportion of these seats will be as far as possible the same which will be obtained in the constituency concerned. The women members and their number will also be one-third of the total seats of these heads. The reserved seats of heads will be allocated by a rotation system at every level.
5. Reservation of seats under Part I and Part II and reservation of seats for women heads under Part IV (which is different from that of Part I and II) will not be effective on the expiry of the term under Article 334.

6. Notwithstanding all this the State Assembly will be entitled to revise the reservation provisions for the SC, ST and women including the positions of heads of Panchayati bodies.

Term of Panchayats

The 73rd Amendment provides that every Panchayat, otherwise dissolved earlier, will have a term of five years since the day it has its first session after elections. The Panchayat body preceding such a new Panchayat will continue to function till it is legally dissolved under Article 243 (d) (i). The Constitution of the Panchayat and dissolution of the old one should take place within the expiry of six months. If the term of the outgoing Panchayat has a period of less than six months, then the election of the new Panchayat for the remaining months will not be necessary. The act further provides that if a Panchayat is dissolved before its term, then the new Panchayat should function for the remaining period of the Panchayat which could have continued if not dissolved.

Eligibility for Membership

The act talks of disqualifications in place of qualifications. The act provides that a member will be ineligible to contest Panchayat election if:

1. he or she has been disqualified for the state assembly elections. But it will not apply in case where the citizen has attained the age of 21 years and is yet to attain the age of 25 years.
2. he or she has been disqualified under any law made by the state legislation. The decision about ineligibility or disqualification will be taken by the official, so empowered by the legislative assembly of the state. He or she will direct the incumbent in writing.

Powers, Functions and Responsibilities of Panchayats

According to 73rd Amendment the state legislative assembly by law can endow Panchayats with powers and functions of a local body as it deems proper. Such rules or laws will direct the Panchayats to use their powers and functions to carry out the legal responsibilities so assigned. These functions and powers are as follows:

1. To plan for economic development and social justice.

2. To implement all those schemes which are assigned to them in the area of economic development and social justice including subjects enumerated in the 11th Schedule.

Power of Taxation and Panchayat Funds

The state assembly can empower the Panchayats to levy taxes on subjects in the manner prescribed by the statute:

1. Taxes, duties, fees within the limits provided can be levied, collected and appropriated by the Panchayat.
2. Grants in aid may be given to Panchayats from the consolidated fund of the state.
3. The Panchayat revenues may be deposited in funds and such funds may be created under the law.

Finance Commission to Review the Financial Condition of Panchayats

The governor of the state under the 73rd Amendment constitutes a Finance Commission after the expiry of every fifth year to review and recommend with regard to the following:

1. Taxes, levies to be collected by the state and distributed between state and the Panchayats. The net proceeds will be shared as per award at every level.
2. All such taxes, fees and levies to be imposed and collected by the Panchayats.
3. The allocation of grants in aid and other measures which may strengthen the financial position of the Panchayats and which the governor may ask from the commission to suggest from time to time.

The state provides that the eligibility and appointment of members of Finance Commission will be determined by the state assembly. The commission will decide about its own procedure of work and will have such powers which the state assembly will vest in the commission. The governor will present before the state assembly all the recommendations of the Finance Commission and all other activities, clarifications and so on which might pertain to commission's functions.

Examination of Panchayat Accounts

The act provides that Panchayats' accounts and audit will be made as per procedures prescribed by rules made by the state legislative assembly.

Election of Panchayats

The constitutional amendment makes a State Election Commission responsible for preparation of the electoral rolls, delimitation of constituencies and conduct of the state. The terms and conditions of service of the members will be determined by the rules made in this regard by the state legislature. Removability procedure of the State Election Commission will be the same as that obtained for the removal of judges of a high court. He will not be permitted to accept any office of profit after retirement and his service conditions will not be altered to his disadvantage. The act further provides that the governor of the state will enable the commission to have the services of the special personnel if and when needed to accomplish his or her job. The act gives general powers to the commission to perform governor's allied and collateral functions related to elections.

Application in Union Territories

The powers of the administrators of union territories have been put at par with the governor of state under Article 239. The union territories having legislative assemblies will make the rules for their respective areas. The union territories without legislative bodies shall obey the presidential directives who may allow exceptions and ask the administration to execute the relevant provisions with regard to Panchayat elections.

The Exceptions

The sub-provisions of Part 9 will not apply to the following areas:

1. Anything under Article 244 (1) will not apply (1) to Scheduled Areas and (2) areas inhabited by Scheduled Tribe people.
2. Nothing in this part will be applicable to Nagaland, Meghalaya and Mizoram states and all those hill areas where Zila Parishads are functioning.

Similarly Darjeeling in West Bengal enjoys a special status and wherever the hill areas are governed by Darjeeling Gorkha Hill

Council, the Panchayati provisions will be inapplicable. But then the Darjeeling Gorkha Hill Council constituted under law may have its impact upon local institutions.

Notwithstanding all this the legislative assembly of Nagaland, Meghalaya and Mizoram can extend the scope of Article 243 (d) (I) to areas in other states, provided the state assembly passes a resolution to that effect by a majority of two-third of members present and voting, establishing absolute majority in the whole house of the state. Similarly, the Parliament of India will be entitled to extend the provisions of Article 243 (d)(I) with regard to Scheduled Areas along with exceptions. It shall not be deemed as an amendment to the Indian Constitution for purposes of Article 268.

Present Laws and Continuance of Panchayats

Any law in prevalence in the state before the introduction of 73rd Amendment will continue till found inconsistent and declared inoperative by the state assembly. Existing Panchayats will not be disturbed if the contrary has not been passed. The old Panchayats will complete their term if each of the two houses of state legislature has not resolved to terminate their existence.

Prevention of Judicial Intervention in Electoral Matters

The act provides that notwithstanding the provisions of the act, any matter pertaining to delimitation of constituencies or allocation of seats under Article 243 (7) will not be allowed to be raised in a court of law. The matters will be raised by an ordinary petition before a competent authority which has been constituted by the state legislature and has prescribed the procedure for the conduct of Panchayat elections in the area.

Amendment of Article 280

The 73rd Amendment adds a duty to the list of duties assigned to the President of India under Article 280 with regard to the National Finance Commission. This amendment adds to Article 280, Part III, Sub-part (B) as under '(BB) Necessary measures to supplement the Panchayati finances from the consolidated fund of state as recommended by the state finance commission'.

Addition of Eleventh Schedule

This new schedule has been added after the 10th Schedule of the Constitution. The schedule includes:

1. Agriculture, including agriculture extension
2. Land development, including land reforms, consolidation and preservation of land.
3. Small irrigation projects, water management and development of water resources
4. Animal husbandry, dairy and poultry
5. Fisheries
6. Social forestry and farms
7. Small forest products
8. Cottage industries, including food processing units
9. Khadi and rural college industries
10. Rural housing
11. Drinking water
12. Fuel and fodder
13. Roads, bridges, transport and water ways
14. Rural electrification
15. Unconventional energy resources
16. Education: primary and secondary
17. Poverty eradication programmes
18. Technical training and secondary education
19. Adult education and informal education
20. Libraries
21. Cultural activities
22. Bazars and fairs
23. Health and cleanliness (primary health centres)
24. Family welfare
25. Women and child development
26. Social welfare, including welfare of deformed and mentally retarded.
27. Welfare of weaker sections, including the members of SC and ST groups
28. Public distribution system
29. Preservation of public property.

Analysis of 73rd Amendment

The positive sides of the enactment are detailed as follows:

1. The constitutionalisation of Panchayati Raj makes it a third tier of Indian federal structure. This makes the local institutions important in the working of Indian polity.
2. The Gram Sabha under the statute acquires a constitutional status. This implies that direct control of rural people over their governance has been accepted in principle as well as in practice. The Gram Sabha was not a part of the legal structure thus far. The act renders grassroots democracy into a reality.
3. One reason for non-development of Panchayati Raj was that elections were not held regularly, which kept the Panchayats under suspension for long spells. The present statute fixes a term of five years and if dissolution comes earlier then fresh elections are be held within a period of six months. This liberates Panchayati Raj from the clutches of bureaucracy and strengthens the real spirit of people's democracy. This continuity will give respect to Panchayati bodies and people will have faith in their elected representatives.
4. The act introduces uniformity in the Panchayati system for all the states within the Indian Union.
5. The statute provides for accounting and auditing of funds accrued by the Panchayati Raj institutions. This will improve the image of institutions and their leaders, and irregularity and abuse of public funds in various schemes will be thwarted to a greater extent.
6. The provisions of the Finance Commission and flow of funds are important because resources have been ensured and their spending will be governed by rules and principles.
7. Social justice characterises the entire arrangement. There is reservation of seats for SC and ST groups and other weaker sections, including women. It is the beginning of a revolution in the countryside where caste and tradition not only dominated but also controlled every aspect of cultural life to the disadvantage of weaker sections.
8. The provision of the State Election Commission is relevant because it is an area where precautions were needed to build a fair democratic image of nascent institutions. They were to be

protected against the onslaught of high-caste lobbies and village mafias of all kinds.

The amendment reserves one-third of all elected positions at all levels for women. The one third seats of Sarpanchs, Pradhans and Pramukhs will also be reserved for women candidates. This means the country will have 800,000 women Panchas and their role in villages and towns will be decisive. Similarly 80,000 women leaders are playing the role of heads of various bodies at village, block and district levels. They will be deciding real matters of rural development. Around 2,000,000 women contested for the posts of heads of Panchayati Raj bodies, which reflects a huge investment in political awareness in the womenfolk of the country. They know their rights and have started participating in the governance of their own rural localities; in Rajasthan state alone, there are as many as 3,064 women Sarpanchs, 80 women Pradhans and 11 women Pramukhs. The 1994 Panchayati elections witnessed a huge popular upsurge and 38,791 women got elected to the positions of popular representatives.

Women's representation has been justified on the ground that women look at social problems with a unique perspective and their participation enhances the quality of decisions. As the system gets stabilized a large number of women leaders will stand trained to handle positions with higher responsibilities, such as MLA or MP. This will help women to break free from the shackles of centuries-old traditions and they will get involved in changing the mainstream of national life which has been essentially patriarchal.

The same applies to the reservation of members of SC and ST groups. They have remained in backwaters for centuries. The opportunities being offered now may be abused here and there, but a new kind of social movement is in the offing. The law could not do much in this area of social justice. But elections will break the ice and build a new ground for social reconstruction.

Notwithstanding all this the amendment has left several very obvious loopholes and inadequacies in the system. Some of them are detailed as follows:

1. It has been taken for granted that the state government wants the disadvantaged to advance and extend support to them. Government will grant powers, resources and responsibilities to local leaders to be elected by the people. The states must act

in their discretion, but the result has been less than satisfactory with state governments acting callously, being apathetic to the cause of Panchayati development. The amendment expect honesty and political will, which the state governments should exhibit; somehow this has not been the case and the reform encounters teething troubles in almost all the states of the Indian Union.

2. One-third of seats at all levels are reserved for women. It covers the reserved and unreserved areas of local population, but in practice this provision has been an apple of discord. The political leadership is obviously jealous and shows rivalry to women leaders, using the backwardness of women and the family values of rural society to abuse this provision; women's representation is criticized with a flimsy reasoning that this might upset the domestic harmony and that their husbands are a better choice for positions of leadership as women's going out of the family realm to actively participate in public activities might upset the family. The rural elites have their sway in Panchayati bodies, and they wish to stall women, and specially women from weaker sections, from coming out to stake a claim on the powers and responsibilities that is legally accorded to them. The husband, father, brother and children of women leaders bring a bad name to the office headed by their women. But this was inevitable to begin with. Actually politics will weaken these ties, and women will come good on their own after some elections when become stronger leaders over time.
3. Although a Finance Commission has been constituted to make resources available to the Panchayati institutions, the insolvent conditions of the states make it questionable whether they will be enthusiastic to help the Panchayats.
4. Critics are apprehensive of the fact that vote politics may hijack the Panchayati institutions and like other democratic institutions at state and union levels they may become dysfunctional.
5. It is also argued that the entire arrangement like Directive Principles of state policy of the Constitution is a moral exhortation. The state will make laws for implementation. Naturally, they will not like to commit suicide by transferring powers to

Panchayats below. The amendment has created a uniform structure, but this does not necessarily lead to rural self-government. Mere regular elections are no guarantee of self-rule, which requires initial support of state government.

6. The 73rd Amendment makes no provision for village courts. It is significant because rural India needs some mechanism to get relief from going through avoidable long-drawn litigations at the courts for legal relief and the harassments that come with it. The absence of Adalati Panchayat or village Nyayalaya is a clear evidence of the glaring omission in the Amendment and the law commission should suggest some viable local structure in this regard.
7. Planning in India, which is too centralized, needs to be decentralized at the level of the district and below. If Panchayats are to be involved in development they should come out with their own plans for incorporation into the master plan of the district.
8. The implementation of Panchayat Raj does not affect union government, and the state governments have to pay dearly from their exchequer at every step of devolution. Naturally, financially weak state governments will not like to get even weaker with the advancement of Panchayati democracy.

Notwithstanding all this, Panchayati Raj adds a new chapter to federal polity of India. It enhances opportunities for economic development and sociocultural changes. The structure will change. What is now needed is the political will to change. The awareness in the area of social justice will strengthen social forces which should ultimately revolutionise rural life.

The 73rd Amendment in the Indian Constitution has not only given constitutional status to the Panchayati Raj but also removed its inadequacies discussed earlier. It has set up a uniform three-tier structure comprising directly elected members. One-third of the offices and membership have been reserved for women. The scheduled castes (SC) and scheduled tribes (ST) have been given reservations in offices and memberships in proportion to their population in the concerned state. The states have been empowered to make reservations for the backward classes as well. The Panchayati Raj institutions have been given powers over 29 subjects listed in the 11th Schedule of the Constitution of India. State

Election Commissions have been empowered to conduct elections regularly and the State Finance Commissions have been instructed to ensure provision of adequate finances. The new Panchayati Raj has been operationalized in all the states and union territories of India.

It may be concluded that the Panchayati Raj system that emerged after the 73rd Amendment to the Indian Constitution in 1992 has a long history behind it. The genesis of Panchayats can be traced to ancient times. Despite some changes in their character in the Mughal era and centralization of administration, these institutions continued to enjoy considerable authority and autonomy even during the colonial period to some extent. The colonial administration, however, destroyed these institutions by introducing a highly centralized system of governance. However, financial compulsions forced the colonial administration to create village Panchayats as local self-government institutions. These acquired a democratic character in the postcolonial period as a result of the introduction of universal adult franchise. The implementation of Balwant Rai Mehta Committee report led to the creation of a three-tier structure of Panchayati Raj, streamlining development administration in the 1960s. Nonetheless, the system became a shadow without substance in the 1970s owing to the erosion of its powers. Thus, the 73rd Amendment has revitalized the Panchayati Raj.

It has not only resulted in broadening the base of democracy in India but also led to the empowerment of women and weaker sections. However, the empowerment is more formal than real because the conditions at the ground level or grassroots level remain largely unchanged. Nevertheless, it is a good beginning and shows great future potential.

5

Empirical Field Study

The study basically pertains to field survey with the general theoretical framework of Indian democracy as enshrined in the Constitution of India and the Gandhian ideology of 'Gram Swaraj'. The concepts used in the study are Panchayat, Panchayati Raj, Panchayat Samiti, Gram Panchayat, elections, voters and so on; however, it is an empirical field study based on primary data and information. The study carries certain research questions or hypotheses and prepositions to examine, test and evaluate. Some of them are listed as follows:

1. Whether reservation granted to population groups such as SCs, STs, OBCs and women in the representation of the Panchayati Raj bodies has brought any qualitative social change (social transformation) in their lives?
2. What has been the impact of reservation policy on development efforts?
3. What has been the impact of reservation on empowering these classes (on the status of these classes)?
4. Is there any change in the social prestige of these classes after providing reservation?
5. Have the Panchayati Raj institutions succeeded in exercising powers granted to them?
6. Or are they merely acting as a dependent politico-administrative departments of the Government of Rajasthan?

It is an empirical field study based on primary data and information. In order to make the study representative, unbiased and empirical, two Zila Parishads out of 33 Zila Parishads of the State of Rajasthan were chosen. These two Zila Parishads are Jaipur and Sikar. Both have their own specific features. Two Panchayati Samitis from each Zila Parishad were selected for the purpose. Each Panchayati Samiti governs five village Panchayats and from each village Panchayat approximately 20 respondents were selected. Thus, the total number of respondents is 400 (2 × 2 × 5 × 20 = 400).

The author has prepared a structured questionnaire (schedule) containing four open-ended sections.

The structured questionnaire contains about 60 questions broadly divided into four sections: (a) introduction, (b) knowledge testing, (c) role and performance, and (d) evaluation and suggestions. The data so collected were edited and processed by proper coding and tabulation to determine the relationships between variables like position in power hierarchy of Panchayat Raj bodies, social status, educational attainments, financial upliftment, development and so on. The author analysed the study data to arrive at findings and draw conclusions. These are discussed in detail in the coming sections.

Question 1. Do you know that our country has adopted a democratic system of government?

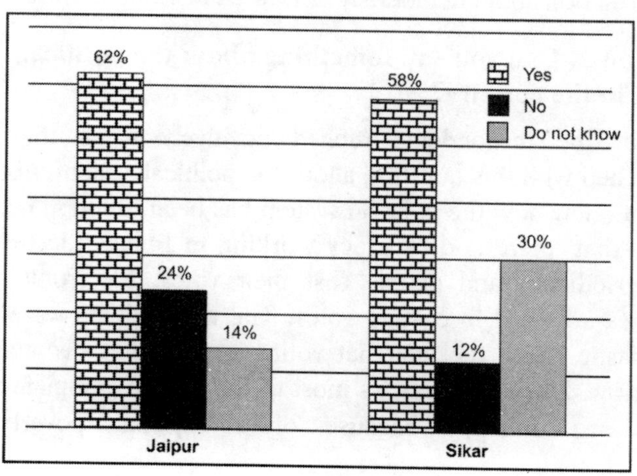

	Yes	*No*	*Don't know*	*Total*
Jaipur	62%	24%	14%	100%
Sikar	58%	12%	30%	100%
Total	60%	18%	22%	100%

To collect primary data about governmental system of the country the question was put to common citizens and office bearers of Panchayati Raj bodies. The response concluded that 60 per cent respondents knew that India has opted for a democracy; when they were further asked to define democracy, very few could explain the essence of a democratic system. The remaining 22 per cent did not give any reply. They replied, 'do not know'. Most respondents neither knew the characteristics of democracy nor could they explain its merits and demerits. They only knew that the country is now a democracy. When they were further asked to identify the source of their information, they revealed that their children gave them this information. As much as 18 per cent of the respondents held that democracy does not exist in the country. They maintained that Englishmen are still ruling India and native states have princely rulers. Our study findings showed that their social background was most backward. They could not recall the date of departure of Englishmen and the advent of freedom in India. Most of these respondents were women and old people.

Thus, analysis of primary data indicated that even after 70 years of independence, 40 per cent of the people in the country have no information about democracy or how its working in the country.

Question 2. Can you say something about the political system in the country?

Most of the respondents replied positively when they were approached with this question about the political system. About 64 per cent knew how the political system has been functioning. They did say that 'there is democracy working in India.' Elections are held periodically and people cast their votes. Electronic voting machines are used in casting votes. The respondents were found enthusiastic about the fact that voting process has become a lot easier now. During interviews most of the people complained that people are unhappy because of corruption, poverty and

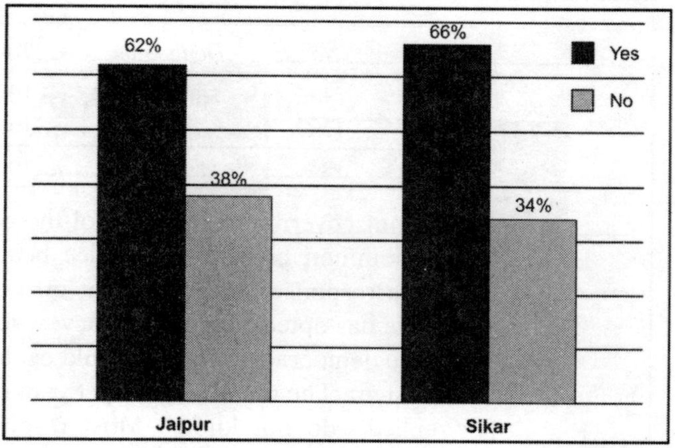

	Yes	*No*	*Total*
Jaipur	62%	38%	100%
Sikar	66%	34%	100%
Total	64%	36%	100%

unemployment. They held the political system and the political leaders responsible for this miserable state of affairs. People were extremely critical of rising prices. Women voters knew little about Sonia Gandhi. Baring a few they knew only this much that she was the daughter-in-law of Nehru family and the president of the Indian National Congress. Some of the respondents mentioned the name of Narendra Modi, but some of them did not know who he is? Educated respondents talked about terrorism, but some 36 per cent people in the sample had no knowledge about the political system and its functioning.

Question 3. Name the Panchayati Raj institutions functioning at present?

It was a relief and moment of happiness to find that 53 per cent people knew the names of Panchayati Raj institutions. Most of the people knew all the three institutions. The rest of them knew the name of the institution concerned. About 47 per cent did not have enough knowledge or information about Panchayati Raj institutions.

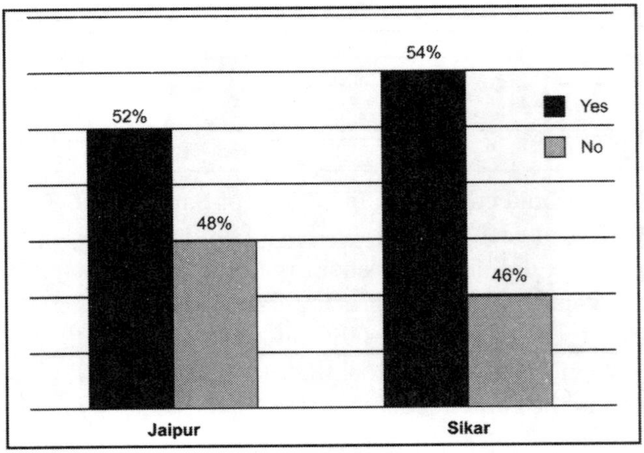

	Yes	*No*	*Total*
Jaipur	52%	48%	100%
Sikar	54%	46%	100%
Total	53%	47%	100%

Question 4. What do you know about village Panchayats, Panchayat Samitis and Zila Parishads?

About 52 per cent respondents maintained that they know about three tiers of Panchayati Raj system, but only 36 per cent of the respondents could explain the working and relationship between the three tiers. They knew the middle and top tiers by name, and

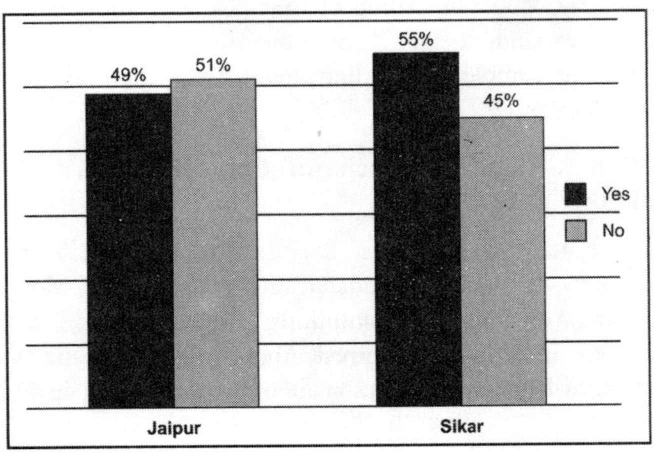

	Yes	*No*	*Total*
Jaipur	49%	51%	100%
Sikar	55%	45%	100%
Total	52%	48%	100%

some of them could enumerate the names of Sarpanchas, Pradhans and Pramukhs at each tier, respectively. As much as 12 per cent of the respondents did not know about the functions at each tier. By and large people had little information about the working of rural institutions. It can be concluded that about 48 per cent respondents were found ignorant about the field-level working of Panchayati Raj institutions in the countryside.

Question 5. When were Panchayati Raj Institutions established in your area?

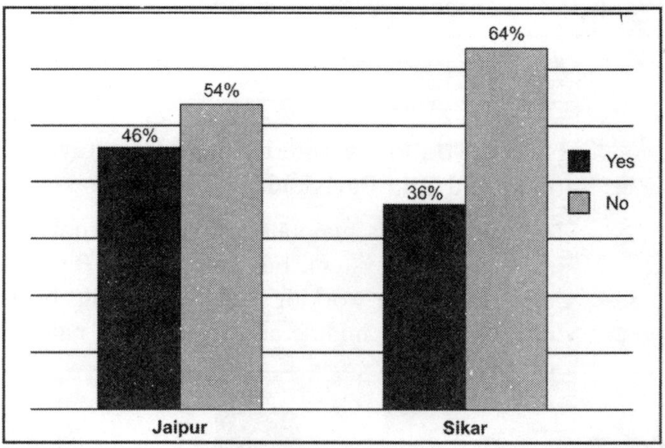

	Yes	*No*	*Total*
Jaipur	46%	54%	100%
Sikar	36%	64%	100%
Total	41%	59%	100%

When posed this question, people could not mention the year of commencement of Panchayati Raj in their district. The majority of them had no information about committee and commissions that recommended rural local self-government. About 41 per cent had some information, but even that information was not correct.

Surprisingly, 30 per cent of these 41 per cent said that Pandit Nehru inaugurated the Panchayati Raj system. Furthermore, 59 per cent were not sure about the year of establishment and could not explain the reasons of its introduction in a satisfactory manner. The educated members of the sample knew that the 1995 Panchayati Raj elections were held after a long period of absence.

Question 6. How are you connected with Panchayati Raj Institutions?

About 36 per cent of the respondents revealed that they were members of these bodies; 15 per cent of them held positions in administration and the remaining 49 per cent were voters. In this category, there were common villagers, farmers office bearers and retired officials. Some respondents contested the earlier elections but had lost. In addition, respondents included teachers, advocates, social workers and members of NGOs also.

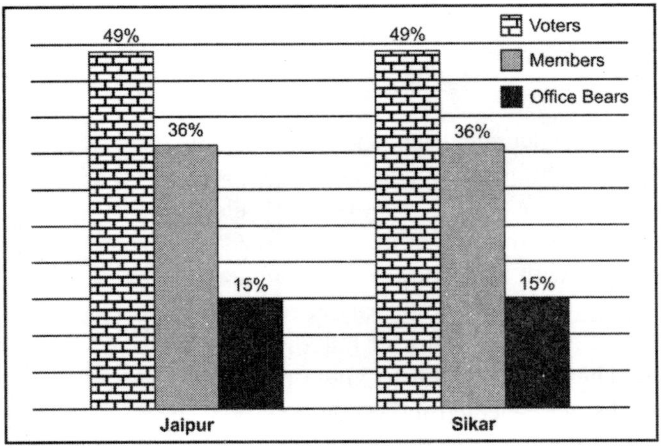

	Voters	*Members*	*Office bearers*	*Total*
Jaipur	49%	36%	15%	100%
Sikar	49%	36%	15%	100%
Total	49%	36%	15%	100%

Question 7. What difference do you find between the Panchayati Raj institutions of yesterday and today?

The question was asked to fathom the depth of their knowledge. Only 43 per cent respondents came out with an answer that there is

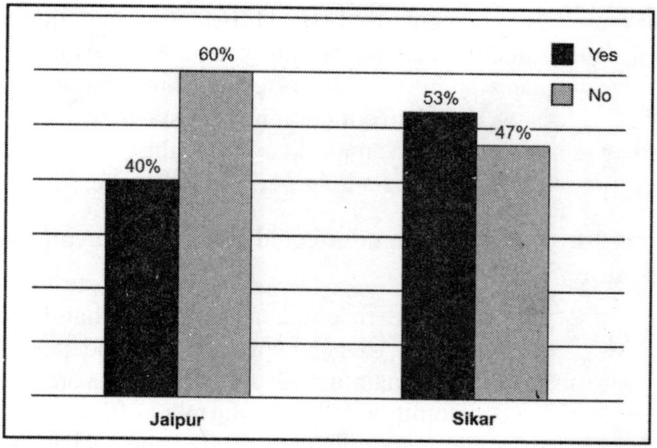

	Yes	*No*	*Total*
Jaipur	40%	60%	100%
Sikar	53%	47%	100%
Total	43%	57%	100%

a real difference between the two systems. We further asked whether this difference made has made a real difference in the lives of villagers? Most of the respondents preferred to stay silent. Only very few knew this difference. They said the present system has been vested with more powers as compared to the past. They also pointed out the lack of regularity in conducting elections in the past and the present regularity in holding elections of Panchayati Raj bodies. They also seemed to know that unlike earlier times when Sarpanchs were elected indirectly now they can vote to elect their Sarpanchs directly. On the whole, some 57 per cent respondents could not explain the difference between institutions at the block and district levels.

Question 8. Name four pioneers of Panchayati Raj in Rajasthan?

About 57 per cent of respondents answered the question and quoted the names of Mahatma Gandhi, Pandit Jawaharlal Nehru and Dr B.R. Ambedkar as pioneers of Panchayati Raj. When asked about Rajasthani leaders they named Mohan Lal Sukhadia, Hari

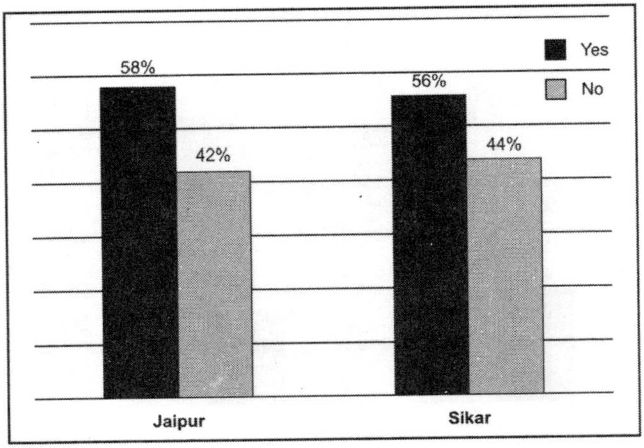

	Yes	*No*	*Total*
Jaipur	58%	42%	100%
Sikar	56%	44%	100%
Total	57%	43%	100%

Deo Joshi, Bairon Singh Shekhawat and Gokul Bhai Bhatt as leaders in the vanguard. About 43 per cent of the respondents had no idea in this regard.

Question 9. What major changes the existing Panchayati Raj has introduced in the constitutional structure of the country?

In this case, 76 per cent of the respondents could not give an answer. They did not know even the year in which the present structure was introduced. To the question whether it has changed the nature of the Constitution, 24 per cent of the respondents preferred to remain silent except the fact that some of them knew that it was inducted by a Constitutional Amendment. They did not know any other details. Only 5 per cent of the respondents in the sample knew that it was 73rd Amendment which added the 9K part to the Constitution. These were students who were preparing for competitive examinations in the cities of Rajasthan.

The analysis points out that there is lack of awareness about Panchayati Raj among the masses; to increase public awareness, perhaps camps must be organised so that people may seek

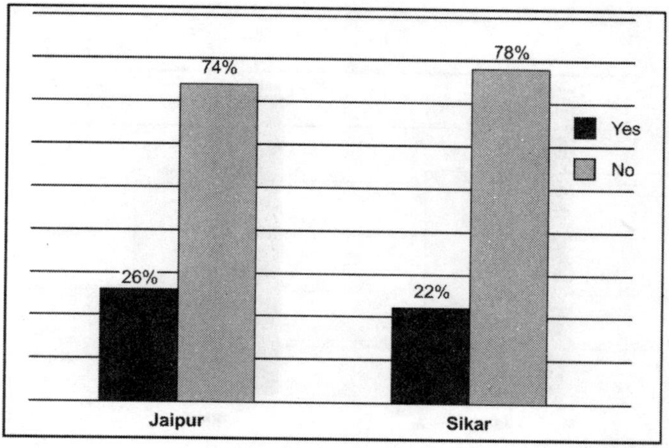

	Yes	*No*	*Total*
Jaipur	26%	74%	100%
Sikar	22%	78%	100%
Total	24%	76%	100%

elementary knowledge about institutions which they elect and which should be vested with more powers.

Question 10. List three functions and powers entrusted to Panchayati Raj bodies under the new dispensation?

When the respondents were asked about the subjects assigned to the Panchayati Raj institutions by the Constitution under 73rd Constitutional Amendment, 53.5 per cent the study respondents had basic knowledge about these powers and functions, but they could not identify the sources of these powers and functions or could point out the legal provisions pertaining to these functions. They only reiterated that Panchayati Raj institutions have these functions. The following classifications of these functions are known to some extent among the respondents:

> 1. Planning, 2. budget preparation, 3. disaster management, 4. welfare programme, 5. development programmes for weaker sections, 6. improvement in agriculture and horticulture, 7. census and surveys, 8. adult education, 9. preservation of ecology, and 10. cottage industries.

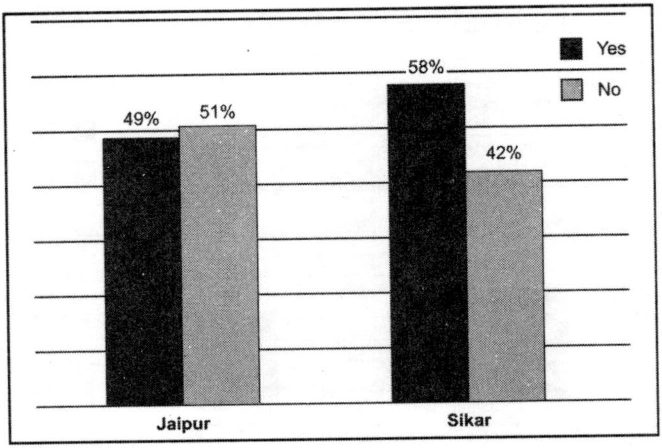

	Yes	*No*	*Total*
Jaipur	49%	51%	100%
Sikar	58%	42%	100%
Total	53.5%	46.5%	100%

As much as 46.5 per cent of the respondents refused to disclose any information in this regard.

Question 11. How many times elections have been conducted in your village Panchayat, Panchayat Samiti and Zila Parishad?

For this question only 26.5 per cent of the respondents knew that elections for Panchayati Raj bodies have been held three times. Almost 59.5 per cent of the respondents knew that Panchayati elections have been held more than four times. The fact is that Panchayati elections in Rajasthan have been held five times. This indicates that people are gradually getting politically aware. As the regularity and periodicity of elections becomes a fact of political life people will develop a positive view of these polls.

About 2.5 per cent of the respondents replied that Panchayati Raj elections have been conducted only two times, and 11.5 per cent of the respondents are ignorant about this.

Here, it may be noted that this political awareness is severely low among women voters. Reservation has positively enhanced their interest in village politics. During informal discussions most of

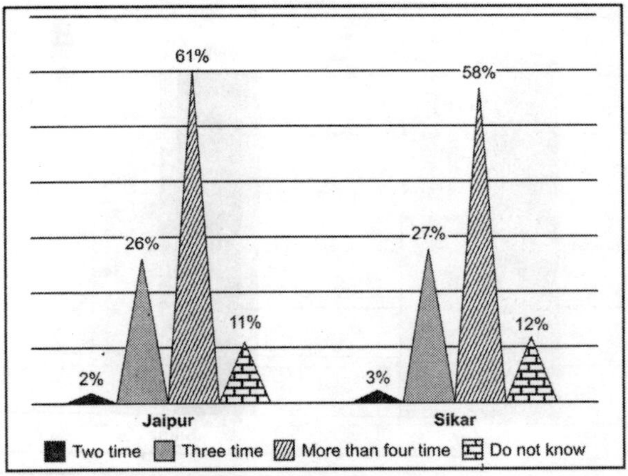

	Jaipur	*Sikar*	*Average*
Two times	2%	3%	2.5%
Three times	26%	27%	26.5%
More than four times	61%	58%	59.5%
Don't know	11%	12%	11.5%
Total	100%	100%	100%

the rural women confessed that politics is a masculine profession and they do not feel much concerned about problems of politics.

Questions 12, 13, 14, 15. Did you vote in Gram Panchayat, Panchayat Samiti and Zila Parishad elections of 2014? If yes, where, and name the booth? If not, why not, and state reasons? What was the basis or determinant of your vote?

Responses to this question generated information about not just voting behaviour; they also revealed many unknown facts in the data which weren't discovered earlier during our analysis. The conclusion is that people have become more aware and majority of the them have begun to participate in the elections and cast their votes. They unhesitatingly mentioned the reasons why their votes were influenced; 62.5 per cent of the respondents mentioned free choice, but the remaining 37.5 per cent checked reasons like caste, neighbourhood, joint family, head of the family influence and so on. Caste was a dominant factor, which explains the caste-based nature

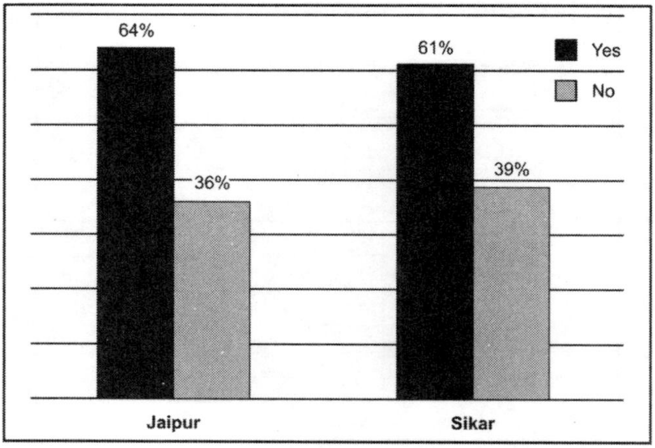

	Yes	*No*	*Total*
Jaipur	64%	36%	100%
Sikar	61%	39%	100%
Total	62.5%	37.5%	100%

of politics in Rajasthan. They confirmed Dr Rajni Kothari's conclusion that caste is an invincible factor and people vote to candidates of their own caste even when they do not like him. It also explains the politicisation of caste rather than caste orientation of politics in Rajasthan.

Question 16. Do you know the figures of budget of your Gram Panchayat, Panchayat Samiti and Zila Parishad? How were the allotments made in the budget?

As much as 66.5 per cent of the respondents answered negatively. They could not figure out the amount or estimates in the budget. When they were told that this information could be sought in the meeting of the Gram Sabha, their reply was that they never attended any such meeting or that they were never informed about these meetings. They could not give any information either about the share of state government or about Panchayats' own resources. They never had any access to Panchayat records as a part of social audit; 33.5 per cent responded positively, but their responses were based on mere guesswork. Correct information about budgets was just not known to anybody in the sample.

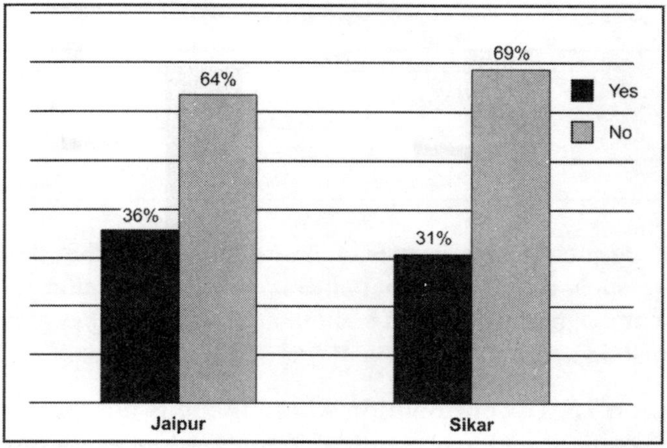

	Yes	*No*	*Total*
Jaipur	36%	64%	100%
Sikar	31%	69%	100%
Total	33.5%	66.5%	100%

Question 17. Name the committees constituted by your Gram Panchayat, Panchayat Samiti and Zila Parishad?

As much as 54.5 per cent of the respondents answered in the negative. They knew that Panchayats worked through a variety of committees, but they could not figure out their names and functions. About 4.5 per cent of the respondents disclosed frankly that there were no such committees. Some 41 per cent had

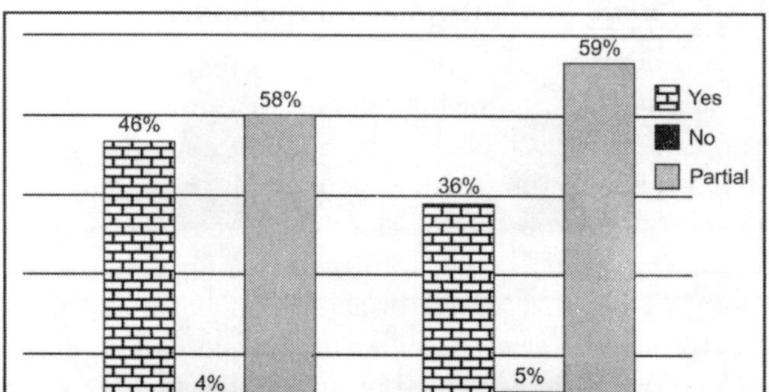

	Jaipur	*Sikar*	*Total*
Yes	46%	36%	41%
No	4%	5%	4.5%
Partial	50%	59%	54.5%
Total	100%	100%	100%

knowledge about the existence of these committees. They did name a few, such as literacy committee, security committee, establishment committee, taxation committee and so on. They had some information about the working of these committees also.

Question 18. In your opinion what functions did the Gram Panchayats, Panchayat Samitis, Zila Parishad carry out in the recent past?

A sizeable section of the sample, more than half, around 54 per cent, specifically mentioned activities in the following areas: irrigation, manure distribution, hand pump digging, housing and water supply systems. These functions were undertaken because poor people were planning to migrate to the cities. Hence, the Panchayat reinvigorated the agricultural schemes, and 22.5 per

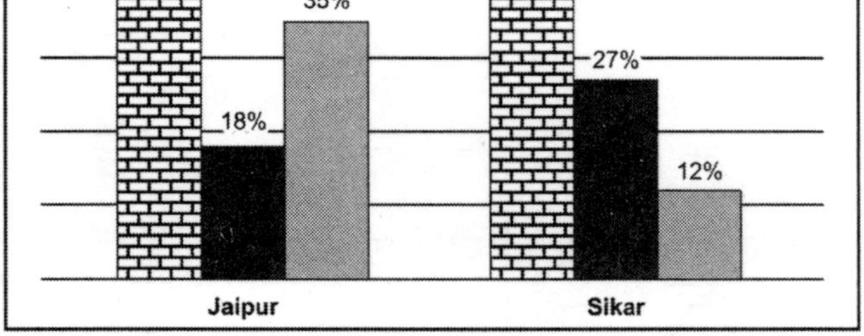

	Yes	*No*	*Don't know*	*Total*
Jaipur	47%	18%	35%	100%
Sikar	61%	27%	12%	100%
Total	54%	22.5%	23.5%	100%

cent of the respondents maintained that villagers were in a pitiable condition and Panchayats did nothing to improve their lot. They take up only very urgent problems. The remaining 23.5 per cent mentioned that they have heard about Panchayat works but that, personally, they have no knowledge of these activities.

Question 19. Do you think Gram Panchayats, Panchayat Samitis and Zila Parishads accomplished something in the following areas (list enclosed)?

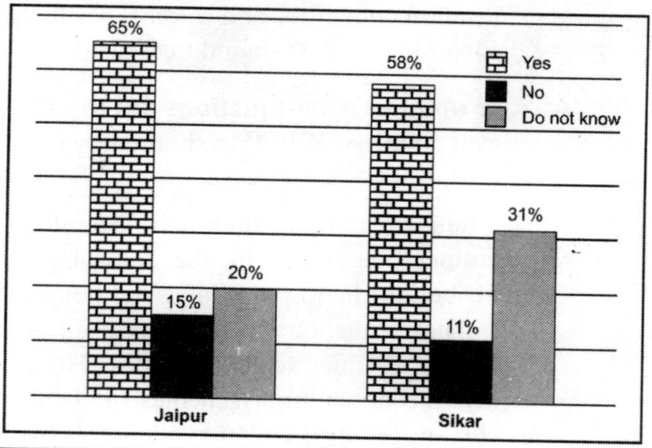

	Yes	*No*	*Don't know*	*Total*
Jaipur	65%	15%	20%	100%
Sikar	58%	11%	31%	100%
Total	61.5%	13%	25.5%	100%

When the study participants were asked about info on activities that were carried out since 2000, 61.5 per cent of the respondents mentioned housing activities for the BPL. They also talked about irrigational facilities, repair of hand pumps and getting the pumps installed in areas with severe water scarcity. Others mentioned activities in areas such as education, social reforms and cottage industries as Panchayati Raj's accomplishments. They have enhanced the percentage of literacy and generated awareness about social reforms taking place with the support of the government. Campaigns against child marriage brought results. However, 25.5 per cent expressed their ignorance about these activities, and 13 per cent just plainly said that Panchayats were inactive and defunct in their areas.

Question 20. What has the state government done to help Panchayats since 1994?

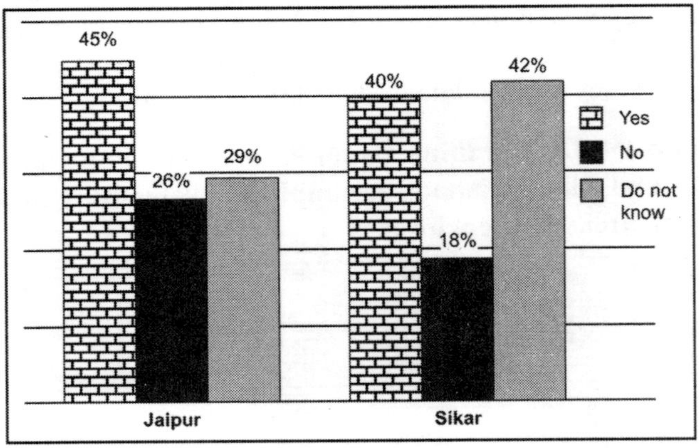

	Jaipur	*Sikar*	*Total*
Yes	45%	40%	42.50%
No	26%	18%	22%
Don't know	29%	42%	35.50%
Total	100%	100%	100%

About 42.5 per cent of the respondents admitted that state government extended liberal grants to the Panchayats and the grants-in-aid per person were also paid in time. The Panchayats spent this sum on developmental work. Some people said that Panchayat staff has been duly trained, and about 36.5 per cent of the respondents said they had no idea what the state government has been doing in this regard. As much as 22 per cent flatly denied the role of state government in development projects. Panchayats did not pay grants-in-aid in time and the sum is still outstanding. This has slowed down developmental works. New work has not commenced, and thus, positions are lying vacant and Panchayat activities are adversely effected.

Question 21. Are the meetings of village Panchayats and Gram Sabha taking place regularly?

The respondents were asked about the meetings of village Panchayats and Gram Sabha to know the level of their knowledge and awareness about the rural welfare initiatives being carried out

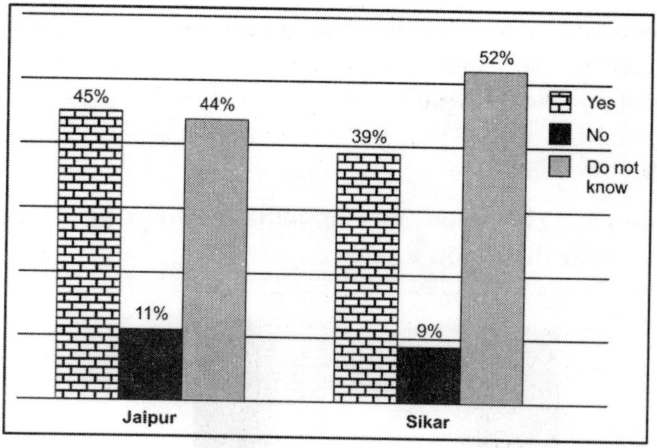

	Yes	No	Sometimes	Total
Jaipur	45%	11%	44%	100%
Sikar	39%	9%	52%	100%
Total	42%	10%	48%	100%

through Panchayati Raj institutions, including about electoral processes and participation.

Most of the people who answered this question replied in the affirmative, but their responses varied widely in terms of the number of meetings they have attended so far. They had little idea of the frequency of Gram Sabha meetings. About 42 per cent maintained that Gram Sabha meetings were in the neighbourhood of 3–4 sessions in a year. When further probed with the question whether they attended and participated in these meetings, their replies were far from satisfactory. Only a few respondents replied that they participated in the meetings and wanted to know whether the decisions taken during the previous meetings were implemented at all. Several people had information about meetings, dates and times, but they could not give any specific reason for avoiding these meetings, except for conveying that they never took the need for participation seriously. They did not know that a Gram Sabha keeps detailed records of rural happenings, including births, deaths and so on. Women respondents did not participate; they said that their domestic chores did not permit to find time to participate in public duties.

As much as 48 per cent of the respondents maintained that Gram Sabha meetings were on paper only. They are neither informed nor the information was displayed on the notice boards. Obviously, the institutions are yet to make their presence felt among rural people.

Question 22. How many Gram Sabha meetings have taken place in your district in a year?

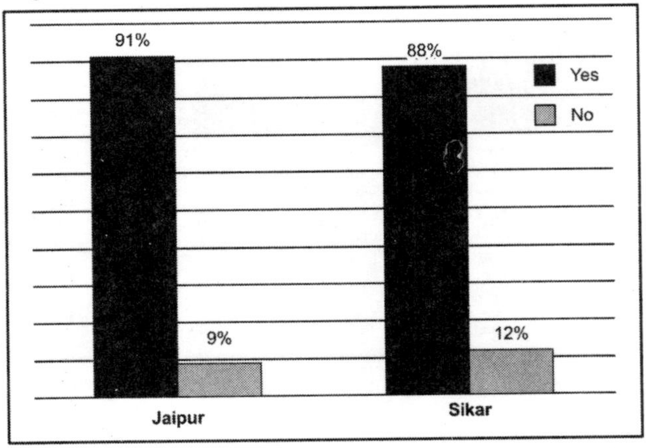

	Yes	*No*	*Total*
Jaipur	91%	9%	100%
Sikar	88%	12%	100%
Total	89.5%	10.5%	100%

Interestingly enough, some 89.5 per cent respondents had adequate information about Gram Sabha meetings. They informed that about two to three Gram Sabha meetings took place in a year. They could not specify the exact dates of these meetings, though. Some respondents said that the Sarpanch issues notices to summon Gram Sabha meetings, but by and large these meetings are not attended by majority of people in the village.

Question 23. Do you think elections are conducted in an impartial and free manner? What is your opinion in this regard?

About 41.8 per cent of the respondents responded positively. They opined that elections were indeed impartial and free, 34.5 per cent

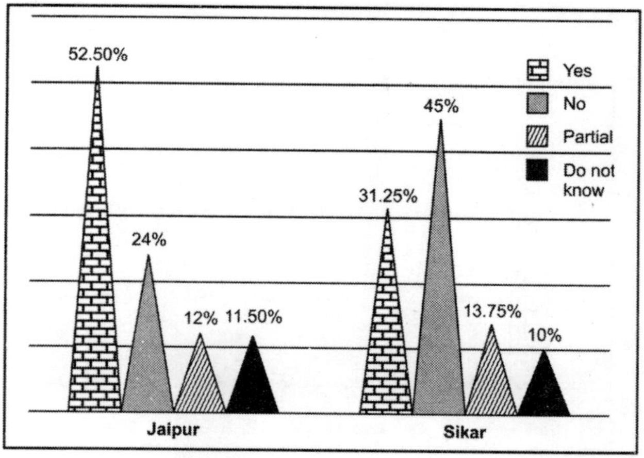

	Yes	*No*	*Partial*	*Don't know*	*Total*
Jaipur	52.50%	24%	12%	11.50%	100%
Sikar	31.25%	45%	13.75%	10%	100%
Total	41.87.5%	34.5%	12.87.5%	10.75%	100%

were of the opinion that elections weren't impartial and free, and 12.87 per cent felt that only partially elections were conducted in a manner that can be termed impartial and free. About 10.75 per cent reported they had no idea; however, study findings showed about three-fourth of respondents have knowledge about elections and, thus, are politically aware. Political awareness is increasing among the rural population. It is a healthy sign and therefore a good and positive step towards building a powerful democratic system.

Question 24. If you contested the elections from where will you get your resources needed to contest?

About 37 per cent of the respondents responded to this question. They maintained that they used their own resources and the expenditure was affordable. 23 per cent members of sample admitted that their caste fellows arranged for their electoral funds. Some 38.5 per cent admitted that money and resources came from varied sources including donations from businessmen and relatives. Even their former colleagues supplied the wherewithal. Only 1.5 per cent of

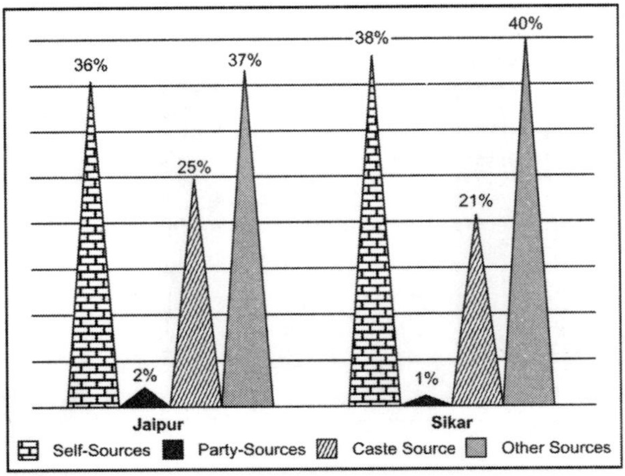

	Jaipur	*Sikar*	*Total*
Self-sources	36%	38%	37%
Party sources	2%	1%	1.5%
Caste sources	25%	21%	23%
Other sources	37%	40%	38.5%
Total	100%	100%	100%

the members maintained that they were given financial support from party coffers to contest local elections.

Question 25. Are you satisfied with the accomplishments of your Panchayat?

The overall conclusion drawn from the answers indicates that most of the people in the villages are neither happy nor satisfied by Panchayat functions; as high as 54.5 per cent members of the sample were found extremely dissatisfied. They narrated stories and said that the situation is exactly the same as it was during the days of their parents and grandparents. They did not have regular electricity, nor has water supply been inaugurated thus far. There are funds for BPL facilities, but much of it is consumed by corrupt officials. That is why people are migrating to cities. Only 38 per cent members expressed satisfaction with the achievements of their Panchayats. They maintained that villages are on the road to progress. Yet 7.5 per cent agreed only partially.

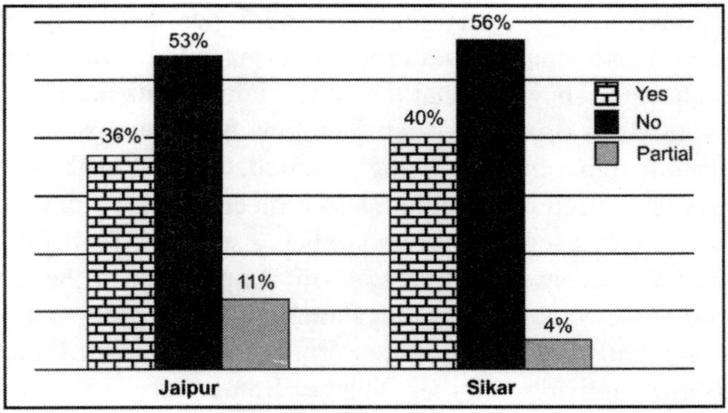

	Jaipur	*Sikar*	*Total*
Yes	36%	40%	38%
No	53%	56%	54.5%
Partial	11%	4%	7.5%
Total	100%	100%	100%

Question 26. What plans have your Gram Panchayat have for your village?

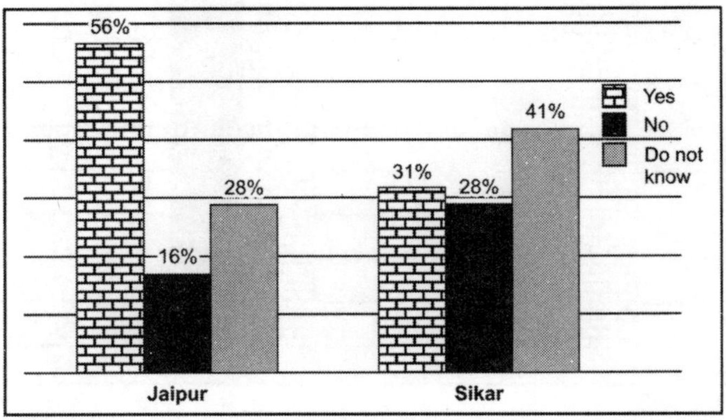

	Jaipur	*Sikar*	*Total*
Yes	56%	31%	43.5%
No	16%	28%	22%
Don't know	28%	41%	34.5%
Total	100%	100%	100%

In response to this question, some 43.5 per cent respondents replied in the affirmative about the programs initiated and launched by Panchayats. They said that the village Panchayats have provided them with clean drinking water. The new hand pumps have been dug up and old ones are being repaired. Several pathways and subways have been constructed, and a mechanism for drainage of dirty water and a sewage system are being set up. Streetlights have been installed at several corners. About 22 per cent of the respondents complained about how they Panchayats have become defunct. The remaining 34.5 per cent were ignorant about Panchayat schemes or activities in their village. Some were well informed about government initiatives like NREGA, and they found the scheme very useful in getting a livelihood. They openly confessed that it has been a blessing and their lives have become somewhat easy and comfortable.

Question 27. What schemes were launched by the Panchayat Samiti in your area?

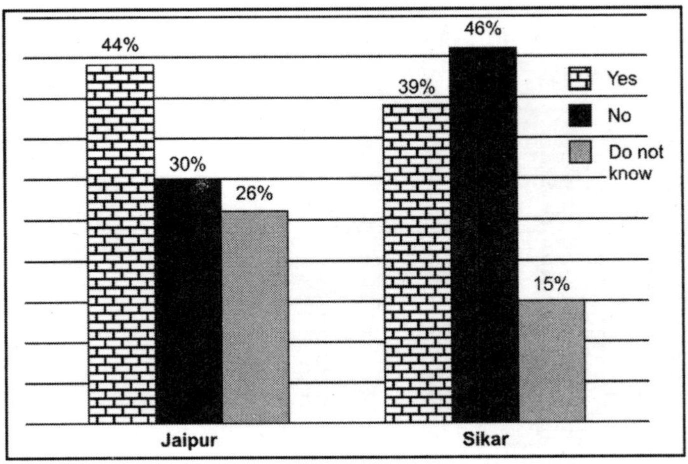

	Yes	*No*	*Don't know*	*Total*
Jaipur	44%	30%	26%	100%
Sikar	39%	46%	15%	100%
Total	41.5%	38%	20.5%	100%

This question could not be answered by 58.5 per cent of the respondents, and the remaining 41.5 per cent had adequate information about these schemes. For instance, they said that the Panchayat Samiti provides an ex gratia amount of ₹ 10,000 if the only earning member of the family living below poverty line passes away. The Samiti has funds for victims of fire and other natural calamities. The Samiti has launched several schemes for planting of trees, protection of water resources, and improving the living standards of people in the weaker segments of rural life. There was a small minority who had no information about these welfare and developmental activities.

Question 28. What schemes or projects did the Zila Parishad prepare for your area?

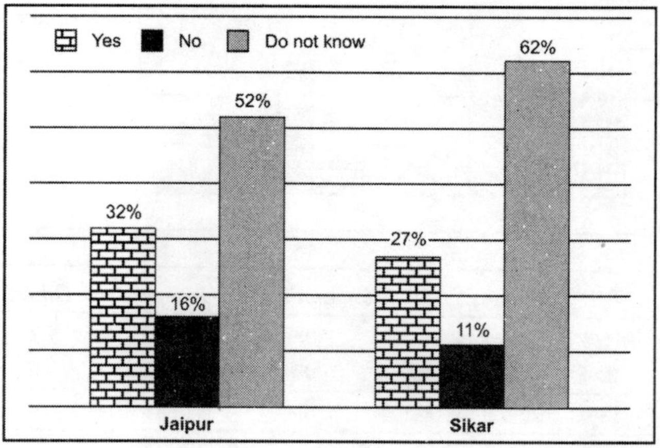

	Yes	*No*	*Don't know*	*Total*
Jaipur	32%	16%	52%	100%
Sikar	27%	11%	62%	100%
Total	29.5%	13.5%	57%	100%

Here again, 57 per cent of the respondents were found to be absolutely ignorant, 13.5 per cent maintained that the Zila Parishad did not launch any new scheme or that if there was any the same might have been buried and forgotten in the bureaucratic maze. They did not witness any development work going on in the field. However, 29.5 per cent had some information, and they confessed that it has come to them without any special effort. These respondents said that the Parishad has constructed a *pucca* (proper) road and that several *kutcha* (unpaved) roads have also been repaired. They pointed out that small and affordable dwellings have been constructed for people living below the poverty line.

Question 29. Have you participated in Panchayati Raj Elections of 2009? Which party with which you had your affiliation?

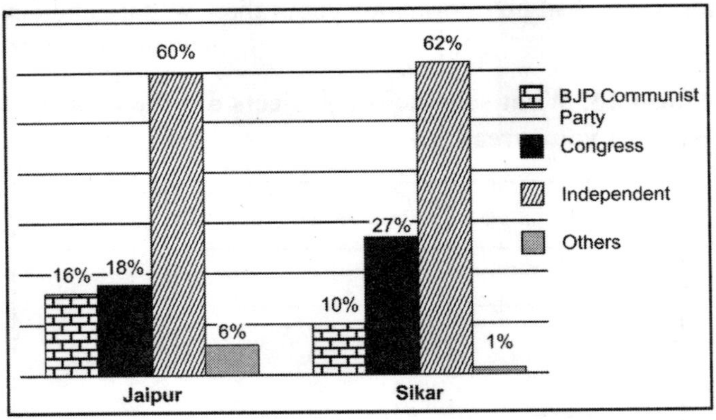

	BJP	*Congress*	*BSP*	*Communist Party*	*Independent*	*Others*	*Total*
Jaipur	16%	18%	0%	0%	60%	6%	100%
Sikar	10%	27%	0%	0%	62%	1%	100%
Total	13%	22.5%	0%	0%	61%	3.5%	100%

The answers to this question revealed that Rajasthan has only two political parties, that is, BJP and Congress; 22.5 per cent of the respondents affirmed their affiliation with Congress, and the figure for BJP in this case was only 13.5 per cent. As many as 61 per cent candidates contested as independents. In other category only 3.5 per cent responded. One reason for this situation was mentioned as non-availability of party tickets at grassroots level. They have to contest on their own and the political parties neither campaigned for them nor offered them funds or resources from the party coffers.

Question 30. What kind of people (caste, class or group) cooperate in Panchayat work?

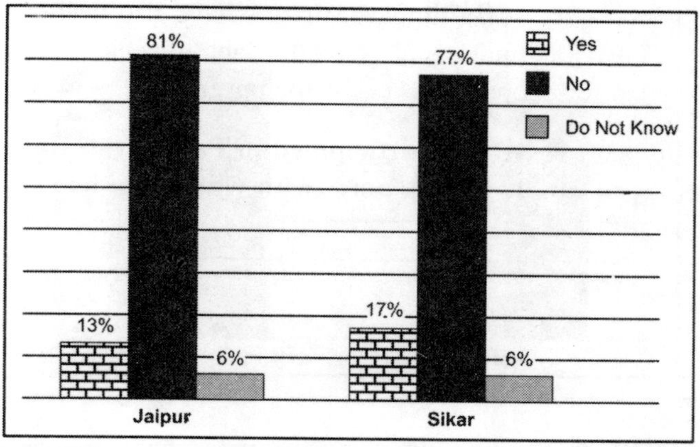

	Yes	No	Don't know	Total
Jaipur	13%	81%	6%	100%
Sikar	17%	77%	6%	100%
Total	15%	79%	6%	100%

As high as 79 per cent of the respondents maintained that masses or common villagers do not cooperate in Panchayat activities. They are generally neutral, and they do not care what the Panchayat does and what kind of popular cooperation it needs. Only 7 per cent felt that younger people help; some people mentioned about SC, ST and OBC groups supporting Panchayat activities. Thus, as much as 15 per cent of the respondents reported about extending cooperation to Panchayat Raj institutions, but 6 per cent had no information about people's cooperation that was based on caste, class or groups.

Question 31. What should be done to enhance popular cooperation in Panchayat politics?

The respondents pointed out several ways by which Panchayats can enhance popular participation; some of them are listed as follows:

1. Panchayats should take interest in the economic life of the villages. This will deepen their interest in Panchayat's activities.

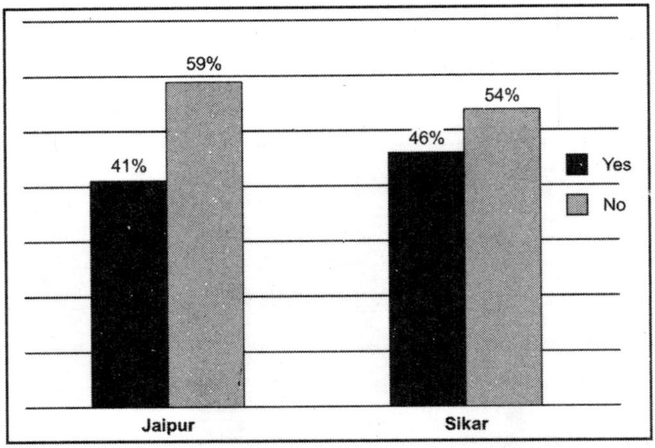

	Yes	*No*	*Total*
Jaipur	41%	59%	100%
Sikar	46%	54%	100%
Total	43.5%	56.5%	100%

2. Awareness campaigns may be launched from time to time so that people may come forward to cooperate.
3. Free food packets may be delivered to participants, such as midday meals in schools.
4. Villagers should be made to realise that their support to Panchayats will ultimately prove beneficial to them.
5. Panchayats should organise camps and meetings, and popular problems and grievances should be resolved in these meetings under the camps.
6. Suitable rewards and awards may be given to those who work for Panchayats on the day of major national events like Independence Day and Republic Day.

As much 43.5 per cent of the respondents answered the question, and they suggested ways how Panchayat can enhance participation of rural population. As much as 56.5 per cent did not respond and most of them stated that they did not know anything in this regard.

Question 32. What is your attitude towards Panchayati activities?

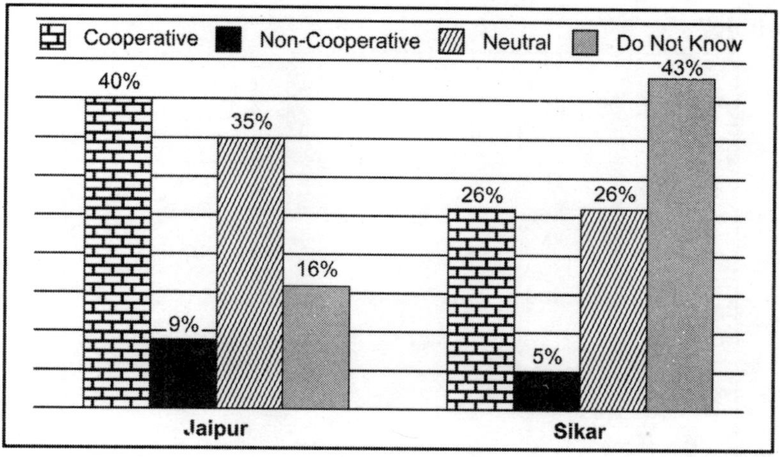

	Cooperative	*Non-cooperative*	*Neutral*	*Don't know*	*Total*
Jaipur	40%	9%	35%	16%	100%
Sikar	26%	5%	26%	43%	100%
Total	33%	7%	30.5%	29.5%	100%

The question received positive responses mostly, and 33 per cent people maintained that they appreciate and support Panchayat endeavours. Only 7 per cent took a strongly negative attitude and condemned the corrupt activities going in the name of development under Panchayats. They openly condemned the leaders of Panchayati Raj institutions and said that those corrupt leaders swallow huge sums of money sanctioned by the central government in order to support rural development and welfare of BPL families.

Some 30.5 per cent respondents were neutral and apathetic in their responses; 29.5 per cent had no knowledge or awareness of Panchayati Raj activities. Most of these people were illiterate, and even some literate members lacked political awareness. The majority in this category was women, who were usually confined to the four walls of their families. They were generally ignorant of political events and, in general, political dynamics in rural life.

Question 33. How do you evaluate the attitude of government officials towards Panchayati Raj functionaries like Panchas, Sarpanchas and Panchayati Raj system as a whole?

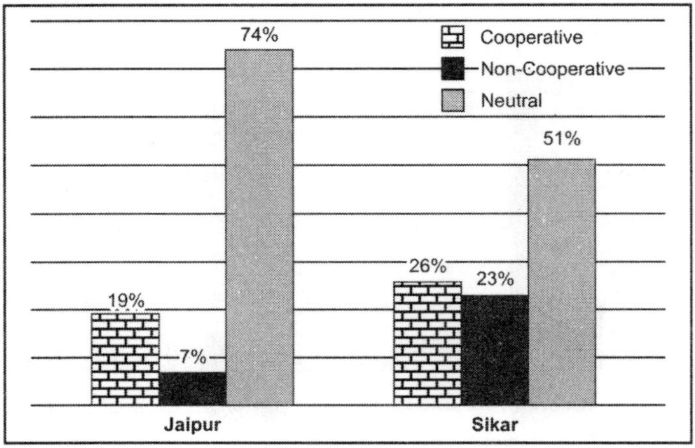

	Cooperative	*Non-cooperative*	*Neutral*	*Total*
Jaipur	19%	07%	74%	100%
Sikar	26%	23%	51%	100%
Total	22.5%	15%	62.5%	100%

As much as 22.5 per cent respondents said that the attitude of these officials is becoming increasingly sympathetic especially village Panchayat seeks popular cooperation, and people respond readily as a call of duty. They were found to be positive and prepared. They helped and cooperated in a variety of functions pertaining to government schemes and projects. Only 15 per cent of the respondents found this attitude hostile or unsympathetic. They could not advance any satisfactory reason for the negative attitude that is an obvious reason for their non-cooperation. The attitude of government officials towards Panchas and Sarpanchas was found 'neutral' by 62.5 per cent respondents of the sample. They feel unconcerned and adopt an apathetic attitude towards Panchayat problems of the village. When pointedly asked if they found Panchayat politics partisan and preferred to be neutral, they wanted to avoid unwanted criticism of political parties and their leaders.

They felt that they should do their duty and that Panchayat functions are not a part of their official duty.

Question 34. Do you know Panchayati Raj elections have provisions of reservation for some castes and classes?

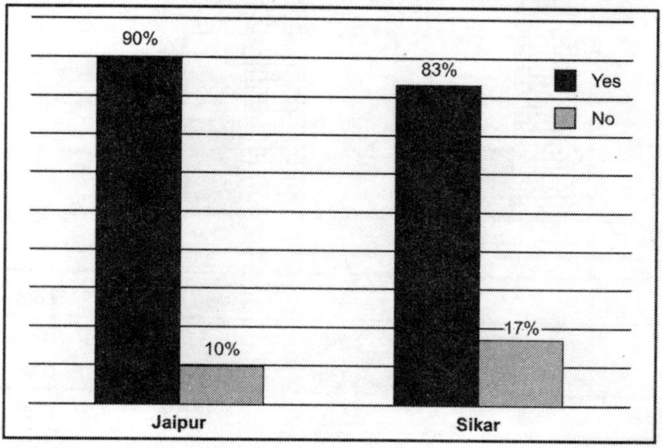

	Yes	*No*	*Total*
Jaipur	90%	10%	100%
Sikar	83%	17%	100%
Total	86.5%	13.5%	100%

In response to this question, 86.5 per cent respondents answered in the affirmative and termed their attitude as sympathetic. A majority of them were aware of the reservation provision for women, SC, ST, and OBC groups. They know that reservation helps these groups to come out of backwardness. Women were especially happy and enthusiastic about reservation provisions. It was a positive step in the right direction. Only 13.5 per cent were ignorant about reservation provisions in Panchayati Raj.

Question 35. Do you know the names of castes and classes which enjoy reservation privileges?

As much as 53.5 per cent of the respondents pointed out that they were aware reservation was given to members of SC, ST, OBC and Women. Most of the people know about this change. About 14 per cent maintained that Panchayati Raj institutions do not have any

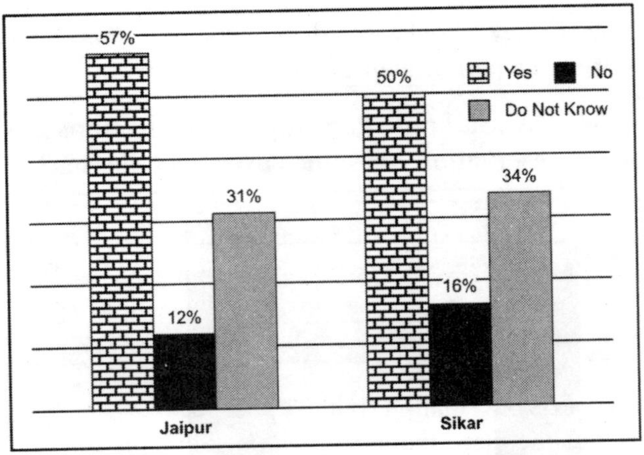

	Yes	*No*	*Don't know*	*Total*
Jaipur	57%	12%	31%	100%
Sikar	50%	16%	34%	100%
Total	53.5%	14%	32.5%	100%

reservation for anybody, and 32.5 per cent knew there was reservation they could not name any caste or tribe who received reservation privileges.

Question 36. How much reservation exists and for which caste or class? Can you provide any information in this regard?

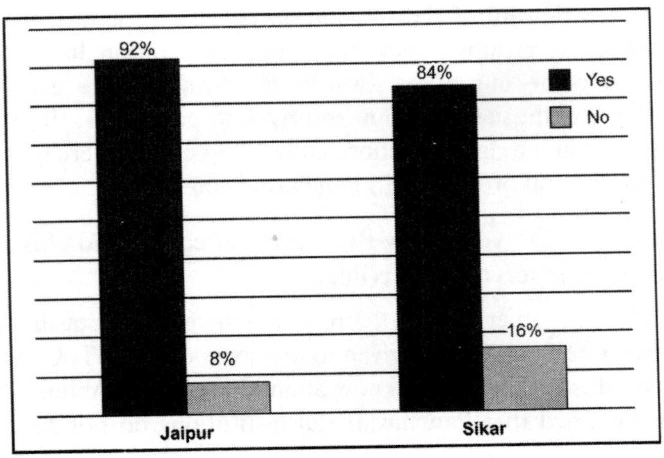

	Yes	*No*	*Total*
Jaipur	92%	8%	100%
Sikar	84%	16%	100%
Total	88%	12%	100%

The answers to this question when analysed led to the conclusion that the respondents did not have correct information about the name of categories of population groups eligible for reservation. Reservation for women reservation was known to all, but about other categories they preferred to remain silent. Thus, 88 per cent had the correct information but 12 per cent were absolutely ignorant about the facts about reservation. Some merely said that there was reservation for posts in Panchayati Raj institutions.

Question 37. Has the 33 per cent reservation given to women caused betterment in the lives of womenfolk in the villages?

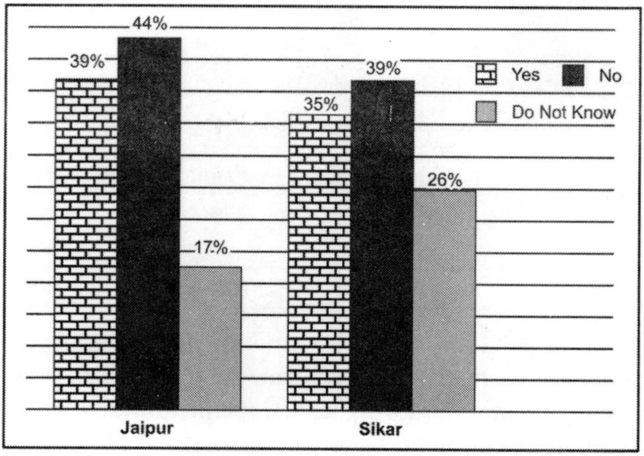

	Yes	*No*	*Don't know*	*Total*
Jaipur	39%	44%	17%	100%
Sikar	35%	39%	26%	100%
Total	37%	41.5%	21.5%	100%

As much as 37 per cent of the respondents said, 'Yes', and they revealed that their interest in political activities has increased and that they feel confident in contesting Panchayati Raj polls. But then

41.5 per cent maintained that the condition of women remained unchanged. Their plight or life situation has not improved at all. In fact, 21.5 per cent of the respondents had no information on this score.

Question 38. How many posts or positions fall under the reservation categories such as caste and tribes in all the three institutions?

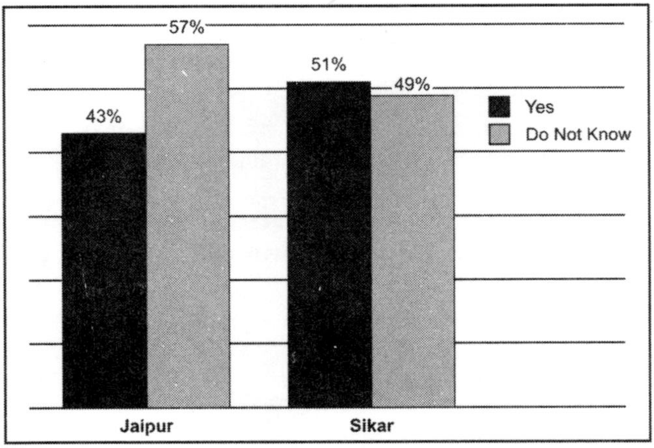

	Yes	*Don't know*	*Total*
Jaipur	43%	57%	100%
Sikar	51%	49%	100%
Total	47%	53%	100%

As much as 53 per cent had no information about the categories or the number of reservations in each category. They knew the name of their representative and who headed the institutions. Beyond this they had no information how the system worked; 47 per cent could specify the names of the candidates and this information was found to be accurate.

Question 39. Which caste or class benefited the most and in which areas and in what matters?

The answer to this question revealed that the general category of villagers has benefited the least. The SC (scheduled caste) members got the lion's share of employment, but the benefits in the area of

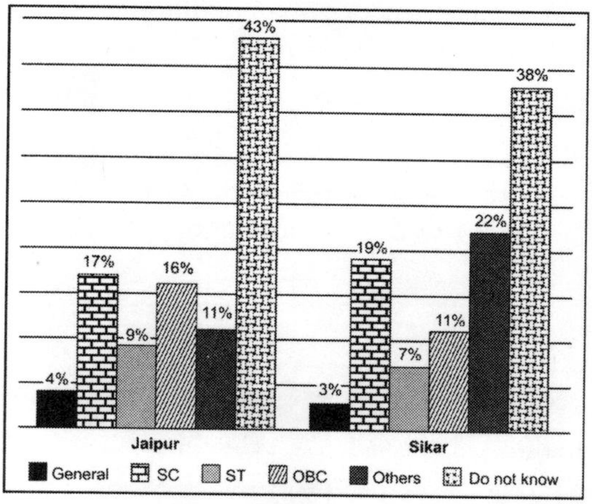

	Jaipur	*Sikar*	*Total*
General	4%	3%	3.5%
SC	17%	19%	18%
ST	9%	7%	8.0%
OBC	16%	11%	13.5%
Others	11%	22%	16.5%
Don't know	43%	38%	40.5%
Total	100%	100%	100%

health went to the ST (scheduled tribe) members. The OBC (other backward castes) category got advantage in matters of employment and education. The various government schemes and projects enabled the rural women to take advantage of facilities in the area of women's health and maternity relief.

Question 40. Which group or caste has benefited the least from reservation?

As high as 53 per cent of the respondents maintained that general category people either got little or absolutely no benefit from Panchayati leaders of reserved category; 8 per cent put ST as the least benefitted category among those eligible for reservation. Similarly 19 per cent put SC and 6 per cent put OBC as the least benefitted categories. They advocated for increased number of seats under reservation. About 14 per cent recommended reservation for various other categories outside the list.

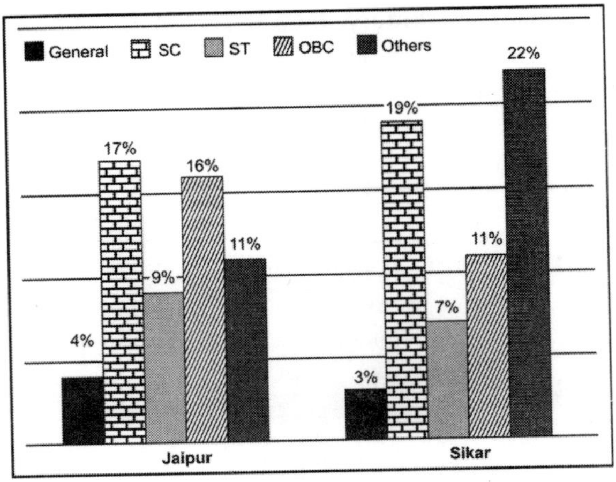

	Jaipur	*Sikar*	*Total*
General	61%	45%	53%
SC	9%	7%	8%
ST	21%	17%	19%
OBC	4%	8%	6%
Others	5%	23%	14%
Total	100%	100%	100%

Question 40 (a). Who plays the critical role in Panchayati Raj decision-making?

Only 13 per cent of the respondents maintained that women played an effective role in decision making. About 46 per cent admitted that male members in general category played a decisive part. Around 21 per cent of SC Panchas played in important role in the decision-making. The Panchas who belonged to the ST group were seen as dominant by 16 per cent of the respondents. Only 4 per cent felt that OBC members of Panchayati Raj bodies played a significant role in decision-making. It indicates that decision-making is influenced by the group which has a majority in the local body.

Question 41. Women's reservation has influenced several fields and which field was influenced the maximum?

The area pointed out in the study was 'the family situation'; in this case family members felt that if some girl or woman in their family is educated and if Panchayati Raj seat comes under woman reservation category by lottery, then they may sponsor her candidature and their family can reach to the position of a village ruler. Very few respondents were against female reservation. Most of them admitted that the status of women has improved and they have become respectable.

Jaipur			*Sikar*		
Family	Positive	31%	Family	Positive	28.5%
	Negative	9%		Negative	8%
Children	Positive	12%	Children	Positive	10.5%
	Negative	8%		Negative	6.5%
Society	Positive	11%	Society	Positive	13.5%
	Negative	9%		Negative	7.0%
Don't know		20%	Don't know		26.0%
Total		100%			100%

Women's reservation has brought a positive change in rural society. Men's attitudes are changing fast. Leadership in patriarchal society and family is gradually being passed onto women, old and young. On average men have begun to realize that women can do it and that with society's support they are capable of performing miracles. There was a mixed reaction about 'nurture of children in the family'; some people said that even children have developed a better political understanding because of the role of their mothers. The opponents felt that children are being politicised unnecessarily.

Respondents maintained that the impact of women's reservation in Panchayati Raj bodies has been seminal or of little consequence. They win elections because of their image and active campaigns by their family members. These family members, like husband, father-in-law or other relations, run their political offices by proxy.

Question 42. Have women leaders like Sarpanch, Pradhan and Pramukh in various Panchayati Raj bodies discharged their responsibilities properly? If not, what are the barriers in their roles?

The 73rd Constitutional Amendment provides one-third of total seats as reserved for women. Women who have been elected to these

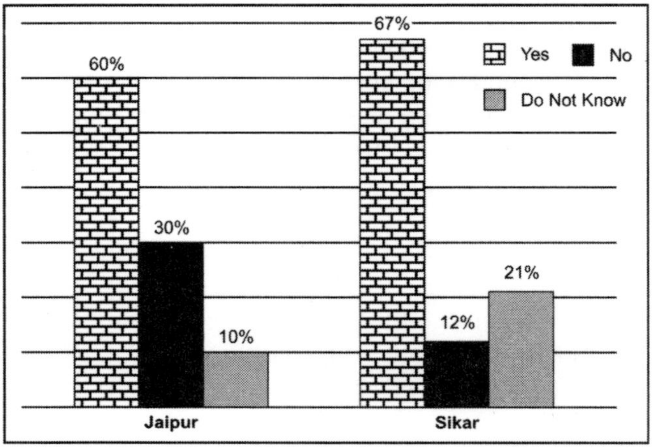

	Yes	*No*	*Don't know*	*Total*
Jaipur	60%	30%	10%	100%
Sikar	67%	12%	21%	100%
Total	63.5%	21%	15.5%	100%

seats are entrusted with responsibilities of running the village government. Regrettably, some respondents felt that these women representatives appear only during the polls and after getting elected they do very little either in their offices or in the field. They neither have the ability nor adequate training to discharge the functions of their office. The barriers and handicaps are innumerable.

As much as 63.5 per cent respondents answered the question positively. They were of the opinion that woman are doing well as Sarpanchs or Pradhans or Zila Pramukhs but that they face certain problems which are typically faced by woman outside of their home. They do need male help in discharging their duties. Therefore, the husband of the woman Sarpanch or Pradhan or Zila Pramukh takes the powers in his hand. About 21 per cent of the respondents were of the opinion that women are not in position to discharge their duties and remaining 15.5 per cent replied that they do not know anything in this regard.

The respondents put 'Parda' or veil wearing as the biggest handicap. Most of these women come out of their homes with their husbands or other kin or relatives. Naturally, rural milieu makes these relatives important and they perform work on behalf of women heading the office. These near relatives do the job and they append their signatures or affix a thumb impression. Moreover, they do not understand problems because of illiteracy and caste ethos of the neighbourhood. The respondents openly admitted the mischiefs of male-dominated patriarchal society and identified this mind-set as a major barrier in the functioning of women leaders in Panchayat Raj bodies.

But then 21 per cent of the respondents felt that this is being exaggerated. They are conducing themselves with honesty and dignity. Best of the sample was either silent or preferred to have no comment on the question.

Question 43. Can you narrate some significant initiatives and projects executed by women representatives of Gram Panchayats, Panchayat Samitis and Zila Parishads?

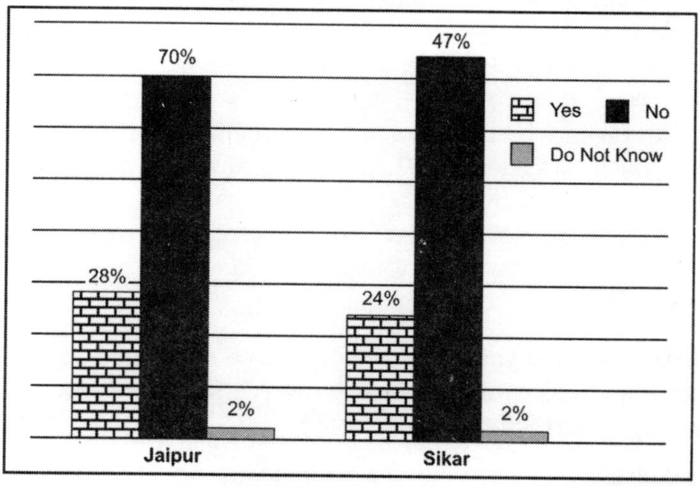

	Yes	*No*	*Don't know*	*Total*
Jaipur	28%	70%	2%	100%
Sikar	24%	74%	2%	100%
Total	26%	72%	2%	100%

After analysing the responses to this question, it was disappointing to note that as much as 72 per cent of the respondents felt that women representatives did not do anything remarkable or noteworthy. They felt that women leaders only attended

Panchayat body meetings and affixed their signatures where needed, acting like mere figureheads with men from their family calling all the shots behind the screen. Only a few women representatives cared to understand or were capable of answering the complex questions posed in relation to decision-making at the local level. They still want to call it an achievement even though they could work only with help from a family member. About 2 per cent of the respondents maintained that the term 'significant' was irrelevant because they felt woman representatives could not execute even routine functions. And 26 per cent of the respondents tried to identify the role of women in Panchayats and they made the following observations:

1. Villagers are training their women folk, and they all agree that as education expands their daughters' capabilities, their daughters will have a better career in Panchayati Raj.
2. Women members have done a good job in arousing popular consciousness against child marriage. Door-to-door canvassing has improved matters.
3. Efforts have been made in the field of environment protection. Some local leaders have taken up rainwater harvesting as a key part of their activities.
4. In Sikar District special efforts have been made to improve the lot of military widows whose conditions have been far from satisfactory.

Question 44. Do you think the condition of women has really improved with guaranteed reservations for them in Panchayati Raj bodies since 1994?

This question was answered in a positive way. About 55 per cent of the respondents felt there is a visible change. Only 34 per cent said that the conditions of people in reserved categories by and large remain the same. About 11 per cent had no information or opinion in this matter. The changes mostly pointed out by protagonists indicated the following:

1. Popular awareness has made the weak and backward groups more confident. Women now feel that they can lead and work outside their homes. They feel stronger and in a Panchayat office they feel one with other members of weaker sections.

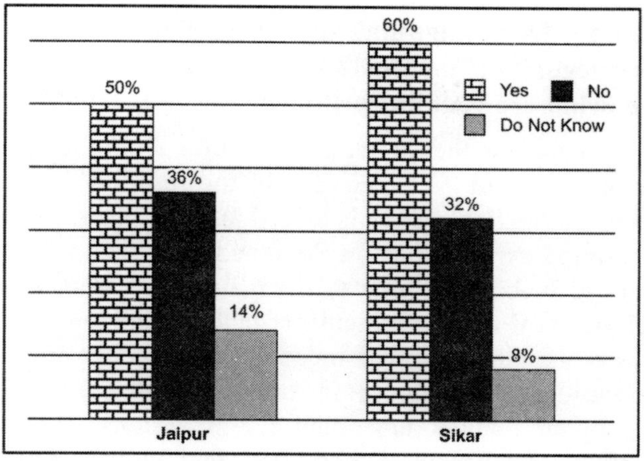

	Yes	*No*	*Don't know*	*Total*
Jaipur	50%	36%	14%	100%
Sikar	60%	32%	8%	100%
Total	55%	34%	11%	100%

2. Weaker sections have started taking interest in politics. They canvass door to door for seeking votes and take pride in their victory at the hustings. They feel equal with their menfolk and the percentage of female vote denotes women and weaker sections are now more enthusiastic about their participation in Panchayati Raj bodies.
3. Weaker sections are becoming less and less fatalist. They say that they have now begun working for ushering in a significant change in their otherwise predictably bleak destiny as was seen in the past. They no longer accept exploitation as a given or an unchangeable situation, which was formerly called the wages of previous actions.
4. They do not support the kin members, and the change that took place in this aspect between 1994 and 2014 demonstrates that this dependence on family members has considerably declined. Women leaders today know reasonably well how the system functions and handle Panchayati decisions on their own and with care and ability. The slow and steady growth of the system makes one optimistic about rural local government.

Question 45. Do young think the reservation accorded to various categories is justified? If you want to revise or improve, what are your suggestions?

Most of the people in the sample were positive about the provisions of reservation. About 78.5 per cent of the respondents found it proper and useful. Reservation is indeed justified in a society which has perpetrated exploitations on these people for centuries. These people are to be brought back to the mainstream of national life. Only 5.5 per cent of the respondents felt that the time has come when reservation is no longer needed and benefits are actually going to those undeserving of reservation.

The opinion about amending the provisions was divided. Some wanted extensions. Others said that women reservation should be 50 per cent given their proportion in the population. A sizeable section wanted a review of the provisions. About 16 per cent showed ignorance about the reservation arrangement. Most of these people were illiterate and had no knowledge about how Panchayati Raj worked.

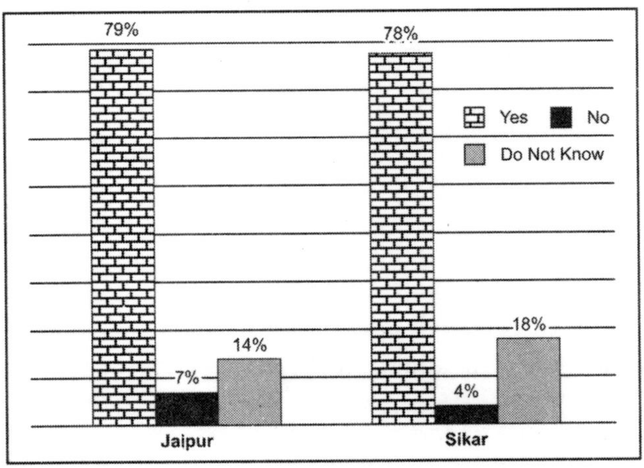

	Yes	*No*	*Don't know*	*Total*
Jaipur	79%	7%	14%	100%
Sikar	78%	4%	18%	100%
Total	78.5%	5.5%	16%	100%

Question 46. Has reservation created new problems in the rural life of India? If so, what are these problems?

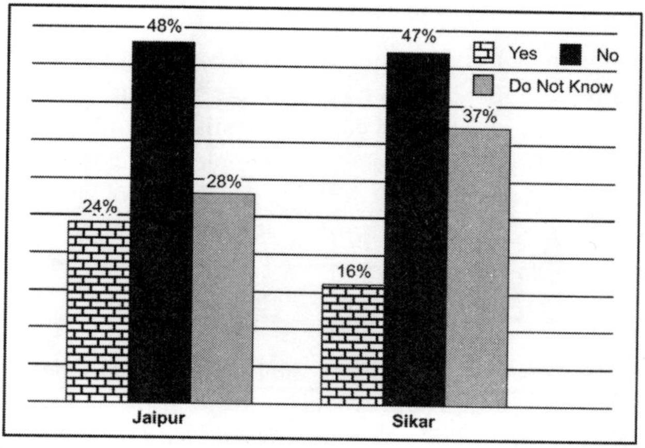

	Yes	*No*	*Don't know*	*Total*
Jaipur	24%	48%	28%	100%
Sikar	16%	47%	37%	100%
Total	20%	47.5%	32.5%	100%

When asked this question, 47.5 per cent of the respondents said that no new problem has cropped up in rural life. However, 20 per cent maintained that some new problems have indeed sprung up. For instance, politics in rural areas has become totally polluted. The groups and cliques keep fighting. Nobody bothers about development and waste their energies in humiliating each other. About 32.5 per cent gave no answer and said they had no information about this matter.

Question 47. Have people been vested with real power in their local affairs by the establishment of Panchayati Raj?

About 63 per cent of the respondents in the sample said 'no'. The negative answer confirm the notion that the powers given are actually pseudo and in fact the Panchayati Raj institutions are powerless. Only 23 per cent took the opposite view. They said that people know that they can remove their elected Panchayat leaders. Gram Sabha really makes them accountable. Only 9.5 per cent said that as compared to past people have more powers and Panchayati

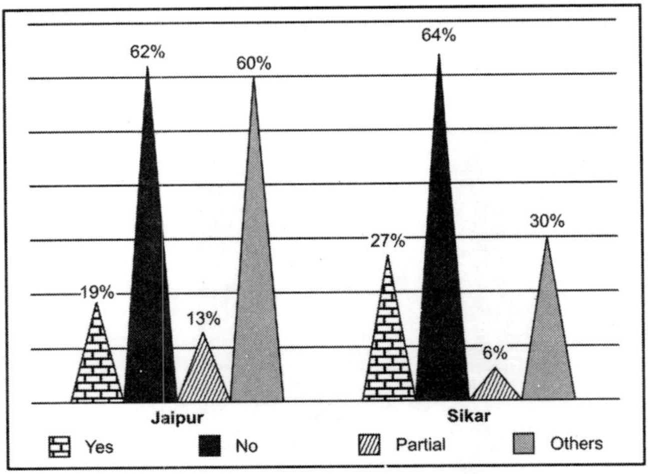

	Yes	*No*	*Partial*	*Others*	*Total*
Jaipur	19%	62%	13%	60%	100%
Sikar	27%	64%	6%	30%	100%
Total	23%	63%	9.5%	4.5%	100%

Raj bodies are in the process of becoming effective. About 4.5 per cent respondents said they were in favour of other categories.

Question 48. Do you think Panchayats are steeped in corruption?

Apparently, as much as 80.5 per cent of the respondents openly maintained that the incidence of corruption was high and terrible. They pointed out that money that is swindled by members comes for various development projects from the state and union governments. These funds are misappropriated through fake muster rolls and forged documents.

The Sarpanchs who verify and attest these documents take bribe money and this further adds to bribery and corruption that already exists in governance.

'Corruption Free Panchayat' was the reply of 5.5 per cent respondents; 7.5 per cent confessed some minor incidents of corruption, but 6.5 per cent claimed to be ignorant of such malpractices. They neither went to the Panchayat office nor had any experience about corruption or bribery.

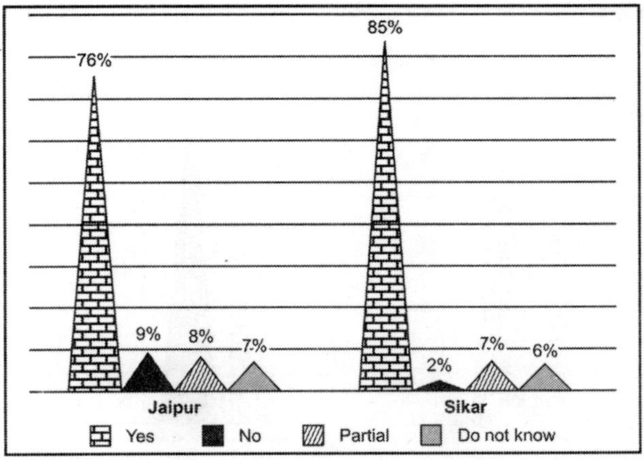

	Yes	*No*	*Partial*	*Don't know*	*Total*
Jaipur	76%	9%	8%	7%	100%
Sikar	85%	2%	7%	6%	100%
Total	80.5%	5.5%	7.5%	6.5%	100%

Question 49. Mention two customs or rituals which oppose the functioning of Panchayats?

Respondents could not easily think of the answer. For them it was a difficult question, and as much as 59 per cent found themselves unable to name any rites or rituals. The rest offered some suggestions and narrated stories from which answers can be deduced:

1. Caste system is the biggest handicap, and even good projects have to be abandoned because they are opposed on caste lines and due to caste consideration.
2. Division of rural society into forward and backward groups. The divide is getting deeper, and powerful groups do not want the weaker ones to emerge. Naturally, opposition leads to a variety of manifestations.
3. Another barrier pointed out was the difference between the males' and females' mind-set; men deny equality and women are scared and refuse to come forward to accept equal positions. The dominant males do not want to sit with women as their equals or discuss issues with them at public places. They honestly believe that they should work only in their households and rule there. Most of the senior women in village

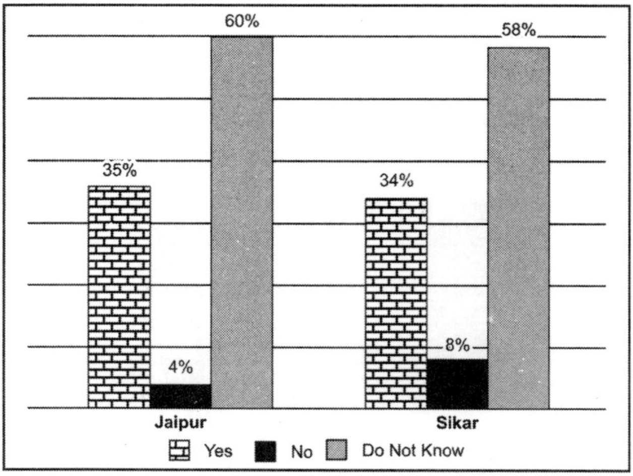

	Yes	*No*	*Don't know*	*Total*
Jaipur	36%	4%	60%	100%
Sikar	34%	8%	58%	100%
Total	35%	6%	59%	100%

oppose the equal role played by younger women specifically when they need to sit with older males or with menfolk from other families who are of equal age. These exclusionary views keep them prisoner of their households.

4. One more reason was the narrowness of local issues. When funds come for the entire village area, the leaders actually want to spend it for improving the area around their houses or for the benefit of their kith and kin or those areas where their voters are a majority.
5. Wearing veils has its negative effect. Women cannot talk freely, and keep their mouth shut and face covered, this is especially case for young daughter-in-laws. This obstructs their participation. Most of the respondents avoided this question.

Question 50. Has any Panchayati Raj body instituted any report or complaint about financial irregularities. Yes or no. if yes, when and why?

Respondents did not know specific cases. As much as 34.5 per cent just said that there had been no financial irregularity in their

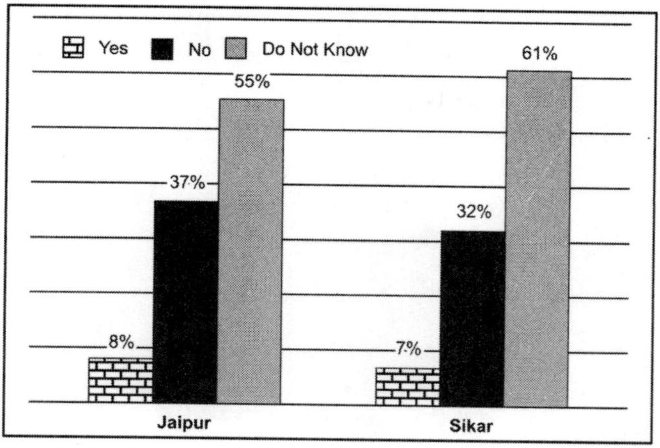

	Yes	*No*	*Don't know*	*Total*
Jaipur	8%	37%	55%	100%
Sikar	7%	32%	61%	100%
Total	7.5%	34.5%	58%	100%

Panchayats. Most of them felt embarrassed and dismissed the question without comments. About 7.5 per cent of them answered in the affirmative and cited some minor cases about which they knew little. About 58 per cent were found to be just ignorant or drew a blank.

Question 51. Has any Panchayat used its powers and functions for supplying information under the Right to Information Act?

About 17 per cent of the respondents accepted that people are more aware and they ask for information. For instance, budget allocation for development works are being sought for. Another common enquiry is about allocations made for road repair. This demonstrates awareness; obviously, such enquiries have made Panchayats act more responsibly.

About 12.5 per cent of the respondents said that the provisions and rights provided through the Right to Information Act remained unused in their Panchayats. About 70.5 per cent were ignorant about whether such rights existed. They did not what is 'right' itself.

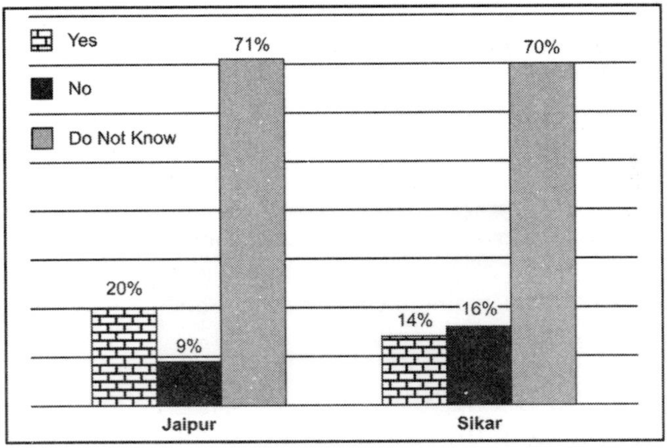

	Yes	*No*	*Don't know*	*Total*
Jaipur	20%	9%	71%	100%
Sikar	14%	16%	70%	100%
Total	17%	12.5%	70.5%	100%

Question 52. Do your Panchayat, Panchayat Samiti or Zila Parishad help people in getting employment under NREGA?

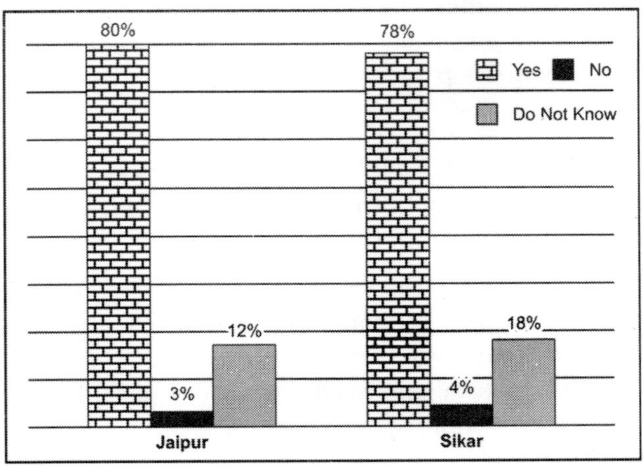

	Yes	*No*	*Don't know*	*Total*
Jaipur	80%	3%	17%	100%
Sikar	78%	4%	18%	100%
Total	79%	3.5%	17.5%	100%

Respondents overwhelmingly subscribed to the view (79%) that their Panchayats are quite active in this field. They also narrated the productive activities going on in the country side. For instance, planting of trees, digging wells, tanks, building of roads are some of the construction activities currently going on. It was appreciated by the people; they said such schemes are useful and supports the poor. Only 17.5 per cent did not know about the project, but they are aware of the fact the government is providing jobs to labourers. About 3.5 per cent maintained that their Panchayats are inactive and are doing nothing for rural employment.

Question 53. Are payments under NREGA made regularly and in time. If yes, how much?

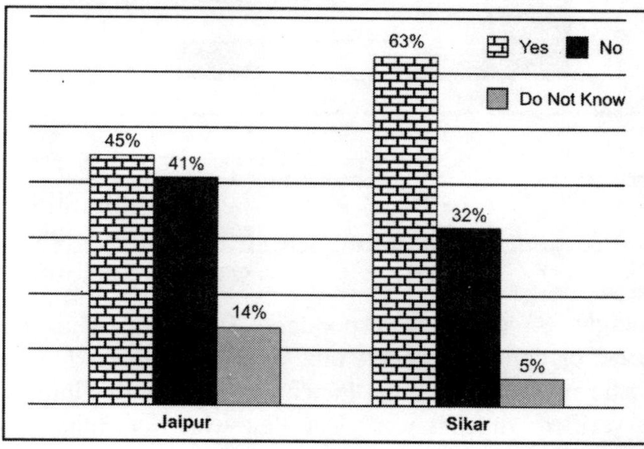

	Yes	*No*	*Don't know*	*Total*
Jaipur	45%	41%	14%	100%
Sikar	63%	32%	5%	100%
Total	54%	36.5%	9.5%	100%

The situation was found to be reasonably satisfactory. About 54 per cent of the respondents said people are paid regularly. However, about 36.5 per cent complained about delays and legal hurdles. Some gave facts about harassments and illegal grafts. Still 9.5 per cent people had no idea how NREGA operates. About the amount, there were wide differences in responses, from ₹ 125–175. In fact, it was made as per the nature of the work and time involved in completing it.

Question 54. How many people do you think can find employment in your Gram Panchayat, Panchayat Samiti and Zila Parishad?

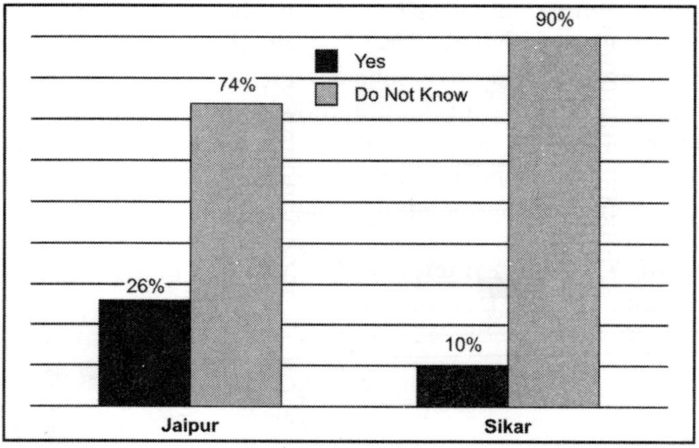

	Yes	*Don't know*	*Total*
Jaipur	26%	74%	100%
Sikar	10%	90%	100%
Total	18%	82%	100%

Surprisingly, 82 per cent respondents said zero. They had no knowledge or couldn't provide any kind of numbers. Even office bearer said that only from the Panchayat records this information can be verified; thus, it was clear that whatever number about employment that was mentioned was just guess work. Only 18 per cent respondents have some information in this regard.

Question 55. What kind of services do your Gram Panchayat, Panchayat Samiti and Zila Parishad offer during famine, floods and other disasters?

Panchayat Raj institutions always seek help from state during emergencies. They undertake relief measures and construction work to provide employment, but funds usually come from the state government. About 82.5 per cent of the respondents stated that repairing of roads, building of tank, temporary housing and so on are some of the restoration activities in which villagers also participate; 4.5 per cent reported that their Gram Panchayat does not do

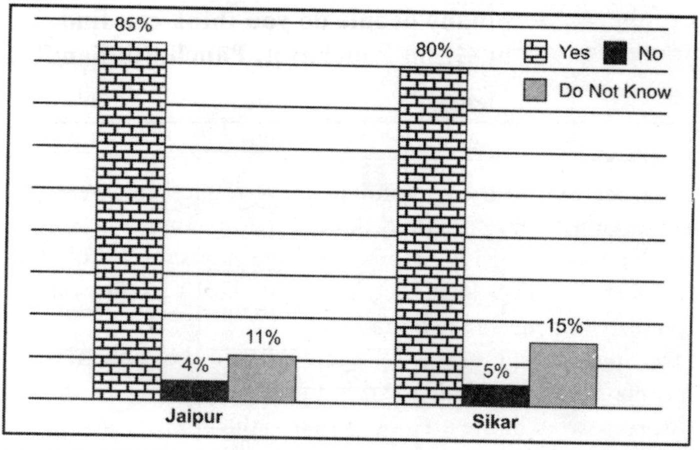

	Yes	*No*	*Don't know*	*Total*
Jaipur	85%	4%	11%	100%
Sikar	80%	05%	15%	100%
Total	82.5%	4.5%	13%	100%

any relief work and 13 per cent stated that they had no information about Panchayati Raj achievements.

Question 56. Identify two areas in which Panchayats should be vested with more powers?

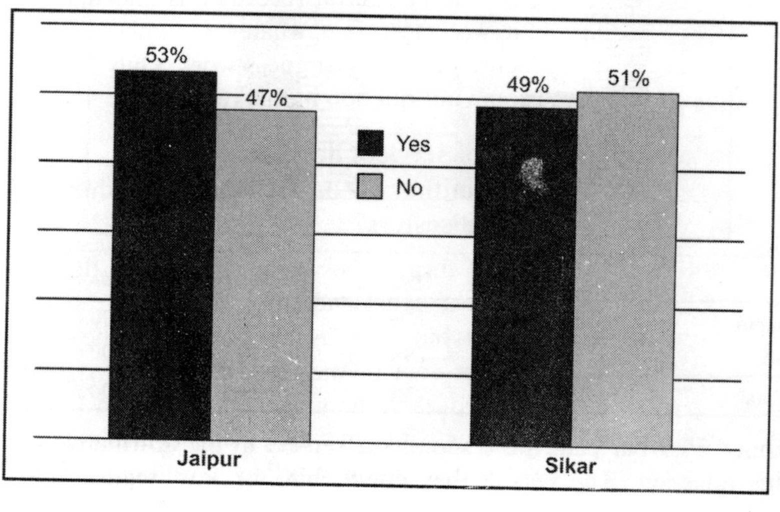

	Yes	*No*	*Total*
Jaipur	53%	47%	100%
Sikar	49%	51%	100%
Total	51%	49%	100%

About 51 per cent of the respondents gave replies that were rather vague. About 49 per cent could not list them; some of the suggestions which could be gather from our discussions are as follows:

1. Powers to deliver local justice in petty cases so that case load on district courts may be reduced
2. The per capita grant by state should be enhanced and grants-in-aid should be paid in time
3. More powers in the area of primary education
4. Powers in the areas of forestry and agriculture
5. More facilities and powers in general.

Question 57. Has the Panchayati Raj become more effective after the constitutional amendments?

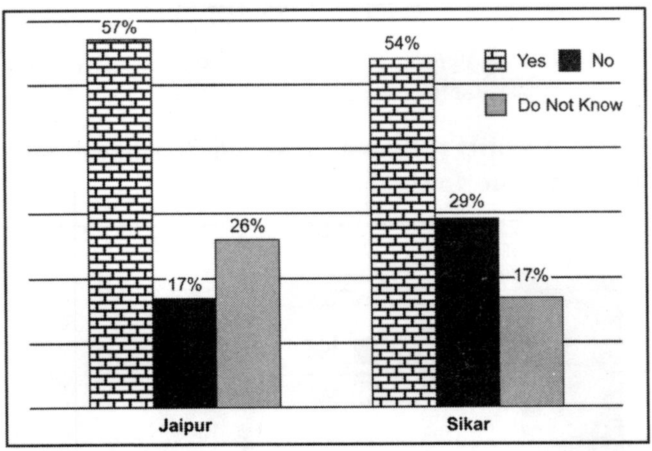

	Yes	*No*	*Don't know*	*Total*
Jaipur	57%	17%	26%	100%
Sikar	54%	29%	17%	100%
Total	55.5%	23%	21.5%	100%

About 55.5 per cent the respondents replied in the affirmative to this question. The reason they could think of was 'regular and

direct elections conducted once in every five years.' Formerly, they starved for funds, but now financial shortage is not a problem. Money comes from various sources. Women are contesting with enthusiasm. It energises Panchayati Raj politics. Only 23 per cent maintained that the change is not visible. About 21.5 per cent did not know how the power structure has changed in terms of functions after the constitutional amendment. They do not even know that such a constitutional amendment has taken place.

Question 58. Have the Panchayats proven themselves to be powerful and effective in providing security to women and Dalits?

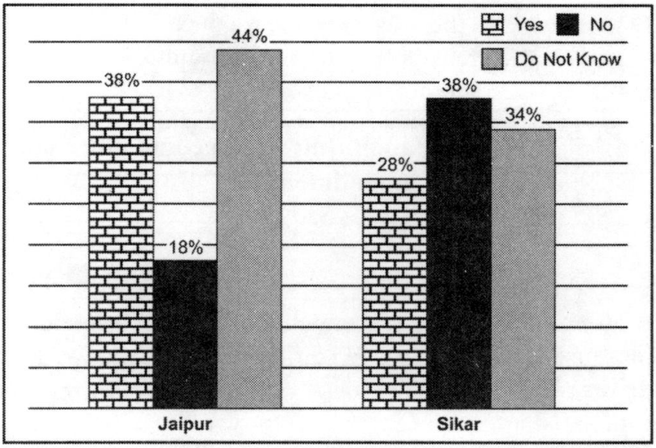

	Yes	*No*	*Don't know*	*Total*
Jaipur	38%	18%	44%	100%
Sikar	28%	38%	34%	100%
Total	33%	28%	39%	100%

About 28 per cent of the respondents felt they had failed to protect weaker sections. The status quo situation remains. And 33 per cent said they are more effective and provide better security. The Dalits have been empowered. They attend Panchayat meetings and solve their problems. About 39 per cent of the respondents claimed ignorance and demonstrated indifference in replying to the question about Dalit security and welfare.

Question 59. What should be done by the Panchayats to empower the Dalits?

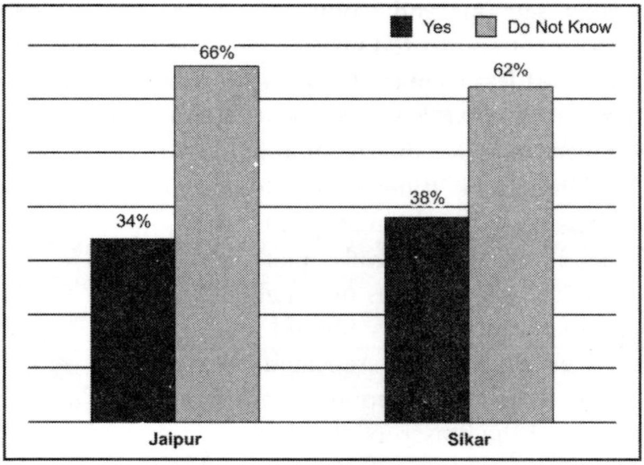

	Yes	*Don't know*	*Total*
Jaipur	34%	66%	100%
Sikar	38%	62%	100%
Total	36%	64%	100%

About 36 per cent of the respondents offered a variety of suggestions because Dalits were viewed differently by Sawarans and Dalits themselves. The analysis of data yielded the following concrete suggestions:

1. Women and Dalit groups should be educated in a formal way. Education will make them enlightened and they will be more aware of their rights. For this, government should open schools and establish literacy centres in rural areas. Absence of education breeds apathy, and therefore, they do not come forward to learn, protect and promote their rights.
2. Administrative training can enhance their participation qualitatively as well as quantitatively. Even those who are politically aware have no knowledge of rules and procedures. Hence, they hesitate and their decisions are not encouraged or supported by higher bodies. Like women, the Dalits also cut a sorry figure in the meetings and look to others for guidance or decision-making. They put thumb impressions and openly ask others to decide on their behalf.

3. Employment-oriented schemes for women and Dalits should be taken up on priority basis.
4. Weaker sections and women should be at the centre of all government-sponsored projects and schemes.
5. Elected leaders from these weaker sections should get help and stringent punitive measures are required to punish those who humiliate them for their station in life.
6. They should be trained in voluntary self-employment, and their economic position should be strengthened.
7. Social functions, festivals, marriages and so on should be solemnised on the basis of equality. Any age-old practice that perpetuate inequalities should be penalised, so that such practices do not get repeated. Social security of weaker sections is a critical requirement for bringing in any positive changes at the grassroots level.

About 64 per cent of the respondents did not offer any suggestion because they felt things are changing and they do not know what are the specific factors to be considered to accelerate social change.

6

Findings and Suggestions

Panchayati Raj system is an instrument of government to connected with the rural population. The essence of democracy is that the top echelons should be linked with the grassroots institutions so that the average citizen may develop his or her capacity for decision-making. India being a huge democracy adopted decentralisation by institutionalising Panchayati Raj at the village, block and district levels of local government. Moreover, India is a country of villages, and the concept of holistic development makes it imperative that rural India should be systematically developed. Hence, the founding fathers of Indian Constitution incorporated Article 40 to give Panchayati Raj its due place in the Constitution. The article mandates that the state should organize and empower village Panchayats. The journey of development ever since the commencement of the Constitution indicates that the governments continuously made efforts in the direction which finally resulted in the 73rd Constitutional Amendment of 1993. This significant landmark of the journey constitutionalises Panchayati Raj bodies in the country. It has established an uniformity in Panchayati Raj structure all over the country, and it has developed three tiers of rural local government institutions. It has regularized the elections of Panchayati bodies, and a State Finance Commission looks after their resources and funding needs. To promote popular participation in the functioning of the Panchayati Raj institutions reservation of seats has been provided for various categories. SCs and STs have been provided reservations as per the provisions of the Constitution; in addition, 21 per cent reservation for OBCs and 33 per cent reservation for women have been given. The 1993 Constitutional Amendment asked the state governments to make their respective local laws in accordance with the 73rd Constitutional Amendment. In Rajasthan, the first elections of Panchayati Raj Institutions as per provisions of 73rd Constitutional Amendment were held in 1994 under the new dispensation. People welcomed this resurrection which infused a new life in the moribund structure of Panchayats in the state.

During the past 23 years five Panchayati Raj elections have been held in Rajasthan. Reservation for women yielded very positive and encouraging results. The present study has been conducted in the two districts of Rajasthan, namely Jaipur and Sikar, between 1994 and 2014. The sample of the study included present and former office bearers of Panchayati Raj bodies and the ordinary citizens of the two districts. The respondents supplied very valuable factual data and information which provided inputs for our analysis. Some of the conclusions which emerged from this analysis are detailed below:

- When people were asked about the political system of the country very few could furnish adequate facts or information even after 70 years of Indian independence. Of course, 60 per cent of the respondents knew that India has opted for a democratic system of government, but 22 per cent showed ignorance about the names of parties and rulers. These people are living in the past and know little about the present. Most of the respondents neither knew the characteristics of democracy nor could explain its merits and demerits. They only knew that the country has democracy. When they were further asked to identify the source of their information, they deposed that their children supplied them with this information. About 18 per cent of the respondents held that they do not know that there is democracy in the country. They maintained that rule of Englishmen and princely states was very good. Their social background when analysed was found most backward. They could not recall the date of departure of Englishmen and the advent of freedom in India. Most of these respondents were women and old people. This situation should change. In far-flung villages rural folks have to walk several miles to fetch drinking water. The main problem in rural areas, even in some big towns like Sikar, being even district headquarter, is the lack of availability of drinking water. Naturally, political awareness is a dream in these areas of quasi-civilized existence. People living in areas closer to cities were reasonably aware and could talk about political change. These people could discuss political issues and behaviour of their political leaders.

- The study posed questions about Panchayati Raj structures and their working. The respondents knew much more about local developments than national or state-level activities. It is because Panchayati Raj institutions are close to their dwellings and daily activities. The Panchayati Raj bodies were related to their lives and showed their familiarity about their problems and prospects. They maintained that state governments should empower these local bodies so that the funds for rural development can directly reach popular welfare activities. This is the reason rural people participate in Panchayati elections and their active participation is highly encouraging.
- The 73rd Amendment has caused positive transformation in rural India. The constitutionalisation has strengthened Panchayati Raj institutions. They are more effective now. With 29 subjects in the schedule assigned to them, the state governments have a constitutional obligation to transfer these 29 subjects to the care of Panchayati Raj. The process may be slow or gradual, but it cannot be reversed. The Rajasthan State has continuously hastened this process and it is an auspicious beginning in the area of local empowerment.
- When the respondents were asked about the subjects assigned to the Panchayati Raj institutions by the Constitution under 73rd Constitutional Amendment, about 53.5 per cent of the study participants said they had basic knowledge about these powers and functions, but they could not identify the sources of these powers and functions or point out the legal provisions pertaining to these functions. They only reiterated that Panchayati Raj institutions have these functions. The following classifications of these functions are known to the respondents to some extent.

1. Planning, 2. Budget Preparation, 3. Disaster Management, 4. Welfare Programme, 5. Development Programmes for Weaker Sections, 6. Improvement in Agriculture and Horticulture, 7. Census and Surveys, 8. Adult Education, 9. Preservation of Ecology, and 10. Cottage Industries.

As much as 46.5 per cent of the respondents denied having any knowledge about these areas.

- Respondents were asked about the meetings of village panchayats and Gram Sabha to know the level of knowledge and awareness of the voters. Most of the people answering this question responded in the affirmative but in terms of the number of times meetings were held theirs answered differed a great deal. They had little idea of the frequencies of Gram Sabha meetings. About 42 per cent maintained that Gram Sabha meetings were in the neighbourhood of three to four in a year. When further probed whether they attended and participated in these meetings, their replies were far from satisfactory. Only few of the respondents said that they participated in the meetings and wanted to know whether the decisions of the previous meetings were implemented at all. Several people had information about meetings, dates and times, but they had no specific reason to avoid these meetings except that they never took the participation seriously. They did not know that a Gram Sabha keeps detailed records of rural happenings, including births, deaths and so on. The women respondents did not participate; they said that their domestic chores did not permit them to find time for public duties. Surprisingly, 10 per cent respondents were not aware at all about the meetings of village panchayats and Gram Sabhas.

  As much as 48 per cent respondents maintained that Gram Sabha meetings were on paper only. They were neither informed nor the information was displayed on the notice-boards. Obviously, the institutions are yet to make their presence felt in the lives of people in the villages.
- Respondents were asked some questions about popular cooperation in the working of Panchayati Raj. As much as 79 per cent of the respondents maintained that masses or common villagers do not cooperate in Panchayat activities. They are generally neutral and they do not care what the Panchayat does and what kind of popular cooperation it needs.

Some felt that younger people help to some extent, and some mentioned about SC, ST and OBC groups supporting Panchayat activities. Thus, in all 15 per cent of the respondents talked about extending cooperation to Panchayat Raj institutions. About 6 per cent had no information about people's cooperation on the basis of caste, class or groups.

- Respondents were also asked to suggest about ways to enhance popular cooperation in Panchayat politics? They pointed out several ways by which Panchayats can enhance popular participation, an some of them are listed here:
  - (i) Panchayats should take interest in village economy. This will deepen their interest in the activities of Panchayats.
  - (ii) Awareness campaigns may be launched from time to time so that people come forward to cooperate.
  - (iii) Free food packets may be delivered to the participants on the lines of midday meals in the schools.
  - (v) Villagers should be made to realize that their support to Panchayats will ultimately prove beneficial to them.
  - (v) Panchayats should organize camps, and popular problems and grievances should be resolved in these camps.
  - (vi) Suitable rewards and awards may be given to those who work for Panchayats on important national events like Independence Day and Republic Day.

  About 43.5 per cent of the respondents answered the question and suggested ways how Panchayat can enhance popular participation; 56.5 per cent did not respond and most of them revealed that they do not know anything in this regard.
- The 73rd Constitutional Amendment provides reservation of one-third of total seats for women. Women who have been elected to these seats have been entrusted with responsibilities of running the village government. Regrettably some respondents felt these women representatives appear only during polls and that they do very little in their offices or in the field. They neither have the ability nor adequate training to discharge the functions of their office. The barriers and handicaps are innumerable.

  About 63.5 per cent of the respondents responded to the question in a positive spirit. They were of the opinion that woman are doing well as Sarpanch or Pradhan or Zila Pramukh but there are certain problems that women face in the field. Some male help is needed in discharging their duties. Therefore, the husband of the woman Sarpanch, Pradhan and Zila Pramukh takes the powers in his hand. About 21 per cent respondents were of the opinion that women are not in position to discharge their duties, and the remaining 15.5 per cent replied that they do not know anything in this regard.

The respondents described 'Parda' or veil-wearing as the biggest handicap. Most of these women come out of their homes with their husbands or other family members and relatives. Naturally, the rural milieu makes these relatives important and they perform work on the behalf of the women elected. These relatives do the job and they append their signatures or affix a thumb impression. Moreover, they do not understand problems because of illiteracy and caste ethos of the neighbourhood. The respondents openly admitted the mischiefs of male-dominated patriarchal society and identified this mind-set as a major barrier in the functioning of women leaders in Panchayat Raj bodies. However, the educational qualification has been fixed for the Sarpanchas and Panchas. Therefore, the problem of signature or thumb impression has been solved automatically. Nonetheless, 21 per cent respondents felt that this is being exaggerated. They are conducing themselves with honesty and dignity. Most of the respondents were either silent or preferred to have no comment on the question.

Respondents were also asked about significant activities executed by women representatives of Panchayati Raj institutions. It was disappointing to hear that as much as 72 per cent respondents felt that women representatives did not do anything outstanding. They only attend Panchayat body meetings and append their signatures wherever asked. Very few care to understand or are capable of examining intricate questions of local decision-making. They call it an achievement when they actually work with the cooperation or assistance of a family relative and not independently. About 2 per cent of the respondents maintained that the term 'significant' is irrelevant because they cannot execute even routine functions. About 26 per cent tried to identify women's role and they observed the following:

(i) Villagers are training their womenfolk and they all agree that as education level goes up their daughters will have a better career in Panchayati Raj.

(ii) Women members have done a good job in arousing popular consciousness against child marriage. Door-to-door canvassing has improved matters.

(iii) Efforts have been made in the field of environment protection. Some local leaders have taken up water harvesting as an important work along with other duties they perform.

(iv) In Sikar District special efforts have been made to improve the condition of military widows.

- The study proves that:

  (i) Popular awareness has given self-confidence to these weak and backward groups. The women feel that they can lead and work outside their household. They feel stronger and in a Panchayat office they feel one with other members of weaker sections.

  (ii) Women in particular have begun to take interest in politics. They canvas door to door seeking votes and they take pride in their victory at the hustings. They feel equal with their menfolk, and the percentage of female vote denotes women and weaker sections are more enthusiastic about their participation in Panchayati Raj bodies.

  (iii) Weaker sections are becoming less and less fatalist. They say their work has brought in a significantly positive change in what they viewed as their rather bleak destiny. They no longer accept exploitation as a given or an unchangeable situation which was formerly called the wages of previous actions.

  (iv) They do not entertain the idea that support of the kin is necessary to perform duties, but changes that took place between 1994 and 2014 demonstrate that this dependence has considerably declined. Women members today know reasonably well and handle Panchayati decisions with care and ability. The slow and steady growth of system makes one optimistic about rural local government.

- The study also suggests that some more powers be vested with Panchayati Raj institutions. The study suggests the following:
  (i) Powers to deliver local justice in petty cases so that case load on district courts may be reduced.
  (ii) The per capita grant by state should be enhanced and grants-in-aid should be paid in time.
  (iii) More powers in the area of primary education.
  (iv) Powers in the areas of forestry and agriculture.
  (v) More facilities and powers in general.
  (vi) Increased provision of latest facilities in medical and health services.
- The study also points out that in order to empower the women and Dalits the following must take place:
  (i) Women and Dalit groups should be educated in a formal way. Education will make them enlightened, and they will have higher awareness of their rights. For this purpose, government should open more schools and set up literacy centres in rural areas. The absence of education breeds apathy and as a result these two groups do not come forward to protect and promote their rights.
  (ii) Administrative training can enhance their participation qualitatively as well as quantitatively. Even those who are politically aware have no knowledge of rules and procedures. Hence, they hesitate and their decisions are not supported by higher bodies. Like women the Dalits also cut a sorry figure in the meetings and look to others for guidance or decision-making. They put thumb impressions and openly ask others to decide on their behalf.
  (iii) Employment-oriented schemes for women and Dalits should be taken up on priority basis.
  (iv) Weaker sections and women should be in the centre of all government-sponsored projects and schemes.
  (v) Elected leaders of these weaker sections should be helped, and the present state of humiliation can be eradicated.
  (vi) They should be trained in voluntary self-employment and their economic position should be strengthened.

(vii) Social functions, festivals, marriages and so on should be solemnised on the basis of equality. Evil practices perpetrating inequalities should be penalized so that they do not get repeated in future. Social security of weaker sections is a key prerequisite to usher in positive changes.

- The study has also shown that women's reservation has brought a positive change in rural society. Men's attitudes are changing fast. Leadership in patriarchal society and family is gradually passing on to women, old and young. Overall, men have begun to realize that women can do it. If the society supports they are capable of doing the miracles. There was mixed reaction in this area, with people specifically voicing their concerns such as 'nurture of children in the family'; some people said that even children have developed better political understanding because of the role of their mothers. The opponents felt that children are unnecessarily being politicised.

  Respondents maintained that the impact of women's reservation in Panchayati Raj bodies has been either seminal or of little consequence. They win elections because of the image and campaigns by their family members. These members like husband or father-in-law or other relatives run their political offices by proxy.

- The new reservation provisions in Panchayati Raj bodies can be called a very positive step in the direction of establishment of social justice and social change, so very vital for the evolution of an egalitarian society. When asked, most of the respondents of the study agreed that reservation should continue. They justified reservation as a necessary evil because it makes Panchayati Raj institutions representative. All sections of rural society get represented and local institutions look more democratic. It is a fact that Indian society has historically kept a large section of its people from the mainstream of national life. Reservation has not only paved the way for these deprived groups to enter into the ruling segment but has also ensured them a life of dignity with human rights. They are gradually developing leadership capability, which portends a bright future. The people in general are not averse to reservation, they only question the abuse of reservation. Those who expressed disagreement with reservation for women felt that enough should be done to make them aware and capable. They have to go a long way in becoming capable participants. Presently, they are not only ignorant but also apathetic and allow their relatives to interfere in administrative affairs of the Panchayats. People had a grouse that the lottery system for reservation of posts has ousted capable people who could give effective leadership and governance. Although social justice continues to be polemical rural people are gradually reconciling to it.

Notwithstanding differences aired about reservations of seats in Panchayati Raj bodies there is a consensus that the present system has yielded positive results. Rural leadership is emerging and elected leaders are exhibiting confidence in local governance. As compared to past leaders know that they cannot monopolise power for a long time. They will have to quit and give place to others for a change. They know that reserved seats are rotated by a system of lottery conducted by the State Election Commission. This rotation system changes the classes and categories. Men, women, members of SC, ST and OBC keep coming one after another to seek a chance to become members. This kind of change makes the leaders aware that they cannot rule for long and others will have opportunity to show their mettle. It is a fact that the rural leadership is far from satisfactory, but the quality of leadership performance is gradually improving for the benefit of the community at large.

- The 73rd Constitutional Amendment has a new schedule which consists of 29 subjects. The state government will transfer these subjects of Panchayati Raj institutions at their discretion. The time frame being not fixed, state governments are taking time in giving effect to this transfer. This being optional even after 23 years, the institutions have not become functional or powerful as was expected. The states are reluctant and practically all elected leaders complained that they do not enjoy adequate powers. This hampers rural development.
- Integrity of administration is a condition precedent for the success of institutions. No plan or program can succeed unless the administrators are people of high integrity and character. This is needed to fix targets and priorities which have to be implemented as desired. Corruption in public life is a complex

and very serious problem in administrative offices. It prevails at all levels and has increased at higher levels. From here it percolates down below. The speed of development can be called commensurate with speed of corrupt practices in public offices. The fictitious muster rolls of workers and loaners is a startling fact which everybody knows. A number of development schemes for the welfare of BPL families have come to Panchayats, but a sizeable amount of this budget is swindled by corrupt bureaucracy at the grassroots level. The deserving beneficiaries suffer the loss and poverty alleviation remains elusive even after decades of efforts. Strong and strict measures are needed to arrest corruption. The Panchayati Raj Lokpal may be strengthened, so that people can bring their complaints to competent officials and get them resolved in time. The Right to Information is a commendable step in this direction.

- The constitutionalisation of Panchayati Raj brings local government as a third tier of Indian Federation. Article 40 exhorted upon the governments to strengthen these bodies. Several measures were taken by the union and state governments since 1950. The union and state governments have taken several steps to strengthen Panchayati Raj bodies, but they have remained mere agencies of development rather than that of governance. The union and state governments decide and routinely implement development programs without considering the complexities of the rural life. Their success is measured in terms of effective implementation of the schemes received from above. The intention of the founding fathers of India was to make them the institutions of self-governance. Local democracy was the idea, which implied people rule at the community level. The present study of two districts tried to discover whether people have a dream of self-governance and to what extent it has come closer to people. The answer is negative, because the Panchas and Sarpanchas do not think beyond development schemes. The concept of self-governance is a far cry. People are afraid of Panchayat functionaries and they do not dare to resist the evil practices of local leaders and petty civil servants. They hesitate to call the corrupt as corrupt, and the state funds allotted to BPL families are swindled by leaders and officials. People know but do not resist because they live in fear and need nothing but peace even at the cost of perpetual exploitation. Elections in rural areas have fallen prey to money and muscle politics. The alliance makes the attainment of power easy and the common man feels helpless in the presence of the rich and powerful. This renders the Panchayati Raj a sham democracy of corrupt elites. People prefer to stay apathetic rather than getting involved in corrupt power mechanism or alliances of the wicked. The knowledge level is low and average people hate the subsystems like district bureaucracy at a higher level.

Apparently, there is need for popular awareness and campaigns are needed to raise the awareness level. People should know about the activities of their local leaders. This will restrain them. For instance, a well-attended Gram Sabha can expose corrupt functionaries. People avoid Gram Sabha meetings. At the same time, elected local leaders also want that the lesser people attend the Gram Sabha. Once people realise that they can change the situation they will make the Gram Sabha functional. Naturally people have to be vigilant.

- Right to information has been awarded to the people of Rajasthan. The objective was to make administration and working of Panchayati Raj bodies transparent and clean. Now any villager or citizen of India can seek any information from Panchayati records after paying a prescribed fee. These records can be reproduced for legal purposes in the courts. People can note the information and seek redressal of grievances. Social audit of development expenditure by Panchayati Raj institutions in Rajasthan has been introduced in 2009. The Gram Panchayat has to prepare an information sheet of all expenditures in development and it will be presented in the Gram Sabha meetings. Its verification by residents of the village will be public and the guilty official will be legally taken to task. The intention of the state government is clear. It wants the Panchayati Raj leaders and officials held accountable in public to the residents of the rural community. This is an earnest attempt to make grassroots democracy functional and real. If people have more powers, the arbitrariness of leaders will get checked. The right to information caused alarm in bureaucracy because people can ask what was done with what results and at what cost. The fake records or manipulations can be physically verified by people. People can know how much money the government has released and how it has been misappropriated by their local leaders and Panchayati Raj sevaks and adhikaris. When asked about right to information, 83 per cent of the respondents replied in the negative. It brings out the fact that people need to be educated on this count. This right is a powerful weapon, and as people gradually start learning more about it the Panchayati Raj politics will get streamlined and people will be relived from the misrule of the rich and the powerful casteist leaders in the village.

- The participatory observation of rural politics in the countryside indicates that Panchayati Raj system has entered into a new era after the 73rd Constitutional Amendment. Now it is more modern than ever before. The criterion of political modernization can be applied, and it can be safely surmised that the process of political modernization is becoming more effective. Past feudal rules of Rajas, Thakurs, Raos, Jamindars and Purohits were quite influential and continued to hold sway. The so-called elections were a farce because nobody could challenge these feudal lords. Common man could not dream of contesting against them in elections. The 73rd Constitutional Amendment has transformed the situation. The common villager not only challenges but wins also.

  There was a time when half of the population of women were behind veils; today they sit in the Panchayat Bhawans and discuss rural matters as members equal in stature to the menfolk. This is political modernization. Responsible participation has enhanced people's interest in politics and they feel happy when their candidate sweeps the polls. They understand the value of their vote and recognize its power also. This causes a change in voting behaviour. The family members and women who used to vote as desired by male elders are free today and they vote for a candidate of their choice. Political assessment of individuals' desire to cast their votes without coercion or influence of any kind is a common thing in most villages. The study reveals that 53 per cent of the voters exercised their franchise without any body's advice or influence.

- Gram Sabha members were found to be somewhat ignorant about their powers. It was expected that this village body will directly control Panchayat government like a parliament (or

Lok Sabha) and will check its malpractices. However, the present study found that this institution could not emerge as powerfully as it was envisaged and thus it is not popular among villagers. It is more a formal affair and respondents felt that they do not want to waste their day in the activities of this dysfunctional institution. The Panchas and Sarpanchas do not listen to the Gram Sabha and its meetings are very poorly attended. It is a pity that this institution of direct democracy survives only on paper.

- It appears that village voters do not have much active interest in Panchayats. They vote once in five years and are usually apathetic during the term of the Panchayats. They attend meetings once a while and their experiences can be termed anything but happy so they avoid attendance.

  A deep analysis of this mind-set of rural folks brings us to the conclusion that rural people are too poor to find time for the luxury of democratic participation. Their poverty prevents them to be active or disagree with people who matter in the village. They accept life as a divine dispensation and their present position in the society is too weak to fight or challenge oppression. Corruption is the most major factor which makes them apathetic and avoid politics.

  It is high time this mind-set has changed. People are to be told time and again that they can change their destiny. Only vigilance is needed and their problem can be solved by the mediation of the Gram Sabha. They should know about poverty alleviation and development programmes of government and should use Right to Information to bring the corrupt to the book.

  'Eternal vigilance in the price of liberty,' says Harold Laski. This vigilance will come by awareness. The process has begun. Panchayati Raj provides the cornerstone. The edifice will be durable and strong if we continue the process with courage and foresight.

Bibliography

Books

Abraham, M. Francis. *Dynamics of Leadership in Village India*. India International Publishers, Allahabad, 1974.

Ahluwalia, M.S. *History of Himachal Pradesh.* Intellectual Publishing House, New Delhi, 1988.

Alderfer, Harold F. *Local Government in Developing Countries.* McGraw-Hill, London, 1964.

Almond, G.A. and G.V. Powell Jr. *Comparative Politics: A Development Approach*, Amerind, New Delhi, 1966.

Altekar, A.S. *State and Government in Ancient India*. Motilal Banarsidass, Delhi, 1962.

Ambedkar, B.R. *Writings and Speeches Series*, Vol. 13, Government of Maharashtra, Mumbai, 1987.

Ananthpur, Kripa. 'Dynamics of Local Governance in Karnataka', *Economic and Political Weekly*, February 24, pp. 667–673, 2007.

Aziz, Abdul. *Decentralized Governance and Planning: Comparative Study in the South Indian States*, MacMillan India, New Delhi, 2002.

Barowalia, J.N. *Commentary on Himachal Pradesh Panchayati Raj Act, 1968 (Act 19 of 1970)*. Minerva Book House, Shimla, 1988.

Banerjee, Pramathanath. *Public Administration in Ancient India*. Uppal Publishing House, New Delhi, 1985.

Berreman, Gerald D. *Caste and Other Inequalities*. Folklore Institute, Meerut, UP, India, 1979.

——. *Hindus of Himalayas*. Oxford University Press, Bombay, 1963.

Baviskar, B.S. and Mathew, George. *Inclusion and Exclusion in Local Governance: Field Based Studies from Rural India*, Sage Publications, New Delhi, 2009.

Bendix, R. and Lipset, S.M. (eds). *Class, Status and Power: A Comparative Perspective*. Routledge and Kegan Paul, London, 1967.

Beteille, Andre. *Caste, Class and Power*. Oxford University Press, Bombay, 1969.

——. *Caste, Class and Power: Changing Patterns of Social Stratification in a Tanjore Village*, Oxford University Press, New Delhi, 1996.

Bhargava, B.S. *Politico-administrative Dynamics in Panchayati Raj System*. Ashish Publishing, New Delhi, 1978.

Bhargava, B.S. *Panchayati Raj System and Political Parties*. Ashish Publishing, New Delhi, 1979.

——. *Grass Roots Leadership: A Study of Leadership in Panchayati Raj Institutions*. Ashish Publishing, New Delhi, 1979.

——. *Panchayati Raj Institutions: An Analysis of Issues Problems and Recommendations of Asoka Mehta Committee*. Ashish Publishing, New Delhi, 1979.

Bhatia, K.S. *Panchayati Raj Administration in Maharashtra*. Popular Prakashan, Bombay, 1974.

Bhatia, S.S. *Indian Democracy at the Grass Roots*. Indian Institute of International Understanding, New Delhi, 1989.

Bhatnager, S. *Panchayati Raj in Kangra District*. Orient Longman, New Delhi, 1974.

——. *Rural Local Government in India*. Life and Light Publishers, New Delhi, 1978.

Brahmanand (ed.). *Jayaprakash Narayan*. Communication Society and Panchayati Raj, Varanasi, 1970.

Brush, Lisa D. *Gender and Governance: The Gender Lens Series*, Rawat Publications, Jaipur, 2007.

Byrne, David. *Social Exclusion*, 2nd Edition, Rawat Publications, Jaipur, 1997.

Charak, S.S. *History and Culture of Himalayan States*. Himachal Pradesh, Vol.II, Light and Life Publishers, New Delhi, 1979.

Chaturvedi, T.N. *Panchayati Raj*. Indian Institute of Public Administration, New Delhi, 1981.

D' Lima, Hezel. *Women in Local Government: A Study of Maharashtra*, Concept Publishing Company, New Delhi, 1983.

Dahl, Robert A. *Modern Political Analysis*. Prentice Hall of India, New Delhi, 1983.

Dahrenndrof, Falf. *Class and Class Conflict in an Industrial Society*. Stanford, CA: Stanford University Press, 1959.

Darshankar, Arjun Y. *Leadership in Panchayati Raj: A Study of Beed District of Maharashtra*. Panchsheel Prakashan, Jaipur, Rajasthan, India, 1979.

Das, Bhagwan. 'Socio-Economic Problems of dalits', in Bhagwan Das and Massey, et al. *Dalit Solidarity*, Indian Society for Promoting Christian Knowledge, Delhi, 1995.

Dayal, Rajeshwar. *Community Development*. Panchayati Raj and Sahakari Samaj, Metropolitan Delhi, 1965.

——. *Panchayati Raj in India*. Metropolitan, Delhi, 1970.

Degler, Carl N. 'Revolution without Ideology: The Changing Place of Women in America' in Robert Lifton, *The Women in America*, Houghton Mifflin, Boston, 1965.

Deliege, Robert. *The Untouchables of India*, Berg Publishers, New York, 2001

Desai, A.R. (ed.). *Rural Sociology in India*. Popular Prakashan, Bombay, 1969.

Desai, Vasant. *Panchayati Raj: Power to the People*. Himalaya Publishing House, Bombay, 1990.

Dey, S.K. *Panchayati Raj: A Synthesis*. Asia Publishing, Bombay, 1961.

Dhaka, Sunita and Dhaka, Rajbir S. *Behind the Veil: Dalit Women in Panchayat Raj*, Abhijeet Publications, Delhi, 2005.

——. 'Women in Grass Root Democracy in Haryana: A Case Study of SC Women', *Kurukshetra*, March 2004, pp. 31–35.

Dube, S.N. and Murdia Ratan. *Structure and Process of Decision-Making in Panchayati Raj Institutions*. Somaiya Publications, Bombay, 1976.

Economic Survey (2008–09) Planning and Programme Monitoring and Statistics Department, Government of Karnataka.

Frolov, I. *Dictionary of Philosophy*. Progress Publishers, Moscow, 1967.

Galanter, Marc. *Competing Inequalities: Law and Backward Classes in India*, University of California Press, 1984.

Gerth, H.H. and C. Wright Mills (ed.). *From Marx Weber: Essays in Sociology*. Routledge & Kegan Paul, London, 1970.

Ghurye, G.S. *Caste and Race in India*. Popular Prakashan, Bombay, 1969.

Gore, C. and Figquiredo (ed.). 'Social Exclusion and Anti Poverty Policy: A Debate', International Institute of Labor Studies Research Series, ILO, Geneva, UNDP, 1997.

Grover, V.P., et. al. *Panchayati Raj Administration in Rajasthan*. Laxmi Narayan Aggarwal, Agra, 1973.

Gupta, Parmeshwar Lal. *Numismatic History of Himachal Pradesh*. B.R. Publishing Corporation, Delhi, 1988.

Haldipur, R.N. and Paramhamsa, V.R.K. (ed.). *Local Government Institutions in Rural India*. NICD, Hyderabad, 1970.

Hutton, J.H. *Caste in India*. Cambridge University Press, Cambridge, UK, 1964.

Inamdar, N.R. (ed.). *Functioning of Village Panchayats*. Popular Prakashan, New Delhi, 1970.

Jacob, George (ed.). *Reading on Panchayati Raj*. NICD, Hyderabad, 1967.

Jain, L.C., Krishnamurthi, B.V. and Tripathi, P.M. *Grass Without Roots: Rural Government Under Government Auspices*. Sage, New Delhi, 1985.

Jain, S.C. *Community Development and Panchayati Raj in India*. Allied Publishers, Bombay, 1967.

Jather, R.V. *Evolution of Panchayati Raj in India*. J.S.S. Institute of Economic Research, Dharwar, Karnataka, 1964.

Jayaraman, Raja. *Caste and Class: Dynamics of Inequality in Indian Society*. Hindustan Publishing Corporation, Delhi, 1981.

Jayaswal, K.P. *Hindu Polity: A Constitutional History of India in Hindu Times*. Bangalore, 1955.

Jogdand, P.G. *Dalit Women: Issues and Perspectives*, Gyan Publishing House, New Delhi, 1995.

Joshi, R.P. and Narwani, G.S. *Panchayat Raj in India: Emerging trends Across the States*, Rawat Publications, Jaipur, 2005.

Khan, Iltija Hussain. *Government in Rural India*. Asia Publishing, Bombay, 1969.

Kamble, N.D. *Atrocities on Scheduled Castes in Post Independent India*, Ashis Publishing House, New Delhi, 1981.

Kanhere, U.S. *Women and Socialization*, Mittal Publications, Delhi, 1987.

Khanna, R.L. *Panchayati Raj in India*. The English Book Shop, Chandigarh, Punjab, India, 1956.

——. *Local Government in Punjab*. Mohindra Capital Publishers, Chandigarh, Punjab, India, 1957.

——. Panchayati Raj in Punjab and Haryana. Mohindra Capital Publishers, Chandigarh, Punjab, India, 1966.

Kothari, Rajni (ed.). *Caste in Indian Politics*. Orient Longman, New Delhi, 1970.

Kumar, Narendra and Raj, Manoj. *Dalit Leadership in Panchayats: A Comparative Study of Four States*, Rawat Publications, Jaipur, 2006.

Kumar, Sushil and Venkataraman, K. *State Panchayati Raj Relations: A Study of Supervision and Control in Tamil Nadu*. Asia Publishing, Bombay, 1974.

Lakshminarayan, H.D. *India's Villages at Cross Roads*. National Publishing House, New Delhi, 1976.

Lasswell, Harold D. *Power and Personality*. W.W. Norton, New York, 1948.

Law, Narendra Nath. *Aspects of Ancient Indian Polity*. Orient Longman, New Delhi, 1960.

Leach, E.R. (ed.). *Aspects of Caste in India, Ceylon and North West Pakistan*. Cambridge University Press, Cambridge, 1960.

Maclean, David. *Karl Marx: Selected Readings*. Oxford University Press, Oxford, UK, 1977.

Macmalion, Arthur W. *Delegation and Authority*. Asia Publishing, London, 1961.

Maddick, Henry. *Panchayati Raj: A Study of Rural Local Government in India*. Longman, London, 1970.

Maheshwari, B. *Studies in Panchayati Raj*. Metropolitan, Delhi, 1963.

Maheshwari, S.R. *Local Government in India*. MacMillan, Delhi, 1971.

——. *Rural Development in India*. Sage, New Delhi, 1985.

——. *State Government in India*. MacMillan, Delhi, 1979.

Majumdar, R.C., et al. *An Advanced History of India*. MacMillan, London, 1970.

——. *Corporate Life in Ancient India.* Calcutta University, Calcutta, 1969.

Malviya, H.D. *Village Panchayats in India*. All India Congress Committee, New Delhi, 1956.

Mannheim, Karl. *Freedom, Power and Democratic Planning*. Routledge & Kegan Paul, London, 1951.

Marx, Karl. *Capital, Vol. III.* Foreign Language Publishing House, Moscow, 1962.

Marx, Karl and Engels, F. *Selected Works, Vol. II.* Moscow, 1951.

Mathur, M.V. and Narain, Iqbal (eds). *Panchayati Raj, Planning and Democracy*. Asia Publishing, Bombay, 1969.

Mathur, M.V., Narain, Iqbal and Sinha, V.M. (eds). *Panchayati Raj in Rajasthan: A Case Study in Jaipur District*. Impax India, New Delhi, 1966.

Mehta, Uday. 'The Impact of Panchayat Raj on Rural India' in Desai, A.R., *Rural Sociology in India*, Popular Prakashan, Bombay, 1978.

Mills, C. Wright. *The Power Elite*. Oxford University Press, New York, 1956.

Mishra, S.N. *Politics and Society in Rural India: A Case Study of Drauli Gram Panchayat. Siwan District, Bihar*. Inter India Publication, Delhi, 1980.

——. *New Horizons in Rural Development Administration*. Mittal Publications, Delhi, 1989.

——. *Panchayati Raj, Bureaucracy and Rural Development*. Indian Institute of Public Administration, New Delhi, 1986.

Mohanty, Bidyut. *Women and Political Empowerment*, ISS, New Delhi, 2002.

Mookerji, Radhakumud. *Local Government in Ancient India*. Motilal Banarsidass, New Delhi, 1958.

Mosca, Gaetano. *The Ruling Class*. McGraw-Hill, New York, 1941.

Mukerji, B. *Community Development in India*. Orient Longman, Bombay, 1961.

Muttalib, M.A. and Alikhan, Mohd. Akbar. *Theory of Local Government*. Sterling Publishers, New Delhi, 1982.

Narain, Iqbal (ed.). *State Politics in India*. Meenakshi Prakashan, Meerut, UP, India, 1976.

Narain, Iqbal, et al. *Panchayati Raj Administration: Old and New Controls*. Indian Institute of Public Administration, New Delhi, 1970.

——. *Panchayati Raj in Rajasthan: A Case Study of Jaipur District*. Implax India, New Delhi, 1966.

Narain, Iqbal, et al. *Rural Elite in an Indian State: A Case Study of Rajasthan*. Manohar Book Service, Delhi, 1976.

Oommen, T.K. Understanding Indian Society: The Relevance of the Perspective from Below, Occasional Paper series, 4, Department of Sociology, University of Pune, Pune, 2004.

Pandey, Suman. *Women in Politics*, Rawat Publications, Jaipur, 1990.

Pant, Niranjan. *The Politics of Panchayati Raj Administration: A Study of Officials and Non-official Relations*. Concept Publishing, Delhi, 1979.

Parmar, Y.S. *Himachal Pradesh: Its Proper Shape and Status*. Director, Public Relations, Shimla, HP, 1965.

——. *Polyandry in Himalayas*. Vikas Publishing, Delhi, 1975.

Potter, D.C. *Government in Rural India*. G. Bell & Sons, London, 1964.

Prasad, R.C. *Democracy and Development: The Grass Roots Experience in India*. Rachna Prakashan, New Delhi, 1971.

Prasad, Sivalinga. *Panchayats and Development*. Life and Light Publishers, New Delhi, 1980

Raghava Rao, D.V. *Panchayati Raj and Rural Developments*. Ashish Publishing, New Delhi, 1980.

Rajput, R.S. and Meghe, D.R. *Panchayati Raj in India*. Deep & Deep, Delhi, 1984.

Rai, Haridwar and Singh, Sakendra Prasad. *Current Ideas in Indian Administration: A Development Perspective*. Uppal Publishing, Delhi, 1967.

Ray, Ajit. *Political Power in India: Nature and Trends*. Naya Prakash, Calcutta, 1975.

Reddy, G. Ram and Seshadri, D. *The Voter and Panchayati Raj: A Study of Electoral Behaviour During Panchayat Elections in Warangal District (A.P.)*. NICD, Hyderabad, AP, 1972.

Reisman, David, et al. *The Lonely Crowd*. UBS Publishers, New Delhi, 1974.

Russell, Bertrand. *Power: A New Social Analysis*. Allen & Unwin, London, 1938.

Sahai, Raghuvir. *Panchayati Raj in India: A Study*. Kitab Mahal, Allahabad, UP, 1968.

Saletora, B.A. *Ancient Indian Political Thought and Institutions*. Asia Publishing, Bombay, 1963.

Sammiudding, Abida. *A Critique of Panchayati Raj with Special Reference to Uttar Pradesh*. Sahitya Bhawan, Agra, UP, 1976.

Seshadri, K. *Political Linkages and Rural Development: A Comparative Study of the Political Process and Interactions between Different Levels of Government in Two Indian States*. National Publishing House, New Delhi, 1976.

Sharma, M.P. *Local Self-Government in India*. Munshiram Manohar Lal, Allahabad, UP, 1978.

Sharma, Ranbir. *Party Politics in a Himalayan State*. National Publishing House, New Delhi, 1977.

Sharma, Ravindra. *Village Panchayats in Rajasthan*. Aalekh Publishers, Jaipur, Rajasthan, 1984.

Sharma, Surjan Singh. *Rural Elites in India*. Sterling Publishers, New Delhi, 1979.

Sharma, Vidya Sagar. *Panchayati Raj*. Vidya Mandir, Hoshiarpur, Punjab, 1962.

Shashi, S.S. *Himachal – Nature's Peaceful Paradise*. Indian Social Supply Depot, Delhi, 1971.

Singh, Chandra Mauli. *Dynamics of Rural Development Administration*. Spick & Span, Delhi, 1988.

Singh, Harjinder. *Village Leadership: A Case Study of Village Mohali in Punjab*. Sterling Publishers, Delhi, 1968.

Singh, Mian Govardhan. *The History of Himachal Pradesh*. Yogbodh Publishing, Delhi, 1982.

——. *Himachal Pradesh – History, Culture and Economy*. Minerva Book House, Shimla, HP, 1990.

Singh, Rajendra Prasad. *Bihar Mein Gram Panchayat*. Bihar Hindi Granth Academy, Patna, 1987.

Singh, Sahib and Singh, Swinder. *Local Government in India*. New Academic Publishing, Jalandhar, Punjab, 1986.

Sinha, Durganand. *Indian Villages in Transaction*. Associate Publishing, New Delhi, 1969.

Sirsikar, V.M. *The Ruling Elites in Developing Society*. Orient Longman, Delhi, 1970.

Srinivas, M.N. *Caste in Modern India and Other Essays*. Asia Publishing, Bombay, 1962.

Srinivas, M.N. *India's Villages*. Asia Publishing, Bombay, 1957.

——. *Social Change in Modern India*. University of California Press, Berkeley, CA, 1971.

Tak, B.L. *Sociological Dimensions of Gramraj*. Vimal Prakashan, Ghaziabad, UP, 1973.

Taylor, Carl C., et al. *India's Roots of Democracy*. Orient Longman, New Delhi, 1967.

Tead, Ordway. *The Art of Leadership*. Whittlerey House, London, 1935.

Tinker, Hugh. *Foundations of Local Self-Government in India, Pakistan and Burma*. Lalvani Publishing, Bombay, 1967.

Tripathi, R.P. *Rise and Fall of Mughal Empire*. Central Book Depot, Allahabad, UP, 1969.

Vankataramaiya and Pittabhiram (eds). *Local Government in India: Selected Reading*. Allied Publishers, Moscow, 1985.

Volkow, M.I. *A Dictionary of Political Economy*. Progress Publishers, Moscow, 1985.

Vyas, R.N. *Creative Leadership*. Ambika Publications, New Delhi, 1979.

Warner, W.L. and Lunt, P.S. *The Social Life of Modern Community*. Yale University Press, New Haven, CT, 1941.

Wasby, S.L. *Political Science: The Discipline and Its Dimensions*. Scientific Book Agency, Calcutta, 1970.

Weber, Max. *Basic Concepts in Sociology*. Peter Owen, London, 1968.

Zaidi, S.M. Ijlal Anis. *Politics, Power and Leadership in Rural India*. Commonwealth Publishers, New Delhi, 1988.

Zamora, Mario D. *The Panchayat Tradition: A North Indian Village Council in Transition, 1947-62*. Reliance Publishing, New Delhi, 1990.

Articles

Arora, Satish. 'Indian Rural Politicians: Two Faces of Power', *Economic and Political Weekly*, 7, 1972.

Arora, Ved Prakash. 'First Panchayat Raj Sammelan: A Resume', *Kurukshetra*, 37(6), 1989.

Arun, Rashmi, 'Role of Women in Panchayat Raj', *Administration*, Vol. 1, April-June, 1997.

Bandyopadhyay, D., Gosh, Saila K. and Ghosh, Buddha Deb. 'Dependency versus Autonomy: Identity Crises of India's Panchayats', *Economic and Political Weekly*, 20 September, pp. 3984–3991, 2003.

Bhalla, Deepak. 'Panchayati Raj – An Appraisal', *Kurukshetra*, 37(6), 1989.

Bhargava, B.S. 'Panchayati Raj and the Janata', *Kurukshetra*, 25(22), 1977.

——. 'Local Participation and Panchayats', *Kurukshetra*, 31(23), 1983.

——. 'Panchayati Raj: Power to the People', *Kurukshetra*, 36(3), 1987.

Bhatnagar, B.S. 'Grass Roots Politics in India: A Caste Study of Kangra Valley', *Asian Survey*, 15(5), 1975.

Bhongle, S.K. 'The Area of Rural Local Government', *Kurukshetra*, 25(8), 1977.

Bora, P.M. 'Democracy and Panchayati Raj, *Kurukshetra*, 23(19), 1975.

Borain, M.P. 'Empowerment of Rural Women: Towards Reversal of Gender Relations', *The Indian Journal of Social Work*, Mumbai, TISS, 64(4), pp. 521–532, 2003.

Chandershekhar, B.K. 'Panchayati Raj Bill: The Real Flaw', *Economic and Political Weekly*, 24(26), 1989.

Choudhary, D. Paul. 'Panchayati Raj and Public Cooperation', *Kurukshetra*, 18(7), 1970.

Dayal, Rajeshwar. 'Village Panchayats in Rajasthan', *Kurukshetra*, 19(11), 1971.

De, Haan. 'Social Exclusion: An Alternative Concept for the Study of Deprivation?', *IDS Bulletin*, Vol. 29, No. 1, 1998.

Dey, S.K. 'Power to the People', *Kurukshetra*, 28(1), 1979.

——. 'Faith in Panchayati Raj', *Kurukshetra*, 9, August 1961.

Dietich, G. 'The Relationship between Dalit Movements and Women's Movements: Cases and Conceptual Analysis', Paper for the *IAWS*, Calcutta, 1990.

Dubey, S.N. 'Organisational Analysis of Panchayati Raj in India', *Indian Journal of Public Administration*, 18(2), 1972.

Dunn, Dana. 'Gender Inequality in Education and Employment in the Scheduled Castes and Tribes of India', *Population Research and Policy Review*, Vol. 12, No. 1, pp. 53–70, 1993.

Duta, Abhijit. 'Constitutional Status of Local Government in India', *Indian Journal of Public Administration*, 30(2), 1987.

Dutta, Vijay Ranjan. 'Decentralisation and Political Development in India: A Gandhian Concept', *Indian Journal of Public Administration*, 28(1), 1982.

——. 'Local Participation and Panchayats', *Kurukshetra*, 32(7), 1984.

'Dynamics of Power and Violence', *Economic and Political Weekly*, 14 September.

Ensminger, Douglas. 'Democratic Decentralization: A New Administrative Challenge', *Indian Journal of Public Administration*, 7(3), 1961.

Fesler, James W. 'Approaches to the Understanding of Decentralisation', *Journal of Politics*, 27, 1965.

Gaikwad, V.R. 'Panchayati Raj and Bureaucracy', *Indian Journal of Public Administration*, 15, 1969.

Gangrade, K.K. 'Revamping Panchayati Raj Institutions', *Yojna*, 34(14 & 15), 1990.

Ghildayal, U.C. 'The Origin and Progress: Community Development in Free India', *Kurukshetra*, 20(20), 1972.

Ghosh, Arun. 'Lessons for the Future', *Seminar Journal 360*, 1989.

Govind, Gowda S. 'Women in Panchayat Raj Institutions: A Case Study in Karnataka', *Journal of Rural Development*, Vol. 17(4), pp. 669–679, 1998.

Guru, Gopal. 'Dalit Women Talk Differently', *Economic and Political Weekly*, 14–21 October, p. 2548–2559, 1995.

Guru, D.D. 'New Economic Policy Initiative: Panchayati Raj Amendment', *Employment News Weekly*, 16(18), 1989.

Haldipur, R.N. 'Relevance of Community Development', *Kurukshetra*, 20(1), 1971.

Harish, R. 'Panchayats – Are They Field for Experiment', *Kurukshetra*, 34(7), 1986.

Hirway, Indira. 'Panchayati Raj at Cross Roads', *Economic and Political Weekly*, 24(29), 1989.

Hooja, B. 'Panchayati Raj versus Decentralization of Administration', *Indian Journal of Public Administration*, 24(3), 1978.

Inbanathan, Anand. 'Affirmative Action and Dalit: Political Representation in Panchayat', *Working Paper*, 138, Institute for Social and Economic Change, Bangalore, 2009.

Iyer, Shekhar. 'Jawahar Rozgar Yojna: Jobs at Doorsteps', *Kurukshetra*, 37(10), 1989.

Jackson, Cicile. 'Social Exclusion and Gender: Does one Size for All', *The European Journal of Development Research*, Vol. II, No. 1, June, pp. 125–146, 1999.

Jain, Avinash Kamal. 'Community Development in Haryana', *Kurukshetra*, 20(20), 1972.

Jain, Laxmi C. 'Democratic Decentralization', *Seminar Journal 360*, 1989.

Jain, Nisha. 'Subjection of Women in India: A Theoretical Perspective on Patriarchy', *Indian Journal of Politics*, Vol. 44, March, pp. 21–35, 2010.

Juneja, S.V.S. 'Panchayati Raj: A Survey', *Indian Journal of Public Administration*, 19(1), 1973.

Kittur, A.T. and Patil, V.T. 'An Analysis of Official–Non-Officials Relations in Panchayats, *Kurukshetra*, 34(6), 1986.

Krishna Iyer, V.R. 'Panchayati Perestroika?', *Economic and Political Weekly*, 16 September, pp. 2051–2054, 1989.

Kothari, Rajni. 'Decentralization: The Real Issue', *Seminar Journal 360*, 1989.

Maddick, Henry. 'Can Panchayati Raj Become the Agency for Integral Rural Development?', *Indian Journal of Public Administration*, 24(3), 1978.

Maheshwari, S.R. 'Whither Panchayati Raj', *Kurukshetra*, 27(22), 1979.

Mahipal. 'Empowering Women through Panchayat Institutions', *Kurukshetra*, 42(9), 1994.

Mall, Sangeeta. 'Women's Civil and Political Rights', *Mainstream*, 27 December, pp. 95–98, 2003.

Mathew, P.M. 'Women in Panchayats: The More Relevant Questions', *Economic and Political Weekly,* 27 December, pp. 95–98, 2001.

Mathur, P.C. 'Remodeling Panchayati Raj Institutions in India', *Indian Journal of Public Administration*, 24(3), 1978.

——. 'Sociological Dimensions of Panchayati Raj', *Indian Journal of Public Administration*, 10, 1964.

Mehta, Balwant Rai. 'Some Recent Trends in Panchayati Raj in India', *Indian Journal of Public Administration*, 8(4), 1962.

Mehta, S.R. 'Some Aspects of Panchayati Raj', *Kurukshetra*, 14(6), 1971.

Mishra, S.N. 'Grass Roots Democracy', *Indian Journal of Public Administration*, 27(13), 1982.

Mishra, Sweta. 'Women and 73rd Constitutional Amendment Act: A Critical Appraisal', *Social Action*, Vol. 44, 16–30, 1997.

Mohanty, Bidyut. 'Panchayat Raj, 73rd Constitutional Amendment and Women', *Economic and Political Weekly*, 30 December, pp. 3346–3350, 1995.

Mukerji, Nirmal. 'Panchayat governments', *Seminar Journal 360*, 1989.

Mukherji, B. 'Administrative Problems of Democratic Decentralization', *Indian Journal of Public Administration*, 7(3), 1961.

Naidu, M.C. 'Panchayati Raj and Rural Development', *Kurukshetra*, 36(3), 1987.

Narain, Iqbal. 'The Administrative Challenge to Panchayati Raj', *Indian Journal of Public Administration*, 22(8), 1966.

Narayan, J.P. 'Problem of Panchayati Raj', *Kurukshetra*, 26(9), 1978.

Omvedt, Gail. 'Women in Governance in South Asia', *Economic and Political Weekly*, 29 October, pp. 4746–4752, 2005.

Palmer, Norman D. 'Experiments in Democratic Decentralization in South Asia', *Indian Political Science Review*, 1966.

Panda, Snehalata. 'Emerging Patterns of Leadership among Rural Women in Orissa', *Indian Journal of Public Administration*, Vol. 42, No. 34, 1996.

——. 'Women in Governance for Development at Grassroots', *Indian Journal of Public Administration*, Vol. L, No. 1, January-March, pp. 347–361, 2004.

Rai, H. and Singh, S.P. 'Panchayati Raj and the Citizen: The Myth of Participation Democracy', *Indian Journal of Public Administration*, 21(1), 1975.

Rao, D.V.R. 'Panchayats and Rural Development', *Indian Journal of Public Administration*, 27(2), 1981.

Rao, L.S. Mathava. 'Panchayati Raj Finance Corporation', *Kurukshetra*, 22(21), 1974.

Rao, V.K.R.V. 'Integrated Rural Development', *Janta*, 32(35), 1977.

Rau, S.K. 'Will Panchayati Raj Institutions Help to Solve the Problem of the Poor?', *Kurukshetra*, 28(10), 1980.

Reddy, G. Ram. 'Decentralization: A Functional Necessity', *Kurukshetra*, 37(6), 1989.

Rudolph, L.I. and Rudolph, S.H. 'The Political Role in India's Caste Associations', *Pacific Affairs*, 33, 1960.

Sah, B.L. 'Panchayati Raj – Its Functioning and Difficulties', *Kurukshetra*, 34(6), 1986.

Sahay, B.N. 'Nagaland Experiment with Decentralization', *Kurukshetra*, 37, 1989.

Samiuddin, Abida. 'Shall Panchayati Raj be Non-Political', *Kurukshetra*, 36(3), 1987.

Sangita, S.N. 'Panchayati Raj Experiment in Karnataka', *Kurukshetra*, 36(3), 1987.

Sharma, Kushal. 'Panchayati Raj, Participation and Rural Development', *Kurukshetra*, 31(9), 1983.

Sharma, S.K. 'Review of Asoka Mehta Committee Report', *Kurukshetra*, 27(3), 1978.

Sheth, Pravin. 'Panchayati Raj for Development and Social Change', *Employment News Weekly*, 14(16), 1989.

——. 'A Renewal', *Seminar Journal 360*, 1989.

Simhadri, R. 'Grassroots Democracy: The Experience of Dalits in PRIs', *Indian Journal of Public Administration*, Vol. III, No. 4, October-December, pp. 788–796, 2007.

Singh, S.K. 'Panchayati Raj: A View Point', *Kurukshetra*, 22(19), 1971.

——. 'Panchayati Raj: Stumbling Blocks in Its Path', *Kurukshetra*, 34(6), 1986.

Singh, Sitaram. 'Revitalization of Panchayats', *Kurukshetra*, 34(6), 1986.

——. 'Panchayati Raj and Rural Safety', *Kurukshetra*, 37(6), 1989.

Singh, Surat. 'Panchayati Raj Institutions – Extent of Coverage', *Kurukshetra*, 37(6), 1989.

——. 'Functioning of Panchayati Raj Institutions in Himachal Pradesh', *Kurukshetra*, 36(3), 1987.

Singh, Vishavajit P. 'Populism or Panacea?', *Seminar Journal 360*, 1989.

Singhvi, L.M. 'Public Opinion Is of Utmost Importance', *Kurukshetra*, 37(6), 1989.

Shinde, Annasahib P. 'Community Development Panchayati Raj, Vehicles of Rural Development', *Kurukshetra*, 14(7), 1966.

Shukla, K.B. 'Panchayati Raj Revisited', *Indian Journal of Public Administration*, 24(4), 1978.

Srinivasa, C. 'Structure and Pattern of Panchayati Raj', *Indian Journal of Public Administration*, 8(4), 1962.

Srivastava, K.B. 'Community and Change in Panchayati Raj', *Kurukshetra*, 26(3), 1987.

Documents, Encyclopedias and Reports

Census of India, 1981.

Encyclopedia of Social Sciences.

Government of Himachal Pradesh: Annual Administrative Report.

Government of Himachal Pradesh: District Gazetteer, Kinnaur.

Government of Himachal Pradesh: Panchayati Raj Amendment Act, 1968.

Government of Himachal Pradesh: Panchayati Raj Amendment Act, 1978.

Government of Himachal Pradesh: Panchayati Raj Amendment Act, 1987.

Government of Himachal Pradesh: Panchayati Raj Amendment Act, 1991.

Panchayati Raj (Hereafter Known as Hardyal Singh Committee), Panchayati Raj Department, Shimla, 1965.

Government of Himachal Pradesh: Statistical Outline of Himachal Pradesh, Economic and Statistics Department, Shimla.

Government of India: Report of the Study Team for Community Development and National Extension Service, Vol. I (Hereafter known as Balwant Rai G. Mehta Committee) Committee of Plan project, Planning Commission, New Delhi, 1957.

Government of India: Report of the Committee on Panchayati Raj Institutions (hereafter known as Asoka Mehta Committee), Ministry of Agriculture and Irrigation, Department of Rural Development, New Delhi, 1978.

Government of India: Report of the Committee to Review the Existing Administrative Arrangement for Rural Development and Poverty Alleviation Programmes (CAARD) (hereafter known as G.V.K. Rao Committee), Ministry of Agriculture, Department of Rural Development, New Delhi, 1985.

Techno-Economic Survey of Himachal Pradesh.

The Constitution of India.

Journals and Magazines

Asian Survey

Economic and Political Weekly

Harijan

Indian Journal Public Administration

Indian Political Science Review

Janata

Kurukshetra

Mainstream

Pacific Affairs

Seminar

Yojna

Newspaper

Employment News

The Hindustan Times

Indian Express

The Statesman

The Times of India

The Tribune

Reviewed Books

Arunachalam, Jaya and U. Kalpagam, *Development and Empowerment: Rural Women in India*, Rawat Publications, Jaipur, Rajasthan, India, 2006.

Baluchamy, S., *Panchayati Raj Institutions*, Mittal Publications, New Delhi, 2004.

Banasode, Chandrashekhar C., *Role of Women in Panchayati Raj Institutions*, Manas Publishers and Distributors, Jaipur, 2012.

Chahar, S.S., *Governance at Grassroots Level in India*, Kanishka Publishers, New Delhi, 2005.

Chalawadi, M.C. and C.A. Somashekarappa, *Dalit Women in Panchayati Raj System*, Prateek Prakashan, Jaipur, 2014.

Das, Purnendu Sekhar, *Decentralised Planning and Participatory Rural Development*, Concept Publishing, New Delhi, 2005.

Duta, Prabhat, *Decentralisation, Participation and Governance*, Kalpaz Publications, New Delhi, 2006.

Gandotra, Rama, *Panchayati Raj Institutions and Rural Development*, Crescent Publishing Corporation, New Delhi, 2015.

Goel, Ravi, *Women and Panchayati Raj*, Sonali Publications, New Delhi, 2014.

Gupta, Jawahar Lal, *Local Government*, Wisdom Press, New Delhi, 2013.

Joseph, T.M., *Local Governance in India: Ideas, Challenges and Strategies*, Concept Publishing, New Delhi, 2007.

Joshi, R.P. and G.S. Narwani, *Panchayati Raj in India: Emerging Trends across the States*, Rawat Publications, Jaipur, 2005.

Khanna, B.S., *Rural Local Government in India and South Asia*, Deep & Deep, New Delhi, 1999.

Kulhari, M.S., *Women and our Panchayati Raj System*, Neha Publicshers and Distributors, New Delhi, 2011.

Mandal, Amal, *Women in Panchayati Raj Institutions*, Kanishka Publishers, New Delhi, 2003.

Menon, P.S.K. and Bakshi D. Sinha, *Panchayati Raj in Scheduled Areas*, Concept Publishing, New Delhi, 2003.

Mishra, S.N. and Sweta Mishra, *Decentralised Governance (Macro and Micro Perspective)*, Shipra Publications, Delhi, 2002.

Mishra, S.N., Shweta Mishra and Chaitali Pal, *Decentralisation, Planning and Panchayati Raj*, Mittal Publications, New Delhi, 2000.

Mishra, Yatish, *Empowering People Grassroot Organisations and Rural Development*, Kanishka Publishers, New Delhi, 2002.

Mohanan, B., *Decentralised Governance and Participatory Development: Issues, Constraints and Prospects*, Concept Publishing, New Delhi, 2005.

Palanithurai, G., B.R. Dwarak and S. Narayanaswamy, *Major Issues in New Panchayati Raj System*, Kanishka Publishers, New Delhi, 1997.

Palanithurai, G., *Dynamics of New Panchayati Raj System in India: Panchayati Raj and Multi-level Planning*, Concept Publishing, New Delhi, 2006.

Palanithurai, G., *Emerging Dimensions in Decentralisation*, Concept Publishing, New Delhi, 2005.

Prasad, R.N., *Governance of India: Issues and Perspectives*, Concept Publishing, New Delhi, 2002.

Prasad, Rakesh, *Panchayati Raj in Action*, Abhijeet Publications, Delhi, 2011.

Ravi, R. Venkata, V. Narayana Reddy and M. Venkataraman, *Empowerment of People: Grassroots Strategies and Issues*, Kanishka Publishers, New Delhi, 2004.

Sharma, Aruna and Rajagopal, *Planning for Rural Development Administration*, Rawat Publications, Jaipur, 1995.

Sharma, Shakuntla, *Grassroot Politics and Panchayati Raj*, Deep & Deep, New Delhi, 1997.

Shukla, N.P., *Local Self Government in India*, Navyug Books International, New Delhi, 2011.

Singh, Anupama, *Bureaucracy at the Grassroots Level in India*, Kanishka Publishers, New Delhi, 2006.

Singh, M.K., *Panchayati Raj System in India: Issues and Challenges*, Centrum Press, New Delhi, 2014.

Sinha, K.K., *Panchayat Dilemma (People's Power and Poverty)*, Serials Publications, New Delhi, 2007.

Sisodia, Yatindra Singh, *Functioning of Panchayati Raj System*, Rawat Publications, Jaipur, 2005.

Soni, Jasprit Kaur, *Governance of Panchayati Raj*, Authors Press, Delhi, 2005.

Srivastava, K.K., *Decentralized Governance and Panchayati Raj*, Kalpaz Publications, New Delhi, 2011.

Tomar, Manohar Lal, *Rural Women and Panchayati Raj*, A.K. Publications, Delhi, 2013.

Verma, B.M., *Social Justice And Panchayati Raj*, Mittal Publications, New Delhi, 2002.

Verma, S.B., S.K. Jiloka and K.J. Kushwah, *Rural Women Empowerment*, Deep & Deep, New Delhi, 2006.

Index